Developing
Teacher
Competencies

Developing Teacher Competencies

JAMES WEIGAND, *editor*
Indiana University

Prentice-Hall, Inc., Englewood Cliffs, New Jersey

This book is dedicated to
teachers and prospective teachers
who contribute so much of themselves
to help others.

Prentice-Hall International, Inc., *London*
Prentice-Hall of Australia Pty. Ltd., *Sydney*
Prentice-Hall of Canada Ltd., *Toronto*
Prentice-Hall of India Private Limited, *New Delhi*
Prentice-Hall of Japan, Inc., *Tokyo*

Printed in the United States of America

The Editor:

JAMES WEIGAND
Associate Professor of Science
   Education
School of Education
Indiana University
Ed.D., Indiana University

The Authors:

RONALD D. ANDERSON
Associate Professor of Science
   Education
School of Education
University of Colorado
Ph.D., University of Wisconsin

ROGER T. CUNNINGHAM
Associate Professor of Early and
   Middle Childhood Education
College of Education
The Ohio State University
Ed.D., Indiana University

ALFRED DeVITO
Assistant Professor
Department of Education
Purdue University
Ph.D., University of Texas at Austin

ODVARD EGIL DYRLI
Associate Professor of Science
   Education
School of Education
The University of Connecticut
Ed.D., Indiana University

DeWAYNE KURPIUS
Associate Professor of Education
School of Education
Indiana University
Ed.D., University of North Dakota

JAMES D. RUSSELL
Minicourse Project Coordinator
Department of Biological Sciences
Purdue University
Ed.D., Indiana University

DORIS A. TROJCAK
Assistant Professor
School of Education
University of Missouri-St. Louis
Ed.D., Indiana University

DONALD LEE TROYER
Assistant Professor
College of Education
Western Illinois University
Ed.D., Indiana University

Contents

Preface

JAMES WEIGAND

Indiana University

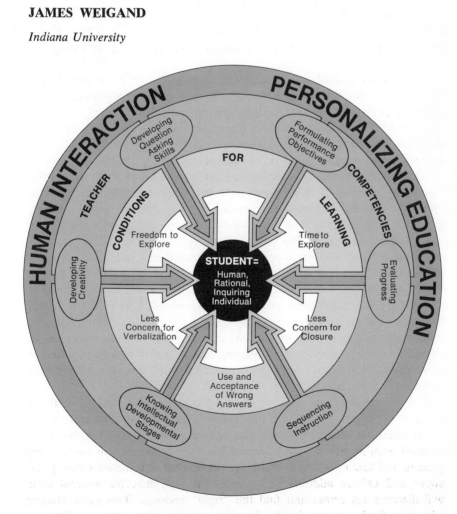

As a student involves himself in the learning process, many external forces are acting upon him. These external forces determine, to a large degree, the value of the learning experience. These external forces can be categorized as (1) conditions necessary for learning, (2) the essential teacher competencies, and (3) human interaction and the personalizing of the educational process. These three forces become the basic input into the student at any stage of the learning process. If the conditions, the competencies, and the teacher-student, student-teacher human interaction are all positive, the output should result in a human, rational, inquiring individual. Very simply this can be described by the model on the preceding page.

Thinking is a thread that permeates all of education. The environment of learning in which a student finds himself will be either conducive or not conducive to the development of the thought process. As shown in the model, the teacher should strive to create conditions that will allow the individual student the opportunity to develop his thinking ability to his maximum capacity. A brief description of these conditions follows:

1. *Freedom to explore.* The learner should have the opportunity to pursue problems by utilizing a variety of approaches. One-solution problems, questions that demand a right answer, and certain types of "busy" work all tend to deny the student the opportunity to explore freely. Examples of this denial are the algebra teacher who demands that the child follow a certain set procedure as he attempts to solve problems even though the child is able to relate other approaches to a solution; the teacher who follows set procedures in a given art activity which remove the possible creativity; and the language arts teacher who teaches a single outlining procedure and demands that the students conform to that procedure.

2. *Time to explore.* The thought process takes time. The amount of time necessary to explore a problem varies with the individual. A child who is denied adequate time to pursue problems tends to give up. This is readily seen in examinations in which the learner may not finish in the time allowed and is penalized for the work not completed. Past research in this area tends to indicate that teachers give students with high ability an abnormally large amount of time to explore and an abnormally small amount of time to the less capable individual. If this is true, we should consciously attempt to reverse this procedure and give each individual student the time that he needs to explore.

3. *Use and acceptance of wrong answers.* Learning can be achieved through our mistakes and bad judgment. Many discoveries have come about through a series of errors. The student whose "wrong" answers are rejected soon formulates a behavior of removing himself from the learning process and teacher-student interaction. A teacher who accepts wrong answers and utilizes additional questions will find that the student soon will discover his errors and find the "right" answers. This same student will very freely engage in the learning process when this condition is established.

4. *Lesser concern for closure.* Students do not learn at the same rate, and as a consequence do not arrive at closure at the same time. Nevertheless, it is common practice for teachers to pull the loose ends together and arrive at closure prematurely. The danger in this is that not all students are ready for closure at a given time and the student who is not ready has a tendency to accept it, not pursuing the learning that actually has not yet taken place. By avoiding premature closure the teacher encourages the student to want to pursue learning in a given area. On the other hand, the student who has reached closure does not have to be informed by the teacher that he has reached closure.

5. *Lesser concern for verbalization.* It is not uncommon for teachers to rank students according to their verbal skills. The learner with low verbal ability recognizes this tendency and often refrains from engaging in verbal activity in the classroom. Rather than utter words that will not receive a positive response from the teacher, he remains silent and disengages himself from the classroom activity. Teachers must recognize that low verbal ability does not mean inability to think. Students have demonstrated over and over through nonverbal or low verbal ability the ability to think; but if this thinking is to continue, the teacher must show acceptance.

If these stated conditions are to be achieved, the classroom teacher must possess certain competencies. Too often in education we hear that someone is a "born" teacher or that he has mastered the "art" of teaching. Actually teaching should become a science and the individual who possesses certain needed competencies is one who has mastered the "science" of teaching. The teacher who knows how to categorize questions, knows how to phrase questions, and knows how to employ strategies in question-asking will find that the previously mentioned conditions will occur in the classroom primarily due to the acquisition of these competencies. This same statement can be made regarding the other competencies shown in the model.

Developing these teacher competencies—knowing intellectual developmental stages, formulating performance objectives, developing question-asking skills, sequencing instruction, evaluating progress, and developing creativity—is essential if effective instruction is to materialize. But these six competencies are not sufficient by themselves. The teacher must also learn positive behavioral skills so that he or she may engage in human interaction with students and to a large degree personalize education. High interpersonal trust must permeate the classroom. Positive human interaction is necessary if high interpersonal trust is to develop.

How does one go about developing these competencies for the pre-service and in-service teacher? In my own teaching, I found that one of the best approaches to the development of these competencies was through programmed instruction. Many of my former undergraduate and graduate students have conveyed to me that they have altered their style of teaching as a result of going through these programs. Because of a firm belief that these competencies are so vital to the teaching act, I decided to search for individuals who could put these competencies into program form. After the seven experts in their respective competencies were located, an eighth member who was an expert in programmed instruction was added to the team.

After the team was formed, initial meetings were held and procedures were described for the writing, testing, re-writing, and re-testing of programs. Each author had the responsibility of writing portions of his programs and testing this material with students at his particular institution. When each author felt satisfied with his program, he sent it to the editor. Field testing of these programs was conducted at all levels of undergraduate instruction as well as with graduate students. On the basis of this testing each program was thoroughly analyzed. A thorough analysis of the field testing pointed out the flaws in the various programs. At the second meeting of the team each program was thoroughly discussed and procedures were formulated to correct all flaws. Each author then proceeded with the job of revising his program. The revised versions were again field tested, either by the individual author or with different groups of students at Indiana University. Upon completion of this field testing the team felt that the programs were ready for use by both prospective and in-service teachers.

The seven programs differ in style. No attempt was made to have the seven authors conform to a particular type of program or style of writing. This freedom allowed each author to pursue the competency in his own unique way. Field testing revealed that students reacted very favorably to the variety of programs. This variety of style was further enhanced by the excellent editorial work of Mrs. October Graham, production editor for Prentice-Hall. The authors are indebted to her for her invaluable assistance.

Hopefully these programs will be beneficial to the user in developing his competencies in the classroom. It must be pointed out, however, that the program in and of itself is not sufficient. It is only a beginning to the fuller development of competency. Each chapter gives the reader selected readings through which he can more fully acquire information and a greater degree of competency. In addition, the eighth chapter describes ways to assess the individual competencies. This chapter gives teachers certain self-assessment techniques they can employ to determine the level of competency they have attained.

We hope this book will cause a change in the teaching act. We hope this book will cause teachers to look upon the teaching act as a science. Specifically, we hope this book will increase the competency level of teachers and establish positive conditions for learning. If the input to the student consisting of competencies and conditions is positive, the output should result in a human, rational, inquiring individual.

JAMES E. WEIGAND, *editor*

Developing
Teacher
Competencies

1 Assessing intellectual development stages of children

ODVARD EGIL DYRLI

The University of Connecticut

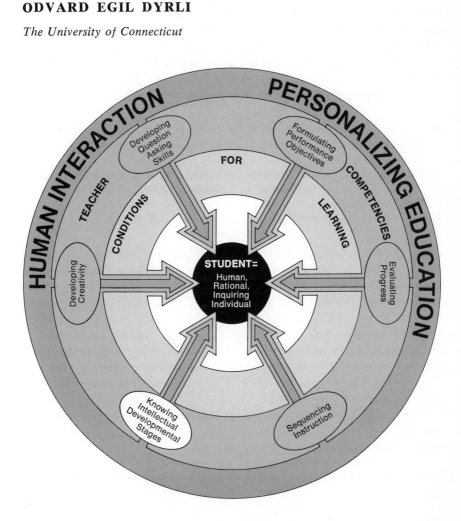

Rationale

To say that the intellectual development of the student is basic to the entire teaching enterprise is certainly not to say anything very profound, yet very little conscious effort is devoted to individualizing instruction so that activities are designed specifically for children with particular capabilities. Although such provisions are often made to some degree at intuitive levels, very seldom are tasks analyzed with respect to the type of thinking required and to the capability of individual students for such thought. If the teacher would become a continuing student of the intellectual development of children, such decisions would become more valid and would also be easier to make. The teacher could then communicate more effectively with *individuals,* could select sequences of experiences better, and could place a greater emphasis on the improvement of logical thought processes in students; in short, he or she would become a more capable and effective teacher. Developing these competencies most efficiently, then, is the purpose of this chapter.

After completing this chapter, you should be able to:

1. List the intellectual development stages of children, and identify the age ranges and describe the major thinking characteristics of children at each level of development;
2. Describe specific tasks, problems, and techniques that may be used to determine the level of intellectual development at which a given child operates in a particular area;
3. Conduct successful problem interview sessions with children.

Central to the completion of this chapter is the preparation of a reference chart that will be useful in gaining a functional understanding of the intellectual development stages of children and will aid in designing tasks well-suited to specific levels of development. It is essential that you *use* your completed chart and some of the tasks suggested in actually working with children. Two sets of materials helpful in this regard are provided in the chapter; we strongly recommend that you assemble these materials and experiment with them in the course of working the program.

In completing the program itself, it is a good idea to cover each page with a sheet of paper, moving it down until the border separating frames is visible; then, when you complete the frame, move the sheet down to the next border. This process will enable you to concentrate on each frame without inadvertently picking up "cues."

Teaching Spotted Lesser Zonks to Freeble

1. There are conflicting theories about how best to teach young Spotted Lesser Zonks to freeble:

1. Some experts say that zonks learn to freeble most quickly if they first observe an adult demonstrate the procedure with expertise (a favorite word in the field). They can then practice freebling themselves, repeating the process until they perfect their technique.
2. Other authorities believe that mature freebling can be best developed if the freeble is first broken down into its component operations. Young zonks can then be given instruction in each of the specific operations in preparation for mature freebling, which should develop in time.
3. Still other theorists claim that since most adults freeble with varying degrees of competence, young zonks will naturally learn to freeble most efficiently when *they* are ready. The emphasis in instruction, therefore, should not be placed upon freebling until the need presents itself (even when readiness is demonstrated, only the *resources* for learning should be provided).

Each of these approaches to freebling has sought to ground itself in some school of psychology. As a result, we are often reminded of the importance of "play freebling," the value of "teaching the whole zonk," and the "problem-oriented," and even the "project-oriented" approach to the freeble. Even you cannot avoid becoming entangled in the controversy. If you were given the sudden responsibility for 25 young zonks, how would you resolve the freeble question? (Check the response selected.)

___A. by implementing theory 1
___B. by implementing theory 2
___C. by implementing theory 3
___D. by first obtaining more information

~~~~~~

2. If you selected one of the three major zonk-teaching strategies described, you might find yourself to be successful, depending, of course, upon how you define "success." But if you decided to resolve the freeble question by first obtaining more information, you would be in a much better position for determining the *best* instructional strategy. What major kinds of information would be helpful?

A. _____

B. _____

C. _____

~~~~~~

3. You would naturally want to obtain more information about

___A. the development of zonks and how they learn
___B. the nature of freebling itself
___C. the resources available for teaching freebling

    In any instructional situation the teacher should carefully consider the learner, the material to be learned, and the resources suited to the task. Consider briefly the implications of these three components of the teaching enterprise for the preparation of effective teachers, and then go on to the next frame.

~~~~~~

4. Suppose you discovered the following information about zonks:

1. A mature zonk is easily recognizable when the primary splotch has darkened into the major splotch.
2. Pre-primary splotches normally appear at 11–12 months of age, giving way to primary splotches at 13–14 months and finally to definite major splotches at 17–18 months.
3. Success in freebling is directly dependent on splotch development. (The pre-primary stage indicates potential for pre-freeble activity; the primary stage indicates potential for completing partial freeble; and the major stage indicates potential for full freeble.)

    The zonks in your group of 25 have an age range of 10 to 15 months. If you prescribe the same freeble instruction for the total group at the same time, you would likely be

___A. creating problems for older zonks
___B. creating problems for younger zonks
___C. creating problems for yourself

~~~~~~

5. With such an arrangement, *everyone* develops problems.
    If you then grouped zonks by splotch development and carefully studied the capabilities of the pre-primary, primary, and major splotch groups in turn, could you prescribe more meaningful freeble instruction?

___A. yes
___B. no
___C. cannot tell from information given

~~~~~~

6. Of course you could! By knowing the capabilities of zonks in each developmental stage in greater detail, you might, for example, provide materials and experiences suited to a particular zonk age range, have older zonks help younger zonks, or even begin to individualize your entire freeble curriculum.

~~~~~~

Piagetian Developmental Stages

7. While human beings do not have easily identifiable splotches to suggest instructional readiness, the Swiss psychologist Jean Piaget discovered that children pass through definite intellectual developmental stages, and that children in each stage exhibit specific intellectual characteristics. If these characteristics are disregarded in instruction, we are in fact trying to teach freebling to all zonks in the same way, even though their *capabilities* for freebling differ greatly. For a teacher, therefore, developing a working knowledge of the intellectual capabilities of children at each developmental state is a(n)

___A. excellent use of time
___B. good use of time
___C. fair use of time
___D. poor use of time

~~~~~~

8. It is clearly an *excellent* use of time. As people interested in becoming the best teachers that we are capable of being, such efforts can lead only to improving our teaching competence. If you answered *B, C,* or *D,* you will have to exert some additional effort to counterbalance your skepticism as we continue.

In order to systematize our thoughts so that we develop a functional frame of reference before we try assessment tasks with children or try to develop appropriate materials, it will be most helpful if we complete a reference chart such as the one that appears on page 7 (you will probably want to make a similar chart on a separate sheet of paper). As each developmental stage is considered, add appropriate lists of characteristics and comments to your "master chart."

In the next frame, we will begin with a brief presentation of the *sensorimotor stage* as an example for completing the chart (note that illustrative characteristics have been filled in for this stage).

~~~~~~

THE SENSORIMOTOR STAGE (from birth to approximately 18 months of age)

9. Although it is true that few teachers work directly with children in this age group, psychologists emphasize the great importance of this stage in the later intellectual development of the child. The value of providing the child with a warm, responsive and stimulating environment cannot be minimized.

Children in the sensorimotor stage encounter objects through random physical movement, without thought. In fact, particular objects "exist" for the child only when he can see, touch, or perhaps hear them in some way. Refer to the sensorimotor portion of the reference chart again and reread the characteristics in light of this brief discussion. Which of the four statements did *not* come from this frame?

___A. Stage is preverbal
___B. An object "exists" only when in the perceptual field of the child
___C. Hidden objects are located through random physical searching
___D. Practical experiences form the substructure for later intellectual development.

~~~~~~

10. As you can see, the illustrative characteristics added to the chart were reworded from the preceding discussion, with the exception of item *A*. We did not feel that it would be necessary to state that the sensorimotor stage is preverbal. From now on, developing the reference chart will be up to you. It will be as useful or as poor as you wish it to be. You might even wish to investigate some additional sources. To begin with, we would suggest:

RICHARD W. COPELAND, *How Children Learn Mathematics—Teaching Implications of Piaget's Research* (New York: Macmillan, 1970).

JOHN H. FLAVELL, *The Developmental Psychology of Jean Piaget* (Princeton, N.J.: Van Nostrand, 1963).

Table 1-1 Intellectual Development Stages *

Developmental Stage	General Age Range	Characteristics of Stage
Sensorimotor	Birth to approximately 18 months	Stage is preverbal An object "exists" only when in the perceptual field of the child Hidden objects are located through random physical searching Practical experiences form the substructure for later intellectual development
Preoperational		
Concrete Operations		
Formal Operations		

* *Chart format adapted from Ronald Anderson et al., Developing Children's Thinking Through Science (Englewood Cliffs, N.J.: Prentice-Hall, Inc., 1970), p. 121.*

HANS FURTH, *Piaget for Teachers* (Englewood Cliffs, N.J.: Prentice-Hall, Inc., 1970).

HERBERT GINSBURG and SYLVIA OPPER, *Piaget's Theory of Intellectual Development: An Introduction* (Englewood Cliffs, N.J.: Prentice-Hall, Inc., 1969).

Go on to the next frame.

~~~~~~

11. A ten-month-old child was lying in his crib and crying loudly. When his mother brought him a rattle and then left him alone again, the crying stopped. From this evidence, it is likely that the child

___A. was crying for the rattle because he liked the touch of it.
___B. was crying for the rattle because he liked the sound of it.
___C. was crying for some other reason (make your own inferences).

~~~~~~

12. The child was not crying *because he wanted the rattle.* Children in this stage do not cry for a specific object since the rattle, in this case, ceases to exist when it is away from him. By the same token, if the child should find a ball in the course of crawling about in a room, it is clear that this would be entirely a random happening and would not involve any conscious search. The answer, therefore, was *C.*

As you continue this chapter, what will you do each time you learn something new about the intellectual development of children?

_____

~~~~~~

13. By now you ought to know the answer: "Add the characteristic to the master chart."

In the next section we will consider how the intellectual development of children progresses as they leave infancy. If you wish to take a break as you work on this program, it is usually a good idea to do so when you have completed the frames dealing with a particular stage. Therefore, either take a breather now or forge ahead to learn some interesting things about primary age children. Go on to the next frame.

~~~~~~

THE PREOPERATIONAL STAGE (from approximately 18 months to 7–8 years)

14. The child learns to think in this stage, but he does not do so by the operation of much logic. Given a physical problem to solve, he will characteristically approach it wholly through trial-and-error. Since he is so bound to his perceptions, i.e., to what he *thinks* he "sees," the preoperational child also lives in an "Alice-in-Wonderland" world where apparent visual contradictions do not cause conflict in his thinking. Consider, for example, this interview with a five-year-old child using a now famous demonstration suggested by Piaget:

Teacher:	(Shows two identical drinking glasses and a pitcher of fruit juice.) "Zac, watch while I pour some juice into each of these two glasses." (Pours the same amount into each.) "Who has more juice, you or I?" (Teacher moves one glass near the child.)
Zachary:	"We both have the same."
Teacher:	"How do you know?"
Zachary:	"Because this juice goes up to here and this juice goes up to here." (Points with finger.)
Teacher:	"All right, now watch while I empty your glass into this new glass." (Teacher produces a third taller and much more narrow glass and empties the child's glass as described.) "Now then, who has more juice, you or I?"
Zachary:	"Me."
Teacher:	"How come?"
Zachary:	"My juice goes way up to here, and yours goes up to there." (Points again.)

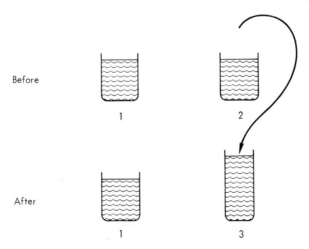

Fig. 1–1   **Conservation of Substance**

From the preceding interview it appears that the preoperational child:

___A. can focus his attention upon the change in liquid height, but cannot simultaneously consider the influence of the difference in glass diameter.
___B. has difficulty in coordinating variables.
___C. has not developed the concept that the total amount of something remains the same even though its appearance is physically altered (in this case the something is the amount of juice).

~~~~~~

15. All three are correct. Read the choices again. *A* was demonstrated in the interview and *B* is really a statement of the same idea in general terms.

Consider *C* carefully. This concept is known as *conservation*. In the interview with Zachary, what type of conservation do you believe the teacher was trying to assess?

___A. conservation of number
___B. conservation of substance
___C. conservation of weight

~~~~~~

16. Perhaps you were able to figure out that this was an example of a problem dealing with conservation of *substance*. In other words, the total amount of juice (substance) remained the same even though it looked different when it was poured into a tall narrow glass. You will find out later why *A* and *C* were not correct. Before we go on, though, we would like you to write a simple and *general* definition for a concept of conservation.

~~~~~~

17. The total amount of something remains the same even though its appearance is altered.

Children in the *preoperational stage* have

___A. developed the concepts of conservation
___B. *not* developed the concepts of conservation

~~~~~~

18. Preoperational children have *not* developed the concepts of conservation. Notice that the plural was used. In addition to conservations of substance, number, and weight, you will soon learn that the child develops several other concepts of conservation as well.

Which of the following characteristics are true, then, of the preoperational child?

___A. He can demonstrate conservation of weight.
___B. An object "exists" for him only when it is in his perceptual field.
___C. He lacks the ability to coordinate variables.
___D. He learns by simple trial-and-error rather than through logic.
___E. He is commonly satisfied with multiple and often contradictory explanations to problems (e.g., an object can be heavy and light, or long and short, at the same time).

~~~~~~

19. *C, D,* and *E* are correct. Preoperational children do *not* conserve weight (*A*), and *B* is a characteristic of the sensorimotor child. Did you really reason out *E* or did you select it only because it was long and sounded impressive? Perhaps we threw a curve since *E* has only been implied. Read *E* again and try to remember to look for this characteristic if you work with preoperational children.

As we go on to the next stage, what are you going to do each time you learn something new about the intellectual development of children?

_____

~~~~~~

20. I think we have made the point by now: *add the characteristic to the master chart.* (All right, we won't mention it again.)

Some very interesting developments take place in the capabilities of children during the next stage. Go on to the next frame when you are ready.

~~~~~~

THE STAGE OF CONCRETE OPERATIONS (from 7–8 years to 11–12 years)

21. As the name of the stage implies, the child in this age range begins to think logically, but this thought is concrete rather than abstract. In other words, while he can now perform simple logical operations, the child can do more advanced thinking if given physical objects to manipulate than he can if he is expected to do the same problems symbolically.

We will illustrate this idea and also give an example of the elementary logical operations that develop in this stage by working with some concrete materials ourselves. The type of operation we will look at more closely is *serial ordering*. This means placing a collection of objects into some *consecutive* arrangement, such as lining children up according to height, or arranging crayons in a box from darkest to lightest colors. If a child in the stage of concrete operations is asked to arrange a collection of objects into various serial orders, will he be most successful

___A. in physically arranging and rearranging the objects themselves?
___B. in completing the problem by symbols using paper and pencil?
___C. by either method, depending on the child?

~~~~~~

22. While he might be successful by either method only if the problem was very simple, the child in the stage of concrete operations would definitely be more successful through working with the objects themselves. In order for you to acquire a better grasp of this idea, prepare the Set I materials in Fig. 1–2 and then go on to the next frame.

~~~~~~

Set I Materials (Serial Order Tiles) *

Items necessary for preparation: Scissors, colored pencils, transparent tape, glue, cardboard

Preparation: Glue pages on cardboard and cut along outside line of each tile. Color all face dots and edge dashes red, and color tile faces and edges as indicated. Bend edges of tile downward and secure corners with transparent tape. Write identifying numeral for each tile on the reverse side.

* These tiles are adapted from Ronald Anderson et al., *Developing Children's Thinking Through Science* (Englewood Cliffs, N.J.: Prentice-Hall, Inc., 1970), p. 123. The tiles are available commercially from Selective Educational Equipment (SEE), Inc., Three Bridge Street, Newton, Mass. 02195.

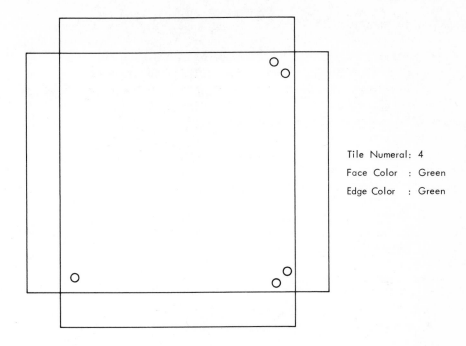

Tile Numeral: 4
Face Color : Green
Edge Color : Green

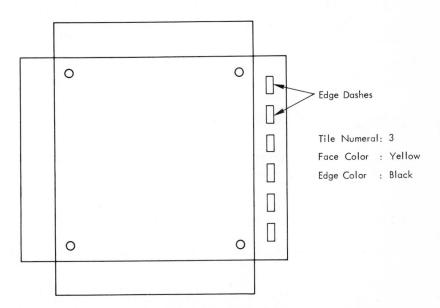

Edge Dashes

Tile Numeral: 3
Face Color : Yellow
Edge Color : Black

Fig. 1–2 Serial Order Tiles

13

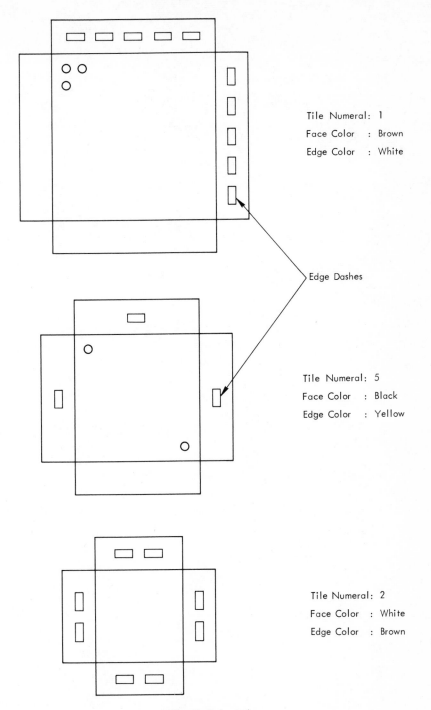

Tile Numeral: 1
Face Color : Brown
Edge Color : White

Edge Dashes

Tile Numeral: 5
Face Color : Black
Edge Color : Yellow

Tile Numeral: 2
Face Color : White
Edge Color : Brown

Fig. 1–2 (cont.)

15

23. The serial order "tiles" that you have assembled can be arranged in a number of serial orders. While this task would be relatively difficult to accomplish symbolically, moving the tiles themselves makes the problem far more manageable. Try this yourself and see how many serial orders you can list, recording the tile numerals as shown (try to list at least 11 *different* types).

1. By size (largest to smallest): 4,3,1,5,2

2. _____

3. _____

4. _____

5. _____

6. _____

7. _____

8. _____

9. _____

10. _____

11. _____

12–22. Repeat 1–11 in *reverse* order, e.g., by size (smallest to largest): 2,5,1,3,4, etc.

~~~~~~

24. How carefully did you observe? Check off the more commonly reported arrangements that you added to your list:

___ 1. By size (largest to smallest): 4,3,1,5,2
___ 2. By ascending order of numerals: 1,2,3,4,5
___ 3. By face color shade (light to dark): 2,3,4,1,5
___ 4. By edge color shade (light to dark): 1,5,4,2,3
___ 5. By number of corners with red dots (fewest to greatest): 2,1,5,4,3
___ 6. By number of corners without red dots (fewest to greatest): 3,4,5,1,2
___ 7. By total number of red dots (lowest to highest): 2,5,1,3,4
___ 8. By number of edges with red dashes (fewest to greatest): 4,3,1,5,2
___ 9. By number of edges without red dashes (fewest to greatest): 2,5,1,3,4
___10. By total number of red dashes (lowest to highest): 4,5,3,2,1
___11. By number of red dashes per dashed edge (fewest to greatest): 4,5,2,1,3
___12–22. Repeat 1–11 in reverse order.

What additional serial orders were you able to report?

_____

_____

∿∿∿∿∿∿∿∿∿∿∿∿∿∿∿∿∿∿∿∿∿∿∿∿∿∿∿

25. You might also have considered weight, or might have specified "size" more carefully as "area" or "length on a side." Children often invent most imaginative solutions to such problems. In order to start gaining some experience in giving assessment tasks to children, then, we recommend strongly that you try the serial order problem with at least one child before going on to frame 26.

∿∿∿∿∿∿∿∿∿∿∿∿∿∿∿∿∿∿∿∿∿∿∿∿∿∿∿

26. The child in the stage of concrete operations also learns to think in terms of *groups,* such as "warm-blooded animals," "legislators," "symphonies" and "verbs." Among the most significant developments in the stage of concrete operations, however, is the idea that the total amount of something remains the same even though its physical appearance is altered. This idea is known as _____.

∿∿∿∿∿∿∿∿∿∿∿∿∿∿∿∿∿∿∿∿∿∿∿∿∿∿∿

27. A concept of conservation.

The concepts of conservation are the key developments in the stage of concrete operations. We will describe each type of conservation in turn and indicate the age range at which the concept usually develops in Column I. You try to match the simple word from Column II that identifies the conservation described.

Column I	*Column II*
___1. The number of items in a group remains the same even though the items are rearranged. (6–7 years of age)	A. Conservation of length
___2. The amount of material in some object remains the same even though its shape is altered. (7–8 years of age)	B. Conservation of volume
___3. The total length of a line remains the same no matter how it is displaced. (7–8 years of age)	C. Conservation of substance
___4. The amount of surface covered by plane geometric figures remains the same no matter how the figures are rearranged on the surface. (8–9 years of age)	D. Conservation of weight

___5. The weight of an object remains the same even though its shape is altered. (9–10 years of age)

E. Conservation of number

___6. The amount of liquid displaced by an object remains the same no matter how the shape of the object is changed. (11–14 years of age)

F. Conservation of area

~~~~~~

28. The preceding frame presented simple definitions for the conservation of number, of substance, of length, of area, of weight and of volume, respectively (*E, C, A, F, D, B*).

The concepts of conservation all develop during the stage of concrete operations. (Check response selected.)

___Yes
___No

~~~~~~

29. No. The conservation of *volume* develops at a later stage. All the other concepts of conservation, however, develop in the stage of concrete operations (with the occasional exception of the conservation of number).

We have been discussing the various conservations in *general* terms. Beginning with the next frame we will consider some *specific* tasks.

Go on to the next frame.

~~~~~~

30. Ten dominoes were arranged on a table so that they formed a large rectangle. A child was asked to observe the pattern, and the dominoes were then rearranged on the table so that they were all far apart. The child was asked whether more of the table was covered by the dominoes in the first arrangement or in the second. He indicated that the same amount of surface was covered in each case. This example was an illustration of the conservation of _____.

~~~~~~

31. Area. The age of the child in the preceding example was most likely

___A. 10 years.
___B. 8 years.

___C. 6 years.
___D. 4 years.

~~~~~~

32. The child would probably have been 8 or 10 years of age. We do not have enough information to make a more accurate estimation.

For each of the following specific examples, indicate the type of conservation illustrated and the age at which this concept usually develops.

A. A straight wire remains the same length even though it is bent into a spiral.

_____

B. A ball of clay submerged in a glass of water causes the water level to rise the same amount whether it is ball-shaped or is fashioned into a pancake-like shape.

_____

C. The number of buttons spread out in a chalk tray remains the same even though the buttons are placed together in a cup.

_____

D. A sealed bag of potato chips weighs the same even though the chips are pulverized.

_____

E. If a container of colored water is used to fill many paper cups, the total volume of water does not change.

_____

~~~~~~

33. The examples illustrate the conservations of

A. length, 7–8 years
B. volume, 14–15 years
C. number, 6–7 years
D. weight, 9–10 years
E. substance, 7–8 years

You may have experienced confusion in distinguishing between con-servation of volume and conservation of substance. By conservation of *volume,* Piaget means the conservation of liquid displacement specifically (reread example *B* in the previous frame). Describe an experiment that you could use with a child to illustrate conservation of substance.

~~~~~~

34. Examples of conservation of substance were described in frames 14 and 32. In addition, you might show two identical spheres of clay and roll one out into a sausage shape and ask the child which of the two shapes then had "more" clay. The child who could conserve substance would respond that the two were equal. How might the child demonstrate that the two shapes were of equal amounts of clay most easily?

~~~~~~

35. The simplest way, though not quantitative, would be to roll the sausage shape back into a sphere and compare its size with the other ball of clay. This idea that the child can return conditions to an original state prior to his actions (in this case rolling the sausage-shaped clay back into a sphere) is termed *reversibility.* As the concepts of conservation develop, the child also learns to demonstrate reversibility in his thought and actions.

If the child upsets a balanced board (see Fig. 1–3) by placing an additional weight on one end, how can he demonstrate reversibility? _____

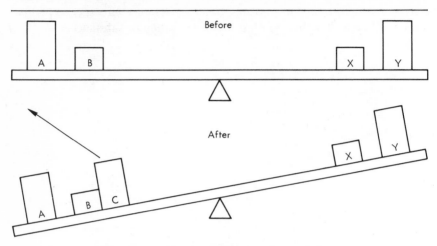

Fig. 1–3   Simple Problem in Reversibility

~~~~~~

36. The answer is simple: by removing the same weight. It should not be necessary to point out that the idea of reversibility is limited, naturally, to physical operations that *can* be reversed.

Indicate a specific example of how a child might demonstrate reversibility for each of the other conservations:

1. number _____

_____

2. length _____

_____

3. area _____

_____

4. weight _____

_____

5. volume _____

_____

~~~~~~

37. As long as you indicated how a child might in effect "undo" the results of his actions and return conditions to their original state, you *know* you are correct.

Which of the concepts of conservation develops in the next stage?

_____

~~~~~~

38. The conservation of volume.

The development of the concepts of conservation is a key characteristic of the stage of concrete operations. (Check response selected.)

__True
__False

~~~~~~

39. True.

If you haven't taken a break recently, you are probably really ready for some conservation of substance of your own by now. After you have had a coffee or a coke, move on to frame 40 to find out about the types of intellectual skills that you yourself have developed. Our next consideration, then, is the most advanced developmental stage.

~~~~~~

THE STAGE OF FORMAL OPERATIONS (beginning at 11–12 years of age and continuing through life)

40. The individual in the stage of formal operations learns to manipulate symbols and deal with ideas verbally without the necessity for always working directly with the physical objects. In other words, he becomes able to think in increasingly abstract terms.

The individual in this stage also learns to hypothesize *before* doing something. He can suggest for example "what might happen if I put an ice cube in a glass of cooking oil," and can then perform the operations necessary to either prove or disprove his suppositions. How would a child in the stage of concrete operations tend to differ in his approach to the same problems?

~~~~~~

41. A child in the stage of concrete operations would tend to be quite closely bound to the manipulation of physical objects. He would probably forge ahead quickly to *see* what might happen, rather than to try to reason out a solution based upon previous experience with liquids and solids.

How would a child in the stage of concrete operations differ from a child in the stage of formal operations in trying to solve the following problem?

A student has a penny, a nickel, a dime, a quarter, a half dollar and a silver dollar on a tray. What two-coin combinations can he select from this collection of objects?

The child in the stage of concrete operations would _____

_____

_____

~~~~~~

42. Once again the child in the stage of concrete operations would be more successful in *manipulating* such a collection of coins than he would be if he were expected to do the same problem more abstractly through symbols.

Also illustrated here is a major development in the stage of formal operations, the establishment of a "combinatorial system" in the logic of the individual. This means that the child in the stage of formal operations becomes able to make systematic *combinations* of objects or symbols. In the problem from the preceding frame, how many two-coin combinations were possible? _____

~~~~~~

43. In order to figure out that 15 combinations were possible, it was necessary for you to make *systematic combinations,* and this ability is a key characteristic of the stage of formal operations. How might the combinations made by the child in the stage of concrete operations differ?

~~~~~~

44. They would differ in that they would not be systematic. That is, while he could name various two-coin combinations at random, he would find it quite difficult to report *all* the combinations possible.

Write a brief problem in some area other than mathematics that requires the establishment of a combinatorial system for solution. For example: a three-part meal is to be served consisting of one kind of meat, one kind of potato and one kind of vegetable. Two kinds of meat are available (chicken and turkey), two kinds of potatoes (boiled and fried), and two kinds of vegetables (squash and turnips). Write all the possible meals that can be served consisting of one meat, one type of potato and one vegetable.

Now it's your turn.

~~~~~~

45. To see how rigorous your problem was, try it out on someone.

In addition to being able to solve problems that require the use of combinations, the individual in the stage of formal operations also learns to perform controlled experiments, where single variables are isolated in turn to observe their effects.

To illustrate, if an individual wished to determine the best conditions of *light, water,* and *soil* for his front lawn, what types of experiments would he make in comparing an "A" plot of grass with a "B" plot of grass.

1. _____

2. _____

3. _____

~~~~~~

46. He would

1. vary the *light* while keeping soil and water conditions the same for both plots.
2. vary the *water* treatment while keeping light and soil conditions the same for both plots.
3. vary the *soil* conditions while keeping the light and water conditions the same for both plots.

This is what is meant by isolating single variables in turn to observe their effects (coordination of variables).

Describe an experiment that could be performed in your major area of teaching interest to illustrate coordination of variables.

~~~~~~

47. We'll leave this one up to you. How about consulting with the person to whom you gave the problem in frame 44?

As a final characteristic, because of the existence of the mental "combinatorial structure," the individual in the stage of formal operations learns to combine propositions (statements). He may reason, for example, in the following ways:

1. "It must be A and B" (conjunction)
2. "It's either A or B" (disjunction)

3. "It's neither A nor B" (negation)
4. "If it's A, then C will be true" (implication)

Some examples of combining propositions are:

1. My sleepiness is due to the lateness of the hour *and* the warmth of the room. (conjunction)
2. My sleepiness is due to *either* the lateness of the hour or the warmth of the room. (disjunction)
3. My sleepiness is due to *neither* the lateness of the hour nor the warmth of the room. (negation)
4. If my sleepiness is due to the warmth of the room, then ＿＿＿＿＿＿＿＿

＿＿＿＿＿＿＿＿＿＿＿＿＿＿＿＿＿＿＿＿＿＿＿＿. (Try to com-

plete the sentence with an implication.)

~~~~~~~~~~~~~~~~~~~~~~~~~~~~~~~~

48. Possibilities include:

1. raising the temperature will increase my sleepiness
2. lowering the temperature will decrease my sleepiness
3. I will be sleepy at this room temperature anytime during the day

Go on to the next frame.

~~~~~~~~~~~~~~~~~~~~~~~~~~~~~~~~

49. By now you should have developed a useful reference chart in your own words. Let's face the facts, though: in learning to become an effective teacher, paperwork can go only so far. If you will try some more of the tasks described in this chapter with children, you will see theory come alive. As one parent stated, "Piaget knows more about my kids than I do."

The importance of developing and trying tasks with children cannot be overemphasized. Working with children will enable you to develop a more functional understanding of their developmental stages, and will enable you to learn to communicate with them more effectively. You will un-doubtedly find yourself greatly inspired by the responses of the individuals you work with. The style of the interview is up to you. After using the serial order tiles you assembled earlier, you might, for example, then try serial order tasks with collections of dowels, nails, washers, and even shells or rock samples. As you experiment in such practical situations, remember to refer to your chart often. In the next section we'll give you a "mystery" to solve for practice.

~~~~~~

"Where's Charlie?"

50. Our "mystery student" is Charlie. Use your reference chart to help determine Charlie's developmental stage based on his responses to some simple problems.

Our interviewer first placed two rows of three coins each on a table. He asked Charlie to observe carefully while the coins in one row were placed in a pile. When questioned, Charlie responded that there were just as many coins in the remaining row as there were in the pile. Charlie is probably in which stage?

___A. sensorimotor
___B. preoperational
___C. concrete operations
___D. (not enough information given)

~~~~~~

51. We can be sure that Charlie is *not* in the sensorimotor stage since he knows his numbers (up to three anyway) and can carry on a conversation. Not only do we *not have enough information,* but something was also wrong with the task itself. What was wrong?

_____

~~~~~~

52. No, this was not a "trick question." The interviewer could not test for conservation of number (as we infer that he was doing) *with only three coins.* The number of elements used was not great enough to make any convincing change in appearance.

The interviewer next took two identical sheets of composition paper and tore one entire sheet into very small pieces. He then asked Charlie which had "more" paper—the shredded sheet or the one that was still intact. Charlie stated that the shredded sheet definitely had more. Now we can say that Charlie is in which stage:

___A. preoperational
___B. concrete operations

__C. formal operations
__D. (not enough information given)

~~~~~~

53. We still do not have enough information. To attempt to categorize an individual based upon only one or two simple tasks is a very poor procedure. Why might this be so?

~~~~~~

54. A particular task might not be well formulated (as was the case when the interviewer tried to use only three coins to assess conservation of number), or perhaps the questioning techniques were such that the interviewer failed to communicate properly with the subject. It is advisable therefore to try *several* related tasks and to try various questioning techniques. Can we conclude then that Charlie does not conserve substance? (Check response selected.)

__Yes
__No

~~~~~~

55. No, we cannot. Perhaps he somehow misunderstood and thought that the interviewer was asking about *surface area* (each time a material is broken apart, additional surface area becomes exposed).

After experimenting with a variety of materials and tasks, the interviewer found that Charlie could conserve length, area, and weight and could demonstrate reversibility for each.

When he was asked to predict what would happen when a solid cylinder made of aluminum was submerged in a container of water and then replaced with a solid (and identical) cylinder made of lead, Charlie predicted that the heavier cylinder would cause the water level to rise higher than the lighter cylinder would. It *appears* that Charlie does not conserve _____.

~~~~~~

56. Volume. Finally, Charlie was given the following written problem to solve:

A chef wishes to observe the effects of three temperatures and three baking times on a new type of pastry. If the different temperatures he will test are 375°F, 400°F, and 425°F, and the different baking times he will use are 30 minutes, 40 minutes and 45 minutes, what experiments must be made to test all the possible combinations? (Write the temperature and the baking time for each experiment.)

To answer the problem, Charlie reported five different experiments apparently selected at random. Indications are that Charlie has developed a combinatorial system. (Check response selected.)

__Yes
__No

~~~~~~

57. No, it does not appear that he has (although some "system" was necessary for even partial success). While additional tasks and problems would be advisable for confirmation, if Charlie had developed a combinatorial system, he should be able to report all of the nine combinations possible in systematic fashion (assuming he interpreted the problem correctly).

Judging from *all* of our observations then, Charlie seems to exhibit the behavior expected of an individual in which stage:

__A. preoperational
__B. concrete operations
__C. formal operations
__D. (not enough information given)

~~~~~~

58. The stage of concrete operations. Of the two age ranges below, it is *more* likely that Charlie is

___A. 7–8 years of age
___B. 10–11 years of age

~~~~~~

59. Based upon the evidence presented (e.g., the ability to conserve area and weight, and partial success with the combinatorial problem), Charlie is more likely to be 10–11 years of age.

It is now time for you to try your ideas for tasks with children. Rather than continue with additional examples, we would like *you* to get involved with more children directly and see what you observe. As we stated earlier, there is no prescribed interview technique, so use your imagination. Try various tasks with the same child and try the same task with different children. You might even wish to tape record your sessions. You will find these experiences to be most enjoyable and highly involving. Share your observations with other teachers and with prospective teachers.

~~~~~~

A Brief Review Using a New Set of Materials

60. As you gain experience in trying the many examples and suggestions presented throughout this chapter in working with children, you will soon find interesting variations to try with the same materials and will soon find yourself using entirely new materials of your own design. To give you some additional ideas for devising tasks, perhaps you would find it useful to observe a number of interview sessions being conducted. Two films that are recommended for this purpose are *Conservation* and *Classification*. Both are available from Davidson Films, 1757 Union Street, San Francisco, Calif. 94123.

If you are a pre-school or kindergarten teacher, you may also find it useful to investigate a complete Piaget-centered program, the *Early Childhood Curriculum,* available from American Science and Engineering, 20 Overland Street, Boston, Mass. 02215. Go on to the next frame.

~~~~~~

Set II Materials (Combinations Problem)

Items Necessary for Preparation: Scissors, colored pencil, transparent tape, glue, cardboard.

Preparation: Glue pages on cardboard and cut along all dashed lines so that you end up with 10 little cards of each of the following geometric shapes: circle, square, triangle, rectangle, parallelogram, and six "extra" cards. Then place all cards face down (so the geometric shape is not visible) and color the margin near *one* edge on the back of each card. If you have done this correctly you should be able to arrange the cards so that the colored margins form a continuous line as shown in Figure 1–5 (see p. 38).

Fig. 1–4   Set II Materials

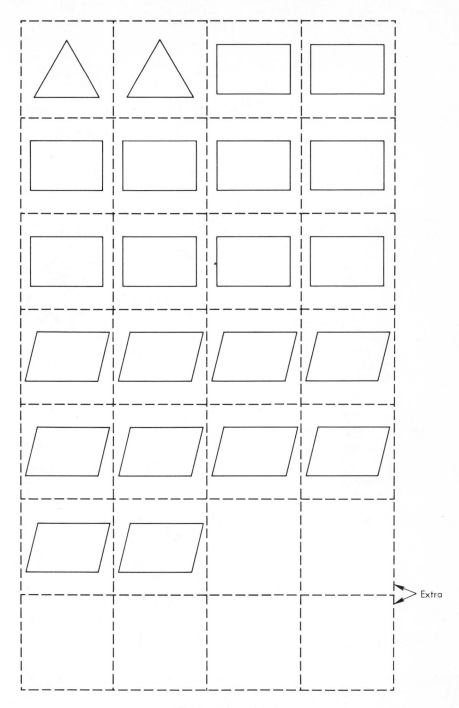

Extra

Fig. 1–4 (cont.)

61. Although the Set II Materials are designed primarily for working with the logic of combinations, they are also useful for a brief review of some of the tasks we have introduced. Prepare the Set II Materials in Fig. 1–4 and try the combination problem yourself:

Select three *different* geometric shapes and clip them together as a set (provide paper clips). Make as many sets as you can so that no two sets are alike. You will have material left over.

How many combinations are possible? —

~~~~~~

62. You were probably able to determine that 10 combinations of three *different* shapes were possible. Of course the problem would be far more difficult if the student could use two or more of the same kind of geometric shapes in a combination.

The Set II Materials can also be used in other ways as well. How might they be used to test for conservation of number?

~~~~~~

63. First, the materials should be used face-down so that the geometric shapes do not distract. If the child is shown two identical rows of 10–15 squares, he can establish that the number of squares in each row is the same through a one-to-one correspondence. If the squares in one row are then placed in a pile, the child can be questioned with respect to the *number* of squares in the pile compared to the number of squares in the remaining row. How might we use the same materials to test for the conservation of length?

~~~~~~

64. We could arrange 10–15 squares face-down with the colored margins of each square forming a continuous straight line. The squares could then be rearranged so that the line forms a zig-zag pattern.

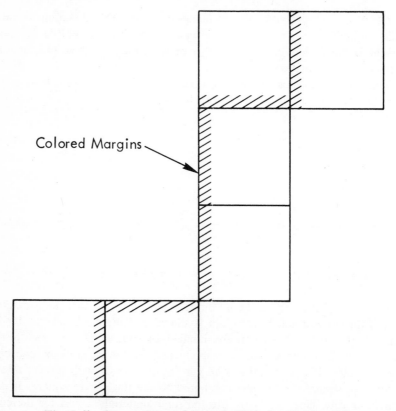

Colored Margins

Fig. 1–5   Conservation of Length With Set II Materials

The child would be questioned regarding whether the total length of the line had changed through moving the squares. How might the squares be used to test for conservation of area?

~~~~~~

65. One possibility would be to arrange 48 squares on a table so that they form two large rectangles composed of 24 squares each. One rectangle could then be rearranged so that all of the squares were spread out. The child would be asked which group covered more of the table, the one remaining in a rectangle or the one that was rearranged.

Go on to the next frame.

~~~~~~

66. Your *introduction* to the intellectual development stages of children has now been completed. We hope sincerely that you will use your reference chart and refer to this chapter again as you continue to work with children. As a sort of "sampling" of what you have gained, we urge you to try the suggestions for self-evaluation that follow. Since working with children is the point of everything that we are preparing for, we would rather not think of this frame as the end of the program. We would rather consider this point as being the beginning. . . .

~~~~~~

Suggestions for Self-Evaluation

1. For each of the following intellectual developmental stage ranges indicate the *name* of the stage and write the *letters* of appropriate characteristics selected from the list below:

A. The child can solve problems in abstract terms without the need for physically manipulating objects.
B. The child learns to demonstrate reversibility in thought and action.
C. Conservation of area develops.
D. The child is simple-goal-directed but does not use logical thinking.
E. The child learns to arrange a collection of objects in a serial order.
F. An object "exists" only when in the perceptual field of the child.
G. The child's answers indicate that the concepts of conservation have not yet developed.
H. Conservation of volume develops.
 I. The child first learns to perform logical operations.
J. The combinatorial system develops.
K. The child develops the capacity to theorize *before* he experiments.
L. The stage is preverbal.
M. The child learns to combine propositions.
N. Apparent visual contradictions do not cause conflict in the thinking of the child.
O. The child learns to perform controlled experiments.
P. Conservation of weight develops.

Birth to approximately 18 months of age
Stage: _____
Characteristics: ___ ___ ___ ___ ___ ___

18 months to 7–8 years
Stage: _____
Characteristics: ___ ___ ___ ___ ___ ___

7–8 years to 11–12 years
Stage: _____
Characteristics: ___ ___ ___ ___ ___ ___

11–12 years through maturity
Stage: _____
Characteristics: ___ ___ ___ ___ ___ ___

2. List the six concepts of conservation in the order in which they develop and suggest an illustrative task of your own device for each that could be used in an interview session with a nine-year-old child to assess his ability to conserve.

3. Describe how students in the stage of concrete operations and students in the stage of formal operations would differ in their approach to the following *type* of problem:

A piece of equipment used in a learning experiment with mice consists of four different tunnels numbered *1, 2, 3,* and *4,* which connect a wooden cage to a metal cage. List all of the possible ways that a mouse can make a "round trip" from the wooden cage to the metal cage and back again by writing the numerals of the two tunnels that might be used on each run.

4. Describe a collection of objects that could be used for serial ordering tasks with children, and list the major variables by which the collection could be so ordered.

Formulating performance objectives

2

DONALD LEE TROYER

Western Illinois University

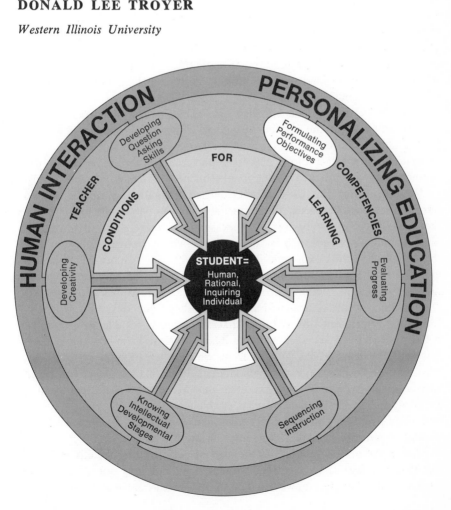

I: Performance Objectives

Who needs performance objectives? We do! All of us have, at some time, enrolled in a class in which we were not sure of just what the instructor wanted us to learn. We sat there, from the very first meeting to the last session, trying to "psych out" the instructor.

Various reasons could account for the lack of clarity regarding course goals which exists in many classrooms. The purpose of this chapter is to examine one avenue which can greatly enhance the clarity of a course, i.e., the explicit stating of course objectives.

If this is your first chance to examine the performance objective, you should gain some ideas that will serve you during your teaching. The performance objective differs from the "traditional" objective in that it is a statement clearly indicating how well a student must perform a given action (behavior) under particular conditions. Thus, the teacher who employs performance objectives is required to earmark carefully certain behaviors which he desires his students to exhibit upon the conclusion of the teaching of that unit or course.

A teacher armed with a knowledge of performance objectives gains in several ways. Once the instructor has developed performance objectives for the unit or the entire course and designated the behavior or behaviors desired, he can select those processes and content topics which he can arrange and rearrange into instructional sequences which maximize learning.

The use of performance objectives aids in evaluation. Since the desired terminal behavior has been stated together with the conditions under which the behavior is to be performed, assessment is merely the arranging of those conditions established in the performance objective. By examining the degree of success experienced by his students, the teacher has objective evidence for his evaluation. In this way he can prescribe additional and/or new and varied instructional procedures and materials as needed.

Individualization of instruction has long been the desire of teachers. Individualizing instruction requires that the teacher be able to assess the behaviors achieved by each student. Once student behaviors have been assessed, the teacher has a base from which a meaningful instructional sequence can be developed for each student. Performance objectives, being specific in the type of behavior desired and the degree of skill with which a student must perform that behavior, enable a teacher to assess his students and then prescribe instructional tasks and sequences. In this way the student progresses at a pace most appropriate for him.

Maybe you are a "veteran" in the area of performance objectives. If so, this chapter might serve as a worthwhile review. You may not need to read further in this chapter, however. Try to answer the pre-test questions: If you can answer the questions at the level designated as acceptable, I suggest that you skip this chapter if you like. If your level of achievement is not at the acceptable level, why don't you work through the program in this chapter and then try the post-test.

II: Pre-test

The purpose of the measure that you are about to take is to determine if you can perform the behaviors designated in the chapter's performance objectives (the chapter's performance objectives are listed on page 48). Read each question and give your answer. After completing the questions, check yourself by comparing your answers with those given immediately following the pre-test.

PRE-TEST QUESTIONS

1. Apart from the rationale, list the three components of a performance objective.

A. _____

B. _____

C. _____

2. Examine the following statements. Are they acceptable performance objectives?

yes   no

___   ___   A. After completing the mapping unit, the student should have an understanding of map reading.

___   ___   B. After completing the unit on division in which the divisor has a value between 10 and 100 and the quotient may have a remainder, the student, given a work sheet of similar division problems, should be able to calculate the correct answer to 80% of the problems.

___   ___   C. After completing the unit on rocks, the student should be able to demonstrate on a test an understanding of rocks.

___   ___   D. Given five shapes (cone, cylinder, cube, pyramid, sphere), the student should be able to name all shapes.

— — E. After completing the swimming class, the student should demonstrate a knowledge of the crawl, backstroke, and the side stroke.

3. Examine the following objective. Identify that portion which constitutes (a) the situation, (b) the behavioral term, and (c) the acceptance level statement.

Given a short story, a paper, and pencil, the student should be able to identify the major theme the author was presenting. The theme will be considered identified when the major idea presented by the author is expressed in one or two complete sentences.

A. Situation: _____

B. Behavioral Term: _____

C. Acceptance Level Statement: _____

4. Change the following non-performance objective so that it is a performance objective.

The student should demonstrate a knowledge of the use of a comma, semicolon, and colon.

5. Write a performance objective on any topic.

~~~~~~

PRE-TEST ANSWERS

1. A. the situation
   B. the behavioral term

   C. the acceptance level statement
   (Answers similar to *A, B,* and *C* are acceptable.)
2. A. No
  B. Yes
  C. No
  D. Yes
  E. No
3. A. The situation is *given a short story, paper, and pencil.*
  B. The behavioral term is *identify.*
  C. The acceptance level statement is the second sentence.
4. Several possibilities exist. Any statement which develops a situation, changes "demonstrate a knowledge of" to some behavioral term which does just that, and adds an acceptance level statement to indicate how well the student must perform is a satisfactory performance objective. If you did this, give yourself credit for having the question correct. Some examples are given below.

A. The student, after completing the programmed instruction booklet on how to punctuate correctly using the comma, semicolon, and colon, should be able to punctuate correctly fifteen of twenty sentences which require these three marks of punctuation.

B. Given an examination consisting of twenty sentences, the student should be able to punctuate each using the comma, semicolon, and the colon. Acceptable level of performance is correctly punctuating fifteen of the twenty sentences.

C. After completing the unit on the usage of the comma, semicolon, and the colon, the student should be able to punctuate correctly fifteen of twenty sentences given him during an examination.

5. Any objective is satisfactory if it contains all three elements of a performance objective. It should be stated so that it is not ambiguous to another person of comparable background and/or a student for whom the objective was prepared.

~~~~~~

How well did you do? If you answered correctly all five of the questions, you did an excellent job. I see no need for you to read further unless you are curious. If you were accurate on four of the five items, you probably know what you are doing but a little review will not hurt you. A score of three or less means you should read through this program.

The remainder of the chapter has three sections dealing with the development of performance objectives; (a) *What is a performance objective?* (b) *How can a performance objective be constructed?* and (c) *Why use performance objectives?* A post-test follows to determine if the objectives for the chapter have been achieved.

Examine the performance objectives listed below so that you will have the behaviors in mind that you will be requested to exhibit at the end of this chapter.

Chapter Objectives

1. After completing this chapter and without aid of reference materials, the reader should be able to list the three components of a performance objective. Acceptable performance would be naming the situation, the behavioral term, and the acceptance level statement.
2. Given several objectives which are stated in performance and non-performance terms, the reader should be able to identify the performance objective. Acceptable level of performance would be selecting 90% correctly.
3. Given a performance objective, the reader should be able to identify the situation, the behavioral term, and the acceptable level of performance required. The acceptable level of performance would be correctly identifying the three components of the objective 90% of the time.
4. Given an objective stated in non-performance terms, the reader should be able to rewrite that objective in performance terms. Acceptable level of performance would be writing an objective which contains all three components of a performance objective.
5. Given the opportunity to select any topic he wishes, the reader should be able to write a performance objective for that topic. Acceptance level of performance would be an objective which contains all three components of the performance objective.

III: What Is a Performance Objective?

What is a performance objective? It is a statement which (a) clearly gives the conditions under which the student will be evaluated (the situation), (b) designates the behavior the student must demonstrate (behavioral term), and (c) indicates the minimum level at which the student must perform in order to be rated acceptable (acceptable level statement).

Instruction needs stated objectives. It does not matter whether the instruction takes place in a formal classroom setting or an informal one, nor does it matter if the instructional level is pre-school or post-graduate. What is important is that all concerned know where they are going.

If we analyze instructional procedure to determine its components we find something like this. First, it is necessary to decide on the objectives; that is, what do we want to accomplish with this instructional unit? It follows that we need to determine which materials and teaching strategies are needed to meet the established goals best. Furthermore, we must decide the minimum level of performance expected from the students as we assess their performance.

Most teachers do state objectives, select materials, and designate the teaching strategy to be followed. Some even consider the type of evaluation to be given prior to teaching the unit. However, many teachers fail to express these objectives so both they and their students are clear as to the type of terminal performance wanted and the level of performance which is acceptable to satisfy the established objective. This is where performance objectives have been playing the most important role.

Probably the best way to clarify your thinking and to develop a greater understanding of just what constitutes performance objectives is to formulate some of them.

IV: How Can a Performance Objective Be Constructed?

Instructions: The following section is made up of separate parts called frames. Read each frame carefully and then, when you are satisfied that you understand the ideas expressed in the frame, answer the question(s) for that frame. Immediately following each frame is a section which gives the answer(s) and an explanation of the answer(s). *Use a separate piece of paper to cover the answer(s)* as you work through the section. Always confirm your answers before going to the next frame.

~~~~~~

1. The first step in any instructional procedure is to decide which traits you want your students to possess at the end of your instruction. Another way of saying this is

___A. that behaviorally-stated objectives should be written prior to initiating instruction. Refer to *A* only under the answer.
___B. that goals or objectives which are broadly stated are adequate for planning lessons. Refer to *B* only under the answer.

~~~~~~

ANSWER

A. If you marked *A,* you are correct; good for you! Proceed to frame 2.
B. Since you marked *B,* let's try again. Remember that it is necessary to decide exactly where we want to go before we can select the best way to get there.

For a teacher this means selecting the traits he wants his students to be able to exhibit upon completion of the instruction.

~~~~~~

2. Broadly stated goals may be helpful in giving an overview of what you desire to "get across," but such statements are so general that they are of little value when selecting the instructional strategies for the course. More specific objectives are needed.

In order to be specific when writing your objectives, you must be sure the statements possess three components. They are

A. the situation,
B. the behavioral term, and
C. the acceptance level statement.

The situation is meant to make clear the conditions your student will be placed under during the time you ask him to perform the behavior being assessed. Therefore, you must be sure that another competent person can establish like testing conditions from the information provided.

Some people prefer to express the type of instruction the student has undergone. This is fine but does not release the writer from specifically stating the testing conditions.

Select from *A, B,* or *C* above that component of an objective which was defined as covering the conditions under which the evaluation measure is administered to the student.

~~~~~~

ANSWER

You should have selected *A,* the *situation.* Depending on the personal preference and upon the particular type of performance objective being written, the situation *may* refer to those experiences, materials, etc., that the student was exposed to during his instruction. It *must* include the materials and/or the environment to which the student is exposed during the evaluation process. Some objectives will contain both the type of instruction undergone and the type of circumstances in which the student is placed during testing.

~~~~~~

3. In order for the teacher to determine how well a student has done, he must elect a performance which is measurable, some capability which serves to indicate the degree of the student's achievement. Since the teacher is unable to look into the mind, he must examine behavior—the actions or the product of the actions of the student being tested.

Check the component of a performance objective which designates the type of action required of the student.

__A. the situation
__B. the behavioral term
__C. the acceptance level statement

ANSWER

The *behavioral term* (B). It is that word or phrase which expresses the type of task required of the student. This word or phrase denotes some action, some performance the student must exhibit. Hence, the presence of a behavioral term enables the teacher to measure how well the student can accomplish the designated task.

4. The level of performance required for any group of students would be unique to that group. For example, the quality of work expected from a seventh grader in woodworking would not necessarily be the same as that required of a high school senior in a similar class. The degree of performance required within a given grade level or even within a given classroom might vary depending upon the potential of the students involved. Therefore, it is important that the instructor specify the minimum level of performance which is acceptable in such a way that both he and his students will know when it is reached.

Check the component of a performance objective which establishes the minimal level of performance.

__A. the situation
__B. the behavioral objective
__C. the acceptance level statement

ANSWER

The *acceptance level statement* (C) is correct. Once the pupil meets this level of performance, he has satisfactorily achieved that objective. If the student does not achieve at the minimum level of performance, more and/or varied instruction is in order. More drill may be required. Review could be the type of instruction which is most appropriate. However, all too often teachers overlook the fact that a new and totally fresh instructional approach may better serve to meet the objective.

~~~~~~

5. Let's take a quick check to see how you are doing. List the three components of a performance objective.

A. _____

B. _____

C. _____

~~~~~~

ANSWER

A. the situation
B. the behavioral term
C. the acceptance level statement

Answers *A, B,* and *C* or similar answers are acceptable.

Did you get all three correct? Very good. If you missed any, you should return to the beginning of part IV on page 49 and review with more care the materials to this point.

~~~~~~

6. Now let us construct some performance objectives. First, write the situation. Remember, the situation is an explicit definition of the conditions you will impose upon the student during the evaluation session. When first attempting to write performance objectives, it may be helpful to start with the words *after, given,* or *having.* However, it is not essential that these terms be used.

Do any of the following meet the definition of a situation?

yes　no

___ ___　A. Given a list of ten United States presidents and a list of fifteen historical events in two different columns . . .

___ ___　B. After reading the chapter on the United States presidents . . .

___ ___　C. Given a paper, pencil, and a list of ten names of United States presidents . . .

— — D. Having a list of United States presidents and while viewing a film strip depicting ten historical events . . .

— — E. After viewing a film strip depicting ten historical events and without any additional materials . . .

~~~~~~

ANSWER

A. Yes. Here we have clearly indicated the materials available to the student. He will have a list of ten United States presidents and fifteen historical events. As of yet we do not know the behavior required of him, but we do know with what he has to work.

B. No. We know what the student had to do prior to being evaluated, but we do not know what the conditions are under which he must perform. Will he be asked to name ten United States presidents with the book opened or closed? May he use notes to answer several essay questions? We stated earlier that the conditions during testing must be given in the situation. You can see that the conditions for evaluation are not clearly stated in *B*. We will have to restate it, but not now. We will work on restating objectives later.

C. Yes. This answer tells us just what is available to the students: a paper, pencil, and a list of ten United States presidents. We don't know what will be asked of the student, but his situation is clear. This is an acceptable situation.

D. Yes. Again, as in *A* and *C* above, we know the conditions for testing. In this item the student will be asked to perform in some way while viewing this particular film strip.

E. Yes. This situation is acceptable because it states "without any additional materials" which satisfies our requirement of stating the testing conditions. It also notes the prior type of instruction (after viewing a film strip depicting ten historical events) which *may* be added but is *not required* to meet our definition of a situation.

If you were correct on all of the above five situations, skip to frame 8. If you are unsure of yourself or missed one or more of the situations in frame 6, move on to frame 7.

~~~~~~

7. Let us try some situations again. Do any of the following meet the definition of the situation?

yes no

— — A. After completing the unit on the various types of stitches . . .

— — B. Given needle, thread, and a small piece of cloth . . .

___ ___ C. After completing the programmed unit on various types of stitches and while examining a piece of cloth with five different stitches . . .

~~~~~~

ANSWER

A. No. It just expresses the prior type of instruction.

B. Yes. If you said yes, good! It clearly states the testing conditions.

C. Yes. Now don't let that "after completing the programmed unit on various types of stitches" fool you. Certainly, that is the prior instruction. Remember, we never said you could not include the prior type of instruction if you like. However, prior instruction alone is not enough. In this item we have more; the part "while examining a piece of cloth with five different stitches" tells the state in which the student is placed. In this way, this item meets the definition of a situation.

~~~~~~

8. Some people feel that both the past instruction and an exact description of the conditions under which the person is being tested are necessary for the situation to be complete. We have not been that rigorous. We stated that the situation should explicitly define the conditions which will be imposed upon the student during the evaluation. It would seem that the best situation is one which explicitly gives the conditions for testing in the minimum number of words. Thus, you may or may not choose to include the previous type of instruction when writing the exact testing conditions.

Now it is time for you to try your hand at writing the situation for a performance objective. Select your own topic. Remember to designate clearly the materials and/or the environment in which you expect to place the student. You may or may not desire to include the type of prior instruction given.

~~~~~~

ANSWER

Check to see if you are correct by asking yourself if the situation is detailed in such a way that one of your students or a fellow teacher could establish the test conditions you intended. If so, you are doing a fine job. If you are not sure of your ability to write a situation maybe you should return to frame 6 on page 52 and review the material on how to write a situation.

~~~~~~

9. Now, which component of a performance objective could come next?

~~~~~~

ANSWER

Either the behavioral term or the acceptance level statement is correct. There is *no rigid order* when writing the three components of a performance objective but frequently the sequence is (1) the situation, (2) the behavioral term, and (3) the acceptance level statement. For that reason alone we will deal next with the behavioral term. However, it is perfectly acceptable to elect a different order when writing performance objectives.

If you could not remember either answer, return to frames 1–5 on pages 49–52. This should clear up any difficulties you are having.

~~~~~~

10. The purpose of the behavioral term is to designate a behavior, an action which is observable and measurable. Not all words used in objectives do express a performance required of the student. The teacher develops objectives in order to clarify. Using a nonbehavioral term results in ambiguity. Thus, it is most important that an unambiguous behavioral term be used when writing performance objectives.

Let's examine some words. Indicate which words are behavioral (B), which are nonbehavioral (N).

A. to know	___	H. to group	___
B. to select	___	I. to write	___
C. to identify	___	J. to have insight	___
D. to understand	___	K. to list	___
E. to appreciate	___	L. to match	___
F. to state	___	M. to feel	___
G. to learn	___	N. to name	___

~~~~~~

ANSWER

A.	N	H.	B
B.	B	I.	B
C.	B	J.	N
D.	N	K.	B
E.	N	L.	B
F.	B	M.	N
G.	N	N.	B

~~~~~~

11. Hopefully you did not miss more than one or two of the above terms. Nevertheless, we should look at behavioral terms some more. We stated earlier that a behavioral term must express some type of activity the student has to perform, something we can observe and measure. We can observe a student *selecting, identifying, stating, grouping.* We cannot directly observe a student *knowing, understanding, appreciating,* or *feeling.*

Do we want our students to know, understand, appreciate, and feel? Certainly. But we also want to be able to determine to what extent they know, understand, appreciate, and feel. Thus, instead of using words which cannot be directly placed in measurable terms, we simply employ behavioral terms that directly measure the degree of knowing and understanding.

Let us take an example of how an objective may be stated so that when an understanding exists, it can be observable. Select the objective which dictates a need for an understanding of map reading yet is expressed in performance terms. Read only the answer with the letter corresponding to the letter of your selection.

___A. Given a map which is color coded to show differences in relief, the student should be able to label the height (give in feet from sea level) of five different areas.

___B. Given a map which is color coded to show differences in relief, the student should be able to show an understanding of map reading.

~~~~~~

ANSWER

A. If *A* was your selection, very good. You noted that in order to "label the heights" an understanding of map reading had to exist. The degree of understanding can be placed in measurable terms. It is only in this way that the teacher can observe the varying degrees of understanding that exist in the classroom and make the needed adjustments in his instructional procedure. Proceed to frame 13.

B. Since you chose *B,* let's try again. It was just stated that understanding was not a behavioral term. Your selection of *B* means you do not possess the ability (behavior) to select a behavioral term. The phrase "to show an understanding" is ambiguous. We have no idea of the action or conduct that the writer of the objective would accept as evidence of an understanding of map reading.

Please refer to answer *A* again. Note that the degree of understanding is placed in measurable terms by asking the student to "label the height" of various locations on the map. We can measure and observe that behavior, a most important thing for the teacher when assessing student progress.

~~~~~~

12. Let's try another one. Select the example which gives us an observable, measurable way of determining how well the students "know" the material.

___A. Given paper and pencil, the student should know the impact that the signing of the Declaration of Independence had on the development of this country.

___B. Given paper and pencil, the student should be able to list three instances where the signing of the Declaration of Independence had an impact on the development of this country.

~~~~~~

Answer

If you selected answer *B* in preference to *A,* good. It is true that both objectives want to determine how much the student knows about the impact that the signing of the Declaration of Independence had upon the early development of this country. However, answer *B* enables us to measure the degree of knowing by requiring the student to list certain pertinent instances.

~~~~~~

13. When developing performance objectives we will try to avoid words like *know* and *understand*. We want words of action for behavioral terms. You should be able to list eight or ten words rather quickly. Try it.

A. _____   F. _____

B. _____   G. _____

C. _____   H. _____

D. _____   I. _____

E. _____   J. _____

~~~~~~

ANSWER

Some behavioral terms you might have listed are *identify, select, list, name, construct, write, measure, distinguish, design, analyze, describe, contrast, transfer, match, select, classify, interpret, demonstrate, evaluate, order,* or *remove.* Many more could be added. Just be sure your choices are action words; that is, that some act is performed and it can be measured.

~~~~~~

14. Now that we have worked with the situation and behavioral terms, let us try writing part of a performance objective which incorporates these two components. A couple of helps to get you started are now in order.

First, what are some words that may be used to start the situation?

A. _____

B. _____

C. _____

~~~~~~

ANSWER

You might have listed *given, after,* and *having.* Many other words could be used. If you are unsure of your ability to write the situation, you might want to refer to frame 6 on page 52.

~~~~~~

15. A second help may be knowing the four words that frequently precede the behavioral term. Refer to the chapter objectives on page 48. Write the four words that precede the *behavioral term.*

_____

~~~~~~

Answer

Right! The words *should be able to* generally are given before the behavioral term. Knowing this helps the novice during the writing of performance objectives. However, you may prefer to use *will be able to, shall be able to,* just *will,* or just *shall.* This is a matter of personal preference.

~~~~~~

16. Now you are ready to try writing the situation and the behavioral term of a performance objective. Suppose the unit to be studied is on the structure of the federal government. You desire to know the degree of understanding your students will have on the characteristics and/or functions of each of the three branches of our federal government. Try writing several performance objectives, each using a different behavioral term, which make it possible to measure the degree of understanding that your students possess on this topic. You may or may not want to include the previous instruction given.

A.

B.

C.

~~~~~~

ANSWER

Maybe your partial performance objectives looked something like this.

A. After completing the unit on the federal government, the student, given paper and pencil, should be able to list for each of the three branches of the government five or more characteristics and/or functions unique to that branch.

B. After completing the unit on the federal government, the student, given paper listing the three branches of the government in one column and fifteen characteristics and/or functions associated with these branches in another column, should be able to match each branch with the appropriate characteristic and/or function which is unique to that branch.

C. After completing the unit on the federal government, the student, given verbally a characteristic and/or function of one of the branches of the federal government, should be able to name (you could use write, circle, underline, identify) the branch of government associated with that characteristic and/or function.

D. Given a paper and pencil, the student should be able to describe in writing three functions for each of the three branches of the federal government.

E. Having completed the unit on the federal government, the student, given a list of topics such as child labor laws, railroad development, and labor union development, should be able to select one topic and compare in writing the type and degree of influence each branch of the government had on the selected topic.

You may have a different situation and/or behavioral term and still be accurate. Ask yourself (1) if the situation is clear enough so that others could establish the conditions, and (2) if the behavioral term does require an act which can be observed directly and thereby measured.

If you could write the situation and performance term in frame 16 and are satisfied with your level of performance, skip to frame 18. If not, proceed to frame 17.

~~~~~~

17. So you are not happy with your present capability to write the situation and the behavioral term and desire a little more help. All right, let us try again. This time we will write a performance objective for a Spanish class. We will suppose that it is a second-year high school class. The students have been assigned to read and discuss a particular story. You desire to know their degree of "understanding" regarding the story and/or their reading capability of the material. Try to write two or three performance objectives in which just the situation and the behavioral terms are given.

~~~~~~

ANSWER

First ask yourself: (a) Is the situation clear? and (b) Is the behavioral term an action word? If both answers are yes, you probably have the start of a good performance objective. Compare them with the ones below.

A. Given a copy of a Spanish story, the student should be able to read the entire story aloud.
B. After reading and discussing a Spanish story, the student, given a copy of the story, should be able to write the English translation for the entire story.
C. After reading and discussing a Spanish story, the student, given a list of ten words in English which are synonyms for ten Spanish words in the story, should be able to match the Spanish word with the correct English word.

D. Having read and discussed a Spanish story in class, the student, given a different story which has no new vocabulary, should be able to read aloud (or maybe write the English translation for) the entire story.

~~~~~~

18. You should feel confident of your ability to handle the situation and behavioral term by now. If not, may I suggest a quick review of frames 6 through 17. You might find a discussion with your instructor beneficial. The trouble you experience most likely is due to a minor misunderstanding, and a brief review should correct any existing difficulties.

Which of the three parts of a performance objective have we still to discuss?

~~~~~~

ANSWER

The acceptance level statement. If you did not remember, it may be necessary to review the sections on the components of a performance objective given early in the chapter (frames 2–5, pages 50–52). The acceptance level word or statement is an important part of a performance objective since it specifies the minimum level of performance which is considered acceptable. In this way both the teacher and student know just what the student must do to meet the minimum standards established.

~~~~~~

19. Since it is true that no two classes are made up of exactly the same types of students, the teacher may desire to adjust the minimum level of performance expected in an acceptance level statement.

List several factors which you feel the teacher should take into consideration when writing the minimum level of performance statement.

~~~~~~

ANSWER

You may have listed such factors as grade level, academic potential, motivational level, background in and out of school, together with any number of other variables which influence classroom achievement.

~~~~~~

20. Suppose we look at the writing of an acceptance level statement in another way. Let us select any *one* particular grade level or class. For example, it could be a sixth grade class, a freshman high school algebra class, or a college class on the principles of economics. Should all the students across the country who enroll in this grade or course meet the same minimum level of performance? Why?

~~~~~~

ANSWER

No. If you said yes, you should refer to all the reasons given in the answer under frame 19. It may be true that in some classrooms students are sufficiently alike that the acceptance level statement would be appropriate for all. Generally speaking, the acceptance level should be adapted to each group.

~~~~~~

21. Who should determine the level of performance which is deemed acceptable?

___A. An individual who is not well acquainted with the persons being evaluated. In this way biases are minimized. Refer to *A* under the answer.

___B. The instructor of the persons being evaluated. He knows the student better than anyone else. Refer to *B* under the answer.

~~~~~~

ANSWER

A. It is generally better that the teacher, the person who should be best acquainted with the students, establish the minimum level of performance.

It is true that some degree of bias would be eliminated if an outsider established the minimum level of performance. However, in most instances these people know little about the students' backgrounds, academic potentials, motivational levels, and many other factors which should be considered when writing the acceptance level statement. Proceed to frame 22.

B. You are correct. In most situations, the teacher is in a position to make the best judgment as to what should be the minimal acceptable performance level. His position is more advantageous because of his knowledge of the students' backgrounds, academic potentials, motivational levels, and the many other factors associated with classroom success.

---

22. Now it is time for us to examine some acceptance level statements. Remember, the acceptance statement designates just how well the student is expected to perform the specified behavior. It may mean giving a quantitative designation on such behavioral terms as *match, name, identify.* With such behavioral terms as *write, describe,* and *evaluate,* a qualification is required so that one can determine when the minimum acceptable behavior has been demonstrated. In a nutshell, we need to qualify the behavioral terms to eliminate ambiguity as much as possible in the reading of the performance objectives.

Select the performance objective which you feel has the minimum level of performance clearly defined.

___A. Given a list of ten United States presidents and a list of fifteen historical events in two different columns, the student should match the names of the presidents with events with which they are associated. Minimum acceptable performance is correctly matching eight of the ten presidents. Refer to *A* under the answer.

___B. Given a list of ten United States presidents and a list of fifteen historical events in two different columns, the student should be able to match the names of the presidents with events with which they are associated. Minimum acceptable performance is correctly matching enough presidents with events to demonstrate an understanding of this unit. Refer to *B* under the answer.

ANSWER

A. Good! You can see that both the teacher and the students know just how much is required to meet minimum standards. In *B* the students (and I suspect the teacher) are not quite sure what constitutes demonstrating "an understanding" of the unit. You apparently have the idea. Why don't you skip to frame 24?

B. If you chose this answer, ask yourself these questions: (1) "What constitutes demonstrating 'an understanding' of the unit?" and (2) "How will the students know that the level of performance they consider satisfactory coincides with the teacher's standard, if one has been established, unless it is spelled out more clearly?" Also, in *B* the teacher has not made a decision, at least in writing, as to what is acceptable. In *A* it is clear that both the teacher and the students know just how much is required to meet minimum standards.

~~~~~~

23. Look at the performance objectives below. Select the objective which has the acceptance level statement most clearly given.

___A. The student, given a color coded map and the key to the color code, should be able to name the heights (in feet) of ten points on the map. Acceptable performance would be naming the height of eight of the ten points within the altitude range specified on the color code key. Refer to *A* under the answer.

___B. The student, given a color coded map and the key to the color code, should be able to name the heights (in feet) of ten points on the map. Acceptable performance would be naming the heights within the range of the color code key. Refer to *B* under the answer.

~~~~~~

ANSWER

A. Your selection is correct. The acceptance level statement is very clear to all concerned. Proceed to frame 24.

B. Your selection is not wrong, but it does not spell out just how many of the ten heights should be named to meet the minimum requirements. You might assume all ten are needed. If ten correct answers are desired, then the acceptance level statement should clearly say so.

~~~~~~

24. Some terms like *match, list,* and *name* can readily be quantitatively evaluated, a fact which virtually eliminates any misunderstanding in reading the performance objective. Of course, this is just what we want, a performance objective which is not ambiguous.

It is not equally easy to write an acceptance level statement for all behavioral terms. Terms like *compare, define, contrast,* and *evaluate* require more thought from the person writing the acceptance level statement so that the minimum performance is clearly indicated. However, do not let difficulty of writing a qualified acceptance statement deter you from using behavioral terms which require students to perform tasks that are more thought-provoking.

Let us examine some acceptance level statements for behavioral terms that are more difficult to qualify. Note the partial performance objective below. Immediately following it are listed several acceptance level statements which were written for the partial performance objective. Read each and then mark it *yes* if it clearly states the minimum level of performance expected and *no* if it does not.

After completing a unit on the vertebrates, the student, given a paper and pencil, will be asked to compare similarities and differences for any of the following classes: fishes, amphibians, reptiles, birds, and mammals.

yes no

— — A. Acceptable performance would be the comparing and contrasting of all five classes with one another.

— — B. Satisfactory comparison is made when three similarities and three differences (morphological and/or physiological) are listed for each of the five classes being compared. Each of the similarities and differences needs to be stated in just one or two sentences.

— — C. Acceptable performance is listing (in a phrase or one sentence) ten characteristics for each class.

— — D. Acceptable level of performance would be achieved when the student could compare each class on the basis of the following systems: (1) nervous, (2) circulatory, (3) respiratory.

~~~~~~

ANSWER

A. No. It is not clear what the writer means by comparing and contrasting. The teacher's expectations would vary a great deal. Consider the response expected from a fourth grader compared to that anticipated from a college zoology major. This acceptance level statement does not tell us any more about what is expected from the student than what is given in the partial performance objective. The term *compare,* although behavioral, needs to be qualified with a statement which expresses what the student needs to do to compare.

B. Yes. You were quick to see that these statements do clarify the behavioral term *compare*. It is necessary to clarify if the student is to know his required performance level.

C. Yes. Again it is clear what will be an acceptable level of performance. You may not feel that the mere listing of characteristics constitutes a comparison. I tend to agree. However, that is beside the point. This teacher has clearly indicated what the student must do to compare (as he views it) the classes of vertebrates listed.

D. No. This example points out the topic which must be covered when comparing the five classes, but nothing is said to clarify the behavioral term "compare." What has been stated is fine. However, this writer needs to complete the job.

---

25. Now that you have examined all three aspects of the performance objective, you should be ready to test your skill in constructing this type of objective. Select a topic which you teach or plan to teach and write *several* performance objectives dealing with your selection. Be sure to keep in mind the model you have been developing during the chapter.

A.

B.

C.

~~~~~~

ANSWER

Whether your performance objectives are correctly written depends on their meeting the established criteria noted below.

Performance Objectives Check List:

A. Does the objective contain a situation, a behavioral term, and an acceptance level statement?
B. Does the objective contain a situation which gives the conditions for testing so that they might be established by another person?
C. Does the objective contain a behavioral term which can be measured?
D. Does the objective contain an acceptance level statement which maximizes or makes totally clear just how well the student must perform the described behavior?

If your objectives meet all these criteria, you have written a satisfactory performance objective. Note that the check list does not state any required sequence of the components of a performance objective (situation, behavioral term, acceptance level statement). Neither does the check list contain any set of terms or phrases which *must* be included. The check list thus offers a great deal of latitude in the style in which performance objectives can be written.

In constructing performance objectives, as in most activities, the competency of the performer increases with practice. Do not be discouraged if you are slow in formulating this type of objective or if phraseology is not to your liking; you will develop these skills as you gain experience. The important thing is not to give up your attempt to develop this type of objective for your lesson.

~~~~~~

26. Many times objectives are written for a lesson or unit, but they are not expressed in performance terms. It might be worthwhile to examine a few objectives which are not written in performance terms and then rewrite them so that they meet the criteria noted earlier.

Rewrite each of the following objectives so that they possess a situation, behavioral term, and acceptance level statement.

A. Given a dry powder, thermometer, water, and a container, measure four tablespoons of water and add it to the powder in the container. Record the temperature on the thermometer. An acceptable response would be that when heat energy is registered on the thermometer, this constitutes an example of a chemical reaction without combustion.

B. Select when it is most appropriate to use the form of the verb lie (lie, lay, lain).

C. The student should be able to type one hundred words without making a mistake.

ANSWER

A. The situation is present. "Given a dry powder, thermometer, water, and a container" clearly constitutes the conditions under which the student will be placed. However, from there on, the statement sounds more like directions for the laboratory than a performance objective. It does not appear that the teacher's intent is to use "measure" and "record" as the behavioral terms. It would seem that the teacher desires for the students to have the concept that whenever substances are combined and heat is given off, this giving off of heat is evidence of the presence of a chemical reaction. The objective is ambiguous so we are not sure of the teacher's thinking. We can only guess. Restated as follows, the objective is expressed much more clearly in performance terms.

> Given a set of substances that give off heat when mixed, the student should be able to recognize that a chemical reaction has taken place. Acceptable performance would be the student's statement that a chemical reaction has taken place and that the evidence to support this assertion is the giving off of heat, as registered on a thermometer.

Was your restatement of the objective something like the one above?

B. This one lacks a situation and acceptance level statement. It does have a behavioral term, *select*. Thus, to complete the objective, we need to add the missing elements. This might be one way:

> After completing the section on the form of the verb lie (lie, lay, lain), the student, given a test composed of 30 sentences with blanks where one form of the verb must be added, shall write in the correct form of the verb on at least 26 of the sentences.

C. This statement suffers from the same problems as the one above *(B);* there is no situation or acceptance level statement. We know the student needs to type, but we do not know under what conditions, nor how fast, nor if more than one chance will be given. Perhaps you had something like the following for your restatement designed to make this objective satisfy the requirements we have established.

> Given any passage from a book, and an electric typewriter with which he is familiar, the student will be asked to type 100 words in two minutes without a mistake. No more than two opportunities will be given.

You quickly note that the changing of an objective involves little more than writing one from scratch. By this point you should be able to construct a new performance objective or rephrase any statement which lacks one or more of the parts found in a performance objective. If you are unsure of yourself at this point, why not return to those frames which cover areas in which you have not demonstrated a satisfactory level of performance.

~~~~~~

27. Before we leave this "how" section of the chapter, we need to look at what is considered by some educators to be the fourth component of a performance objective. This is the *rationale*. Although the rationale is frequently not incorporated into the performance objective, it is an exceedingly important statement.

The rationale is a statement which explains, states, or justifies the relevance of the behavior being taught. That is, it expresses why the student should spend his time developing the stated performances. Some experts think that stating the rationale will aid the student by informing him of the worth of the particular performance, thus giving him motivation to learn the stated behavior because he knows the use this particular learning will have for him.

Possibly the most obvious impact that the rationale can have on classroom instruction is to force the teacher to justify the course content. Some of the "sacred cows" of the course may not stand the test and may have to be dropped. Teachers should be willing to examine each of their objectives on such grounds since the resulting course would be of greater value to their students.

The rationale can be developed in two ways. First, a *topical rationale* may be written to cover a concept, topic, or behavior which can be easily subdivided into several sub-behaviors. In this instance the rationale is developed for several performance objectives that have a common component on which the rationale is based.

Let us construct a topical rationale for some performance objectives that have been established.

The biology teacher knows that a student enlightened in the use of the microscope has extended his senses and thus has the capability to gain information. He may decide, for the sake of simplicity, to construct several performance objectives on the topic instead of just one. Rather than repeat a like rationale for each, he precedes all performance objectives with a topical rationale, one common to all objectives. Examine the illustration below.

> It is important for each person in the class to develop his skill in the use of the microscope, since this instrument will enable us to examine that world which our natural eye cannot view. Not only will viewing this microworld help our overall understanding of living things, but it is both fascinating and just plain fun.

A. Given a compound microscope, the student should be able to identify and name the objectives (high and low powers), eye piece, coarse adjustment, fine adjustment, diaphragm, and mirror. The student will be expected to point to and name each of the above listed parts to attain acceptable performance.
B. Given a compound microscope and light source, the student should be able to adjust the microscope so that light passes through. Acceptable performance is achieved when a totally white, fully round light can be viewed through the eye piece under both low and high powers.
C. Given a compound microscope and a prepared slide, the student should be able to focus the object on the slide for both high and low powers. Acceptable performance will be achieved when the teacher can get a clear view of the object by moving just the fine adjustment.

As can be seen, all three performance objectives deal with the use of the microscope. Thus, the teacher develops a topical rationale to precede these performance objectives.

Another example of a topical rationale is the first section of this chapter. Here an attempt is made to demonstrate a need, that is, to justify, the development of the behaviors stated in the performance objectives on page 48. This type of topical rationale, because of its length, is generally impractical for the classroom teacher.

Let us look at the second type of rationale. Here a brief statement justifying the use of the objective is added to each performance objective and in this way each performance objective has its own rationale. There may be times when the teacher will find this type of rationale more appropriate. Examine the following examples.

A. Given a balance, some weights, and an object, the student should be able to determine the mass of the object. Acceptable performance would be determining the mass of the object to within ± 0.1 gram in no more than three minutes. The ability to determine the mass of an object to ± 0.1 gram will enable you to be more precise in collecting data, and this increased precision should increase the accuracy of the inferences and predictions drawn from the data.
B. After completing the program on the slide rule, the student, given a slide rule and a list of problems (multiplication, division, square root, squaring), should be able to calculate the correct answers. Acceptable performance is achieved if 95% of the answers are correct and the student uses only the slide rule to obtain the requested results. The slide rule is a handy tool both in and out of the classroom. It is a great time saver for the person who is skilled in its use.

Now it is time for you to construct a rationale for a performance objective. Refer to the three performance objectives you wrote in frame 25, page 67, and write a rationale for each. If you wish, it is perfectly all right to write one or more "new" performance objectives and develop a rationale for them.

A.

B.

C.

~~~~~~

ANSWER

If you developed any "new" performance objectives, determine your accuracy by referring to the performance objective check list on page 68. To check your rationale ask yourself:

1. Is the statement written so that the student can comprehend its meaning and, as a result, be encouraged to develop the stated behavior?
2. Does the stated rationale justify the time needed to develop the stated behavior?

If the answer is yes to both questions, your rationale is acceptable.

Your choice of using the topical rationale or a rationale for each performance objective is not nearly as important as whether or not you employ a rationale. A well-constructed performance objective which cannot be justified on the basis of its value to the student is of no consequence and should be discarded.

~~~~~~

28. Which of the following statements best expresses your feelings about performance objectives?

___A. I have been exposed to the role that performance objectives play in instruction and therefore I do not feel that I would gain a great deal by reading the section, *Why use performance objectives?* Refer to *A* under the answer.

___B. I have an interest in the role that performance objectives play in maximizing instruction and desire to learn more. Refer to *B* under the answer.

~~~~~~

ANSWER

A. If you have been exposed to performance objectives and feel confident that you know their value in the classroom, why don't you skip to the end of the chapter and take the post-test. If you are not sure of yourself just stay with us.

B. Good! Let us continue.

~~~~~~

V: Why Use Performance Objectives?

Most of our prior discussion has centered on the formulation of performance objectives. Some time was spent on the advantages to the classroom teacher of using performance objectives. In this, the "why" section, we will return to the discussion of the role that performance objectives have in classroom instruction.

Performance objectives are neither good nor bad. Their value, like that of the automobile, depends on the way they are used. None of us wants to give up the auto because it is nearly a necessity in many of our lives. However, when improperly driven, the auto can cause damage. The performance objective is like the auto: When it is properly used, it serves a vital role in planning classroom instruction. If it is improperly employed by the teacher, however, it can be a detriment to learning.

In our discussion of the ways that a performance objective can be applied so that it is an asset to classroom instruction, we must not forget that performance objectives are written to include specific and measurable behavior. It is this characteristic of the performance objective that gives it its worth. Here are some of the ways that the performance objective can aid the teacher.

A. *Motivation.* All of us desire to know where we are going and just how well we must perform to get there. Students are no different. Objectives which make clear the behaviors expected and how well they must be performed stimulate students to do better. A student who is more highly motivated should learn more.

B. *Establishing Problem Areas.* The use of the performance objective pinpoints much more specifically many problem areas which exist for the student, the teacher, and the curriculum.

C. *Instructional Design.* Once the teacher has the method to measure the presence or absence of certain traits, instructional design is then a matter of trying out various teaching styles and aids, and the sequencing of these instructional variables to determine the best way for that teacher to get his students to attain the desired behaviors. So, if we want to know the best instructional strategy, we need to know when the desired behavior has been attained. That requires clearly spelled-out performance objectives.

D. *Simplification of Evaluation.* To assess pupil progress, the teacher is required to make a determination of the number of objectives the student has attained. The best way to make this determination is by developing a list of performance objectives which serves as a standard for both the teacher and student. Once the performance objectives have been established, the construction of an assessment measure is little more than the restating of the required behaviors.

~~~~~~

29. There is one point regarding performance objectives and evaluation which should be brought out. It simply amounts to congruence between the behavior stated in the objective and the behavior requested of the performer in the evaluation.

Check yourself to see if you have the idea. Select the evaluation question which is congruent with the performance objective listed below.

OBJECTIVE

The student, given a paper, pencil, and protractor, will be asked to construct and to name the size of an angle between 0° and 180°. Acceptable performance would be correctly constructing and naming four of the five angles. The angle must be accurate to within ± 3 degrees.

EVALUATION ITEM

___A. Using the paper, pencil, and protractor supplied, describe in writing the procedure for constructing a 45° angle. Refer to *A* under the answer.
___B. Using the paper, pencil, and protractor supplied, construct a 45° angle. Refer to *B* under the answer.

〜〜〜〜〜〜〜〜〜〜〜〜〜〜〜〜〜〜〜〜〜〜〜〜〜

ANSWER

A. Are you trying to be tricky or did you forget that we said the skill designated in the performance objective is the same skill described in the evaluation item? Return to the other selection and its corresponding answer.

B. So you said he should construct an angle. Good! That is congruent with the skill stated in the objective. Suppose you decide that the student should possess the skill of describing how to construct a 45° angle. That is all right, but you should write a performance objective for that skill. Thus, for each skill you should construct a separate performance objective. Then you may select from the different skills when evaluating, or use them all.

Be very careful not to be a tricky teacher. There are enough problems in instruction without bringing in the element of trickery, consciously or unconsciously.

Beware! Performance objectives are a great aid but there exists a danger of which you should be aware. That is, performance objectives can be more easily developed for some behaviors than for others. Behaviors such as naming, listing, constructing, and matching, plus many physical skills, such as running and jumping, are good examples. As a result, these types of behaviors frequently are emphasized to a greater degree than perhaps they should be. Their over use is principally due to the ease with which these behaviors can be numerically qualified in the acceptance level statement.

You, like most teachers, want your students to learn more than skills which require lower levels of thinking. You want your students to develop behaviors which demand the higher levels of thinking such as making application of ideas to new and varied situations, and analyzing, synthesizing, and evaluating problems of all types. You also want students to develop an appreciation for certain things. To write acceptance level statements for this type of performance objective, however, is much more difficult. The minimum level of performance can rarely be stated in numerical terms and, as a result, more thought is required to develop an unambiguous acceptance level statement.

To encourage this type of thinking, you must construct a number of performance objectives which involve the higher levels of thinking and the development of appreciation in some areas. Only in this way can you hope to stimulate and develop this type of student activity.

Would you like to refine your ability to write performance objectives? If so, I would recommend the two books in the reference list. For one reason, they give a comprehensive coverage on the writing of performance objectives at different intellectual levels. Another reason is that they cover extensively the writing of performance objectives for physical skill, intellectual skills, and the development of attitudinal traits.

VII: Post-Test

This measure should help you determine whether or not you possess the behaviors stated in the performance objectives on page 48. Read each question and give your answer. After completing the questions, check yourself by comparing your answers with those given immediately following the post-test.

POST-TEST QUESTIONS

1. Apart from the rationale, name the three components of a performance objective.

   A. _____

   B. _____

   C. _____

2. Examine the following statements. Identify any which would be considered a performance objective.

   yes   no
   ___   ___   A. Given any resource materials, the history, the laboratory test results, and an opportunity to examine five patients each inflicted with a different disease, the student should be able to name the diseases and state reasons for his decision. Acceptable performance would be correctly naming each of the five

different diseases and stating no less than two characteristics unique to each disease.

— — B. After completing the unit on Shakespeare, the student should demonstrate a knowledge of this material. Acceptable performance would be achieved when the student correctly answers 75% of the 40 questions covering this unit.

— — C. After visiting the planetarium, the student shall name 10 constellations. Eight of the 10 constellations must be correctly named to meet acceptable performance.

— — D. Given thirty-five preserved specimens of birds of the area, the student will be asked to identify each by writing its common name. Acceptable performance consists of correctly naming 25 of the specimens.

— — E. Given a paper, pencil, and an audio tape with five musical selections which have not been played in class, the student must correctly identify the composer of each piece.

3. Examine the following objectives. Identify that portion which constitutes the (A) situation, (B) behavioral term, and (C) the acceptance level statement.

Given a solution containing more than one ion and the assigned laboratory materials, the student should be able to identify the ion present. Acceptable performance consists of correctly identifying each ion within a two-hour period. Only one opportunity to identify the ion will be given.

A. Situation: _____

B. Behavioral Term: _____

C. Acceptance Level Statement: _____

4. Change the following non-performance objective so that it *is* a performance objective.

The student should demonstrate his capability as a mechanic by being able to correct a set-up mechanical problem in less than twenty minutes.

5. Write a performance objective on any topic.

~~~~~~

POST-TEST ANSWERS

1. A. the situation
   B. the behavioral term
   C. the acceptance level statement
2. Refer to the check list for performance objectives (page 68) if you are unsure of any of the answers after checking your selection.
   A. Yes.
   B. No. It lacks a behavioral term. The phrase "demonstrate a knowledge of" is nonbehavioral. We do not know if the student will be asked to "match," "select," "write," or some other behavior. Note, too, that the situation is given last and is acceptable. Remember, we stated that the order of the component of a performance objective is not important; we need only to meet the requirements of the check list.
   C. No. The situation is lacking. We do not know which materials and/or conditions will accompany the testing.
   D. Yes.
   E. Yes. If you question whether an acceptance level statement is present, ask yourself if the student knows at what level he must perform. It seems this statement clearly intended for each student to meet a minimum standard of identifying all five composers.
3. A. The situation is *Given a solution containing more than one ion and the assigned laboratory materials.*
   B. The behavioral term is *identify.*
   C. The acceptance level statement is the last two sentences.
4. As always, several possibilities exist. When checking your answer, just be sure all three of the components of the performance objective are present. Refer to the check list on page 68. You might have restated the objective something like this.

   Given a complete set of tools and an automobile with a set-up engine problem, the student should be able to correct the problem within twenty minutes. The problem will be considered corrected when the engine can be started and continues to run for two minutes with no outside aid.

5. Any objective is satisfactory if it contains all three elements of a performance objective. It should be stated so that it is not ambiguous to another person of comparable background and/or a student for whom the objective was prepared. Again, refer to the check list on page 68 if necessary.

Did you get each question correct? You should have scored 100% in order to meet the acceptable level of performance. If you missed just one, you did a fine job. So you missed more! Perhaps we should start again . . .

References

BLOOM, BENJAMIN S. (Ed.), *Taxonomy of Educational Objectives, Handbook I: Cognitive Domain*. New York: David McKay Company, Inc., 1956.

KRATHWOHL, DAVID R., BENJAMIN S. BLOOM, AND BERTRAM B. MASIA, *Taxonomy of Educational Objectives, Handbook II: Affective Domain*. New York: David McKay Company, Inc., 1964.

Developing question-asking skills

3

ROGER T. CUNNINGHAM

Ohio State University

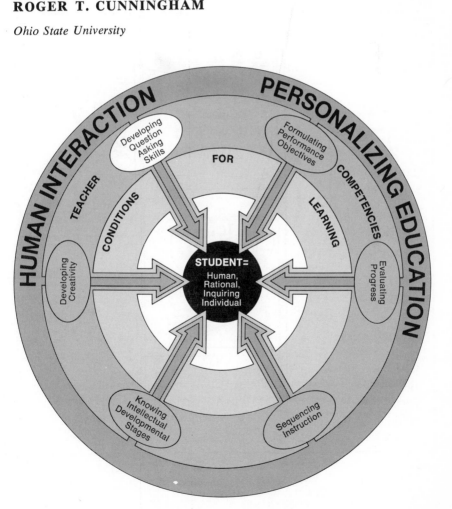

Fig. 3-1

Questions

The question Snoopy asks might also be asked of questions that are used for classroom instruction: "What kinds of questions do teachers ask?" More important, however, might be "What kinds of questions should teachers ask?" This chapter seeks to answer both of these concerns.

Teachers spend as much or more time asking questions as using any other kind of verbal utterance. Studies have shown that teachers spend 70 to 80 per cent of their time asking questions. "Questions have always been the 'stock in trade' of teachers." [1] Questions are used to give directions, correct misbehavior, manage classroom activity, initiate instruction, create learning situations, and evaluate learning. The most disappointing factor is that the least common use of questions is to stimulate thinking. Despite the teacher's good intentions, critical thinking is the least common outcome of questioning. This happens even though most teachers perceive developing the ability to think as the major goal of education.

What is a question? A question is a verbal utterance that seeks a response from the person to whom it is directed. It is a means of finding out and interpreting information. However, it is more than a logical grouping of words punctuated by a question mark. It is one of the first things that arouses the curiosity and mental activity of a child. Its most important offering is its value for stimulating and directing thinking. As Bossing points out, "it is an effective stimulus and it is readily available to teachers." [2] A well-developed understanding of the characteristics and potentials of the question, as well as skill in using it effectively, becomes one of the most valuable devices with which the teacher can assume his responsibilities as a manager of learning.

This chapter is designed to help you to become more aware of types of questions used for instruction and to develop your question-asking ability. Reading and working with the material in this chapter will help you to focus on how you can phrase more effective questions and use more diversified question-asking techniques. These are only initial steps; utilizing the premises of this material is by far the most important step.

Specifically, the objectives of this chapter are:

A. Given one or more instructional questions, you will be able to identify these questions with different levels of thinking.
B. Given one or more instructional questions at one level of thought, you will be able to rewrite (rephrase) these questions for other levels of thinking.

[1] Norris M. Sanders, *Classroom Questions: What Kinds?* (New York: Harper and Row, Publishers, 1966), p. ix.
[2] Nelson L. Bossing, *Progressive Methods of Teaching in Secondary Schools* (Boston: Houghton Mifflin Co., 1942), p. 329.

C. Given one or more poorly phrased questions, you will be able to rewrite (rephrase) these questions so that they are phrased in a more effective way.
D. Given one or more questioning strategies, you will be able to identify those strategies associated with an effective approach to questioning.

To help you reach these goals we will point out some advantages to be gained from analyzing questions and question-asking procedures, describe the characteristics of effective questions and question-asking strategies, provide some practice in recognizing and constructing better questions, provide practice in evaluating questions and question-asking procedures, and finally, provide you with an opportunity to see just how well we have succeeded.

Therefore, the chapter will focus on developing your skill at recognizing, evaluating, and constructing effective questions and question-asking strategies. Emphasis will be placed on developing this skill as a means of stimulating and guiding the thinking of children. To keep this discussion from becoming purely theoretical, we have drawn many of the questions used as examples from actual classroom settings.

The Importance of Questions

Recent developments in education have placed much emphasis on helping children learn how to learn, to become independent in their learning, and to think for themselves. One of the teacher's most effective instruments for stimulating and guiding this initiative is the question. In order for children to be independent in their learning, they too must learn how to question. The teacher's questions serve as a model.

In order for elementary school children to be successful in their learning, the teacher must be able to set the stage, initiate the process, sustain the activity, and give direction and purpose to the children's learning. The teacher must also be skillful at diagnosing individual progress in the learning process. The most effective agent of instruction for accomplishing these purposes is the question. The question-raising part of teaching, however, remains one of the major communication dilemmas for teachers.

Effective questioning is not an innate talent that only a few possess; it is a skill that can be developed with practice. It is one of the teacher's basic tools of communication. Teachers who are not adept at questioning, who do not develop a questioning attitude, and who do not pose questions as they prepare for teaching will have difficulty directing the learning of children.

Teaching itself is a process of learning. It involves recognizing and, if necessary, changing one's behavior to become more effective. This learning process on the part of the teacher can begin by focusing on the kinds of questions the teacher uses. The greatest effect of the question is the way and extent to which it causes the pupil to think. The data available from research demonstrate that the teacher's questions and way of using questions are crucial in helping students learn how to think. A study by Taba, Levine, and Elzey [3] found an almost perfect correlation between the levels of thought pupils displayed in their answers to teachers' questions and the types of questions asked by their teachers. In addition, the study showed that questions asked by the teacher have a very strong influence on other behaviors performed by the pupils. The way you ask questions can be one of the most influential parts of teaching.

The questions used in a teaching strategy directly affect thinking skills developed by children. Therefore, the impact of question-asking on the teaching-learning process is evident. If teachers are stressing factual recall in their questioning, children are not expected to do much creative thinking. From the evidence gathered in studies on questioning, it appears that teachers' questions, whether oral or written, are, in fact, stressing the recall kind of answer most often.

If you doubt the importance of questioning, try to envision a classroom or any other teaching-learning situation without questions. Teachers often ask too many questions. The real concern, however, as illustrated above, is not the amount of question-asking but the method of asking and using questions. Traditionally, the use of the question has been confined to the purpose of finding out what pupils have learned. Good questions and good question-asking procedures go beyond this purpose.

Good questions make provisions for different levels of thinking. A good question can be judged by its clarity. A question that is clearly posed, leaves no doubt of its purpose, and is stated with a sensible word order is much more successful than one without these characteristics. Of course, clarity is important for any level of thinking. A good question provides for reflective and critical thinking; to do so, it should relate meaningfully to the experiences of the persons being questioned—familiar terms and examples make this possible. Good questions facilitate the accomplishment of goals set by the teacher. The attainment of behavioral objectives for an instructional unit by a group of learners depends very heavily on the quality of questions in the program, since a good question provides suitable guidelines for the pupil to form a meaningful response. Therefore, the quality of a question is very much a part of the way it is phrased.

In addition to the previously mentioned purposes, questions asked and used in an effective way facilitate development of desirable attitudes, develop and sustain interests, provide new ways of dealing with the subject matter, and give quality and purpose to evaluation. Their importance in

[3] Hilda Taba, Samuel Levine and Freeman Elzey, *Thinking in Elementary School Children* (Cooperative Research Project No. 1574, San Francisco State College, San Francisco, California, April, 1964), p. 177.

developing the ability to think cannot be overlooked. Development of this ability is almost entirely dependent on the teacher's skillful use of questions.

Classifying Questions

To be an effective question-asker you should know the kinds of questions that can be asked for different levels of thinking as well as the purpose served by each kind of question. Two important factors influence the effect that a question has: One is the level of thinking it stimulates; the other is the kind of response the question elicits because of the way it is worded. Studies of classroom activities show that both of these factors have a strong influence on the kind of learning that takes place and on how children learn to think for themselves. To be able to ask the "right" kind of questions will make a big difference in how effective you are as a teacher.

This part of the chapter is designed to help you develop your ability to identify and construct questions for different levels of thinking. Therefore, the objectives you will seek to accomplish for this part of the chapter are as follows:

A. Given four basic categories for classifying questions and a series of questions, you will be able to classify questions by the level of thinking that they require.
B. Given questions that can be identified with one of the four basic categories, you will be able to rewrite (rephrase) these questions so that they require a different level of thinking.

Questions that teachers ask children during the learning process can be thought of first as belonging to two general types. Basically, these two general types provide a way of grouping questions according to what they ask of the learner. Each of these two general categories can in turn be divided into two subgroups on the basis of the level of thought elicited by the question. We will be primarily concerned with these four categories. You should be able to classify questions into each of them.

~~~~~~

NARROW QUESTIONS [4]

The first of the two general categories is narrow questions. Questions that require low-level thinking, short factual answers, or other predictable responses including "yes" or "no" are classified in this category. The answers to narrow questions are predictable because they are specific,

[4] Adapted from Edmund Amidon and Elizabeth Hunter, *Improving Teaching: The Analysis of Classroom Verbal Interaction* (New York: Holt, Rhinehart & Winston, Inc., 1967), pp. 11–12.

allowing for only a very limited number of acceptable or "right" answers. These questions require little thought by the pupil. The kinds of questions that are used in drill sessions by teachers are typically narrow. Questions of this type are often used to test children's reading comprehension. "Where was Judy?" "What was Judy doing?" "What color dress was Judy wearing?" "Who was wearing the green dress?" or "When did Judy go home?" are examples of the probing for comprehension with narrow questions.

Some examples of narrow questions follow:

A. How many points do you need to identify a triangle?
B. What is the largest city in Ohio?
C. What is a force? What is the definition for force?
D. Why are its people called America's human resources?
E. Why don't we use the word "ain't" today?
F. Do the words you were given fall into the category you studied?

As you can see, the answers to these questions can be predicted. This characteristic of narrow questions does not suggest that they should be avoided; they do serve a purpose. Narrow questions are used to collect information, to verify ideas and understandings of material, or to review previously studied material. They can also be used to identify, group, and note relationships. This information gathering, facilitated by narrow questions, can be the first step to developing concepts. However, the questions should be used in such a way that this information-gathering process leads to higher levels of thinking rather than to time spent giving pat answers. The danger in the use of narrow questions is in their overuse. Too much time spent answering narrow questions deters development of higher-level thinking skills.

~~~~~~

From the questions listed below select those that are narrow by placing an N in the blank space provided. After you have identified those you think are narrow, turn to the next page to see if you are correct.

___A. What kind of animal is this?
___B. What is the effect of the conjunction on the total sentence?
___C. Suppose you were trying to convince someone that air is real; how might you do it?
___D. How might life in the United States be different if England had won the Revolutionary War?
___E. Does the symbol 45 consist of two numerals?

~~~~~~

If you classified either of the questions labeled *C* or *D* as narrow, you goofed! You had better go back and re-examine the description of narrow questions. This category will become much clearer to you, however, as you examine more questions. Both questions *C* and *D* require more thought and permit more than one acceptable answer. These questions are discussed under the topic of *Broad Questions*.

If you classified *A, B,* and *E* as narrow questions, you are correct. Good start! These questions must all be considered narrow since they require a specific or "right" answer. Questions *A* and *E* require a very low level of thinking. Question *A* requires only naming an observed animal, and question *E* demands only a "yes" or "no" response. Question *B* is at a higher level but asks for a *best* explanation, so it must also be considered narrow. This point will become clearer to you as you proceed.

If you identified these correctly, you are off to an excellent start. Proceed to the section on broad questions.

~~~~~~

BROAD QUESTIONS [5]

Broad questions are just what the name implies. They are questions that permit a variety of acceptable responses. For this reason, the answers to broad questions are not predictable. They are questions designed to be thought-provoking. Broad questions cause the person responding to hypothesize, predict, or infer. They also include answers that involve expressions of opinion, judgment, or feeling. For broad questions, the one *best* answer is not a concern. When a teacher asks a broad question, he seeks a longer, more thoughtful answer than he would get from a narrow question.

Broad questions may be used to motivate children to explore the subject matter more deeply or to experiment. They may lead to the development of new insights, ideals, appreciations, or desirable attitudes. Broad questions may also be used by the teacher to stimulate and guide interests in a new learning experience or problem-solving situation.

Broad questions can be the means by which the teacher enhances development of intellectual skills. The use of broad questions should encourage pupils to become more independent in finding and using information. Because broad questions allow more than one acceptable answer, children should move away from developing habits of trying to guess what the teacher wants or to recall textbook information. They should go beyond this recalled information to develop higher levels of thinking. Some examples of broad questions follow:

[5] Adapted from Amidon and Hunter, *Improving Teaching,* pp. 11–12.

A. If you had chosen another field of interest, how might you have viewed this chapter differently?

B. Suppose you could not ask a single question in a classroom; how would you communicate?

C. What is your opinion on the importance of questioning as a teacher competency?

D. Why do you think a study of teaching competencies is important?

E. If all elementary teachers were men, in what way do you think education at that level might differ from what it is now?

Notice that these questions permit different answers and require a higher degree of thinking than narrow questions. However, this higher degree of thinking may depend on the background knowledge you have obtained. The questions labeled *A, B,* and *E* offer a hypothetical situation to which there may be many suitable answers. Obviously, there is not any "one right" answer; you are permitted to form alternative answers. To form such answers demands a higher level of thinking. The questions labeled *C* and *D* call for selecting criteria and making judgments or expressing your opinion on the basis of your self-selected criteria. To do so requires more than one thinking operation.

~~~~~~

From the questions below identify those that are broad by placing a B in the blank provided. If the question is narrow, label it with an N. When you have identified those you think are broad, turn to the next frame to see if you are correct.

___A. How do you define the word "questioning"?

___B. What do you think are some of the things that might happen if you began to teach a group of children a lesson without planning any questions?

___C. What kind of question is usually limited to recall or rote memory?

___D. Suppose that children were to ask all the questions in a classroom situation; in what ways do you think teaching might differ from the present method?

___E. Do you agree with the emphasis educators are placing on the individualization of instruction?

~~~~~~

If you identified the questions labeled *A* and *C* as broad, we've both failed. You should go back and review the discussion on narrow questions.

If you identified *B, D,* and *E* as broad questions, you deserve a pat on the back. Both questions *B* and *D* permit alternative responses. If these questions were asked of a group of your peers, it is likely that there would be several acceptable answers. Hopefully, these questions would stimulate discussion and interaction among members of the group.

If you identified the question labeled *E* as narrow, you were doing some thinking but not enough. True, this question could be answered with a "yes" or "no," but it implies justification or demands that you select criteria to take a self-selected position. This mistake is understandable now; it will become clearer as you progress. However, this misunderstanding may be avoided if the question is rephrased to say "How do you feel about the emphasis educators are placing on the individualization of instruction?"

Where have we been?

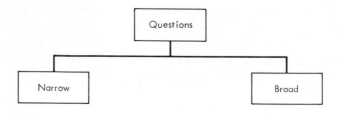

Now try your new skill on the four basic categories. If you feel a need for a break in your work with this chapter, however, this would be a logical stopping point.

The sections that follow will ask you to construct or rewrite questions. Therefore, this would be an appropriate time to obtain pencil and paper.

So far we have seen that questions can be categorized into the two general categories of broad and narrow. Each of these categories can be subdivided into two specific groups. These more specific categories will permit you to develop your skill for identifying types of questions more closely with the thought levels they require.

COGNITIVE-MEMORY QUESTIONS [6]

Cognitive-memory questions are narrow questions that are limited to the lowest level of thinking. This kind of question calls for answers that

[6] Adapted from James J. Gallagher, *Productive Thinking in Gifted Children,* Cooperative Research Project No. 965 (Urbana, Illinois: Institute for Research on Exceptional Children, University of Illinois, 1965), pp. 24–25.

are a reproduction of facts, definitions, or other remembered information. A cognitive-memory question often requires the person responding to reply with a one-word answer or to give the name of something. Therefore, when a pupil responds to a cognitive-memory question he may recall a fact, define a term, identify something he observes, or give an answer he has learned by rote memory. The following are examples of cognitive-memory questions:

A. Define: What is gravity?
B. Name: What is the subject of the sentence?
C. Yes or no: Does the square root of 25 equal 5?
D. Identify—observe: What numeral is below the blue line and to the right of the red line?
E. Designate: How many classes of words can you find?
F. Recall: From what country did Columbus sail? [7]

Notice that all of the questions are limited to very narrow answers. They require only low-level (rote-memory *or* recall) thinking by the person answering the question. If you were a teacher in a classroom and you asked these questions of a group of children, the responses you would get would be very similar to one another.

So that you can more clearly identify a cognitive-memory question and apply the criteria that identify this type of question, read *each* question listed below. Next, label it with a C-M if you determine it to be a cognitive-memory question. After classifying *each* question move to the next frame and check your answer by reading the paragraph identified by the letter that corresponds to the letter of each question.

___A. What did you observe in this demonstration?
___B. What is meant by a natural resource?
___C. Does all communication have to be spoken?
___D. Why is fishing important in New England?
___E. What do they call the mineral from which iron is made?

A. If you identified this question as a cognitive-memory question, you are correct. In this question, the pupil is asked to typify verbally what he has seen. If he were asked to associate the events of the demonstration

[7] This question is quoted from Claudia Crump, *Self-Instruction in the Art of Questioning* (unpublished program for pre- and in-service teachers in social studies, 1969), p. 15.

to construct an explanation for what he observed, then it would not be a cognitive-memory question.

B. If you said that the question calls for defining and must be classified as a cognitive-memory question, you are right. Good show! If you missed this, refer back to page 90 and read the paragraph immediately following the heading.

C. As it is phrased, this question is best answered with a "yes" or "no." Because it gives the pupil a 50-50 choice, not much thought is required. It can be only a cognitive-memory question. If you disagreed on this one, return to the second paragraph in the discussion on cognitive-memory questions and be sure you have the criteria clearly in mind.

D. This question is not a cognitive-memory question. The key word that distinguishes it from a cognitive-memory question is "Why?" This word implies a level of thought higher than recall, defining, or naming. Although the pupil may respond with a brief answer, he does have to give a reason or explain. Even though he may recall a textbook explanation, he gives a response in his own words. Constructing this kind of answer requires more thought than merely answering "yes" or "no." To change it to a cognitive-memory question you could ask, "Is fishing an important industry in New England?"

E. If you classified this as a cognitive-memory question on the basis of its demand for factual information or naming, you are right again. The pupil is *not* asked to explain, give a reason, or evaluate in this question. Give yourself another pat on the back and proceed.

~~~~~~

Try Your Skill.   See if you can write three cognitive-memory questions. If you need some sort of a context you might go to a textbook. You might also recall some questions you asked recently or that one of your professors asked in the past (they may be good examples of cognitive-memory questions). If you feel really challenged, you might try to change some of the previous questions so that they require a higher level of thinking.

~~~~~~

Where have we been?

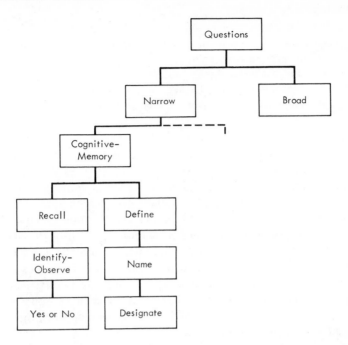

All the operations that follow require higher levels of thinking than do any of the cognitive-memory criteria. Please proceed to the next section on *convergent questions.*

~~~~~~

CONVERGENT QUESTIONS [8]

Questions in this second category are also narrow, but they are broader than cognitive-memory questions because they require the person answering the question to put facts together and construct an answer. These questions are narrow because there is usually one "best" or "right" answer. When a child responds to a convergent question asked by a teacher, he must know certain facts, be able to associate or relate these facts, and give an explanation, usually in his own words. To state or explain relationships or explain concepts, the respondent must carry on a higher level of thinking than that required by cognitive-memory questions. Therefore, to respond to a convergent question a child may be expected to perform the operations of explaining, stating relationships, associating and relating,

[8] Adapted from Gallagher, *Productive Thinking,* p. 25.

or comparing and contrasting. Examples of this kind of question include the following:

A. Why can't these two lines be made into a rectangle?
B. Why do plants grow toward light?
C. How does a magnet affect the iron filings?
D. How are the people of Australia like the people of the United States?
E. Why aren't languages all the same if they all come from one source?

As you can see, even though convergent thinking questions call for one answer, they require an explanation or statement of relationship of previously learned facts or concepts. As you can see by the examples, the cue word "why" suggests explaining and is used often in convergent questions.

Teachers may use convergent questions to get children to compare, discriminate, or illustrate in search of the "best" answer. This kind of question is very typical of the majority of those found in textbooks. Some educators have proposed that "how" and "why" questions are good questions. However, research shows and observations of classrooms bear out that there is real danger of making children's thinking too fixed by asking convergent questions consistently. Children develop an obsession about finding the "right" answers or are inhibited about responding when they are not challenged to form and test their own ideas.

~~~~~~

In the list of questions that follow, identify each of the questions as cognitive-memory, convergent, or neither by labeling them C-M, C or N. After you have classified *each* question, read the paragraph identified by the letter of the corresponding question.

___A. What are some of the ways you might use to stop a forest fire?
___B. Why does the sun appear to move in the sky?
___C. How are present methods of communication different from those in the past?
___D. What is the name of the force that causes the iron filings to stick to the magnet?

~~~~~~

A. You are mistaken if you labeled this question as cognitive-memory or convergent, but do not be disturbed; it is new. To answer this question, the child has to go beyond the operation of recall. He will also have to do more than relate factual information to form a response. This question is characteristic of what we commonly refer to as "open-ended." It permits a diversity of answers. If you asked, "What *way?*" then it could be classified as a convergent thinking question. If you don't understand, hold on, this type will be discussed next.

B. This question *does* satisfy the criteria for a convergent question. Rather than requiring the pupil to recall a fact, this question asks him to put together concepts about the relationship of the sun and earth as well as the earth's rotation, and explain the reason for its apparent movement across the sky. Of course, when you identify it as convergent, you must assume that the pupil has not previously learned the answer to the question. For the pupil who has read this information in the textbook, the question may be no more than recall and therefore, cognitive-memory.

C. If you classified this question as convergent, good for you. The criteria for a convergent question are satisfied by its request for a comparison. If you did not correctly identify this question, refer back to the first paragraph on convergent questions.

D. This question is best labeled as cognitive-memory. When the child identifies the force, he is using the operation of *naming*. A higher level of thought is not necessary. The pupil is not asked to explain, cite relationships, or compare; therefore, the criteria for classification as a convergent thinking question are *not* satisfied.

How are you doing? If you scored perfectly on this last set of questions, you are progressing very well. Give yourself a gold star. If you didn't, return and review the criteria for the two categories.

~~~~~~

Try Your Skill.   See if you can write three convergent questions. Perhaps you have noticed that the level of thought expressed can be changed by rephrasing the questions. You might rewrite some of the previously examined cognitive-memory questions.

~~~~~~

Where have we been?

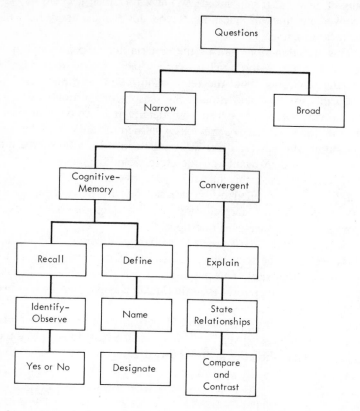

To this point you have worked with the two subgroups under narrow questions. The two categories under broad questions will truly test your skill.

DIVERGENT QUESTIONS [9]

The questions in this third category are broader in nature than the preceding types. They permit more than one acceptable response. The answers to these questions are not necessarily predictable; these are thought-provoking questions. A divergent question asks the person responding to organize elements into new patterns that were not clearly recognized before. A teacher asking this kind of question would allow a child to be original in his response. Divergent questions might create new problem situations and require him to synthesize ideas and construct a meaningful solution. In responding to divergent questions the child may

[9] Adapted from Gallagher, *Productive Thinking*, pp. 25–26.

perform the operations of predicting, hypothesizing, or inferring. Examples of these kinds of questions include the following:

A. What predictions can you make about what is going to happen to the marbles?
B. If you saw a native of a strange planet, how would you communicate to him that you were friendly and meant no harm?
C. What are some numbers that will make this sentence true?
$$\square + \triangle - \square = 5$$
D. What do you think would happen if the balls had a different mass?
E. How might our country be different today if we had never had slavery?

As you can see, the above questions encourage responses that are more creative or imaginative. They are more thought-provoking than the narrower types of questions. This kind of questioning stimulates interest and provides motivation for exploration and experimentation. Using divergent questions is also more likely to lead to development of insights, appreciations, and desirable attitudes. Too often teachers are preoccupied with covering the content of a subject, and fail to utilize this level of questioning to help children develop their ability to think and handle new problem situations.

~~~~~~

Identify each of the questions below as cognitive-memory, convergent, divergent, or none of these, using the symbols C-M, C, D or N. As you categorize *each* question check your answer by reading the paragraph that corresponds to the letter of each question.

___A. How do you explain why the green ball did not float?
___B. What are some ways a fish might live differently if the type of water in which he lives is changed?
___C. In the decimal numeral 33, what number does the first 3 name?
___D. Which type of government do you think is the best devised by man? [10]
___E. How might life in the United States be different if the South had won the Civil War? [11]
___F. Suppose you were a caveman trying to write a message about your recent hunting trip using nothing but a picture; how would you do it?

~~~~~~

A. If you didn't classify this question as convergent, you have forgotten already. It is hard to make the distinction at first. Glance back at

[10] Crump, *Self-Instruction in the Art of Questioning*, p. 48.
[11] *Ibid.*, p. 36.

the previous section and note the operations for convergent thinking. In this question the child is to give the *one* correct explanation for what he has observed. It cannot be classified as divergent because the possibility of diverse responses has been eliminated. If the pupil were asked to report what he saw, then the question would be cognitive-memory.

B. If you categorized this question as divergent, very good. Notice that the question asks for *ways* that a fish *might* survive. These and other cue words such as "what if" are common to this category. These words imply a request for a diversity of responses.

C. If you classified this question as anything but cognitive-memory, something has gone wrong between the beginning of this chapter and this point. The question asks the pupil to name something. In other words, it demands the lowest level of thinking. He is not required to employ any of the criteria characteristic of convergent or divergent questions. If you did not get this correct, turn back to the descriptions of cognitive-memory questions.

D. If you classified this question as any of the previously described categories, you have been fooled by the wording. This question asks for a judgment. The pupil would have to make a selection and justify that selection. So far, this has not been discussed, but you can look for it next.

E. You are correct if you placed this question in the divergent category. This question is likely to produce many different responses from the children. It does not require factual recall or one right answer; therefore, it allows the pupil to function at a higher level of thought than cognitive-memory or convergent.

F. This, too, is a divergent type. You use the same criteria as you did in *E*. Many answers are possible. If you missed here, refer back to the beginning of the section on divergent questions.

~~~~~~

Try Your Skill.   Try your hand at writing some divergent questions. It is much more of a challenge but worth the effort. You might try to rephrase some of the previously listed cognitive-memory and convergent questions.

~~~~~~

Where have we been?

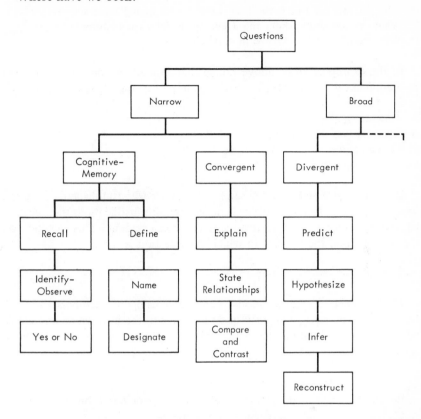

If you have had little difficulty with the questions so far you are making excellent progress. Proceed to the final category on *evaluative questions.*

~~~~~~

EVALUATIVE QUESTIONS [12]

The evaluative question requires the person responding to judge, value, justify a choice, or defend a position. It is the highest level of questioning. It involves the use of the cognitive operations from all three of the other levels. An evaluative question causes the pupil to organize his knowledge, formulate an opinion, and take a self-selected position. In order to make a judgment he must use evidence. He makes a judgment of good or bad, right or wrong, according to standards he sets or someone else sets. Because they can be either broad or narrow, these questions are sometimes difficult to classify. The following are some examples of evaluative questions:

[12] Adapted from Gallagher, *Productive Thinking,* pp. 26–27.

A. What makes this picture better than that one?
B. Why do you say this is the best order for arranging these objects?
C. What do you think about the accuracy of John's conclusions?
D. Why would you like to live in Australia?

In the examples given above notice that evaluative questions can often be identified by certain phrases. Some examples of these phrases are:

A. How do you feel about . . . .?
B. What do you think about . . . .?
C. Do you agree . . . .?
D. In your opinion . . . .?

It must be stressed that where criteria are clearly established (the pupil has a fixed guide to judge by) and do not require justification, the question will be no more than cognitive-memory or convergent. This depends on the wording and the context in which the question is used.

~~~~~~

Identify each of the questions that follow using the symbols C-M, C, D, or E. As you categorize *each* question move to the next frame and check your answer by reading the paragraph that corresponds to the letter of each question.

___A. Is tuberculosis an infectious disease?
___B. Which president do you think did the most for our country?
___C. Why is a symphonic poem like a narrative?
___D. In your opinion which folk singer is the best?
___E. What might your day be like if there were no gravity?

~~~~~~

A. If you did not classify this question as cognitive-memory, maybe too much time has lapsed since you last dealt with these questions and you have forgotten. Turn back to the section on cognitive-memory questions and review the criteria. This question could be answered by a "yes" or "no" with little room for an opinionated response.

B. If you identified this question as an evaluative question, you're on the ball. Good thinking! Notice that it asks the respondent to make a choice. To justify that choice would be a natural follow-up.

C. This question asks for a comparison. To do so one would have to relate elements to identify similarities or differences. Therefore, this question must be classified as a convergent question. If you labeled it otherwise, it would be wise to review the criteria for convergent questions. If you didn't answer correctly don't worry, you will master it.

D. This question also fits the criteria for an evaluative question. If you labeled it correctly you're really with it. Keep it up! If you missed this, turn back to the discussion on evaluative questions and note the cue phrases. Understanding will come; these questions are a bit harder.

E. Like several of the previous examples, this question permits original responses. Because of its open-ended nature, it is best classified as a divergent question.

~~~~~~

Try Your Skill. Try writing three evaluative questions according to the above criteria. This is more difficult than writing other kinds of questions. Give it a try!

~~~~~~

As a summary, refer to the questions below. Examples are given for different areas of the curriculum for each level of questioning. Notice how the wording of a question can be changed to place it at a different level of thinking.

COGNITIVE-MEMORY

A. Language Arts: How do you define the word *communication?*
B. Math: What do the symbols 5, 7, 12, +, −, and = mean?
C. Science: What does the fish have which helps him to move about?
D. Social Studies: Where is the city of Chicago?
E. General: Who was the famous person who recently spoke about censorship of the news?

CONVERGENT

A. What is the difference between language and communication?
B. How would you construct a mathematical sentence using the symbols 5, 7, 12, +, −, and = ?
C. How are the goldfish and the turtle alike or different when they move?

D. What is there about the location of the city of Chicago that accounts for its importance?
E. How does censorship work?

DIVERGENT

A. If you were a creature of the sea, how would you communicate with other sea creatures?
B. If you were given the symbols 5, 7, 12, +, −, and =, what are some mathematical sentences you could construct?
C. What would happen if you gave the turtle fins and a tail like the fish and took away his legs?
D. How might the lives of the people of the city of Chicago be different if it were located close to the equator?
E. What might happen if we had complete censorship of the news?

EVALUATIVE

A. How do you feel about the argument that both uses of the words *language* and *communication* are acceptable as long as they are understood by the group?
B. What is your opinion on the importance or unimportance of mathematical sentences?
C. Which animal, the fish or turtle, do you think is better equipped to move about in the place which he lives?
D. Why would you or wouldn't you like to live in the city of Chicago?
E. What is your opinion of censorship of the news?

Try Your Skill. A true test of your skill for phrasing questions for different levels of thought would be for you to rephrase some of the questions previously described under each of the question categories. Give it a try! You have come a long way since we began.

Where have we been?

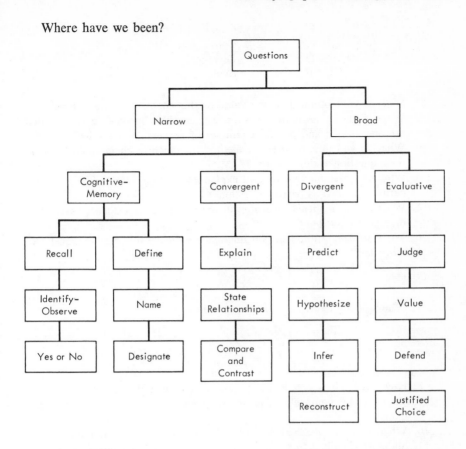

On the pages that follow, you will find a brief self-test by which you can check your skill in classifying questions into the four categories. Answer *all* of the questions in the space provided and then check the correct answers on the page that follows the self-test. You may want to turn back to the chart above as you take the test.

Self-Test

Classify each of the questions listed below into the appropriate category using the following symbols for each category.

CM . . . . .Cognitive-Memory
C . . . . .Convergent
D . . . . .Divergent
E . . . . .Evaluative

___ 1. What is your opinion on the value of this chapter on questioning?
___ 2. What is the name of the question category that includes questions that are open-ended and permit a number of acceptable responses?
___ 3. What do you think is the best method by which teachers could improve their question-asking abilities?
___ 4. Why are questions that require explaining, stating relationships, or comparing classified as narrow questions?
___ 5. What might happen to learning in the classroom if teachers asked only divergent questions?
___ 6. What are some numbers you might use to make this mathematical sentence true?

$$\square \times \triangle = \triangle \times \square$$

___ 7. Which of the figures are simple closed curves?

(a)   (b)   (c)   (d)   (e)

___ 8. How does $4/9 = 4/9 \times 1$ help you to rename $4/9$ as $16/36$?
___ 9. Which major peninsula in northern Europe is mostly forest and woodlands?
___10. What would be the best way of reducing noise in our cafeteria?
___11. Should the United States abandon all means for involvement in war?
___12. What are some ways we might classify these postage stamps?
___13. Why is racial segregation a good or bad practice for insuring equality of education for all races? [13]
___14. What story might you tell about this picture?
___15. What is the *explanation* for the cause of the water rising in the tube?
___16. What are some ways you could get this light bulb to light using a piece of aluminum foil and a flashlight battery?
___17. How do you *explain* the difference between a conversation carried on by humans and the sounds that animals seemingly make in response to each other?
___18. What is the name given to the word in a sentence that shows action?
___19. What happened to the drops of water on the waxpaper when you brought them near one another?
___20. How do you account for the fact that many of the things the Greeks learned were forgotten for hundreds of years?
___21. What do you think is the best method for solving this problem?

[13] Crump, *Self-Instruction in the Art of Questioning*, p. 49.

___22. What is the simplest numeral for $(6 \times 4) \times 5$?

___23. How would life in a Russian city compare with your life?

___24. What kinds of problems might occur if the ice at the two poles of the earth were to melt?

___25. What are some ways you could get on the roof of your home that have not been used before?

~~~~~~

Answer Key

1. E	8. C	14. D	20. C
2. C-M	9. C-M	15. C	21. E
3. E	10. E	16. D	22. C-M
4. C	11. E	17. C	23. C
5. D	12. D	18. C-M	24. D
6. D	13. E	19. C-M	25. D
7. C-M			

Score

23–25 Excellent. Happiness is a good grade.

20–22 Close counts in more than horseshoes! Good!

17–19 You had better check those you missed and note the criteria that are not clear.

 0–16 Whoops! Not so good. How about one more try?

~~~~~~

If you scored in either of the first two ranges, proceed to the next section on phrasing questions. However, if you have been working on this section for some time, now would be an appropriate spot to break.

If your score fell into either of the last two ranges above, it is strongly recommended that you review the criteria for each category, identify the cue words and phrases, try writing some more questions and then take the second self-test found below.

~~~~~~

Follow-Up Self-Test

___ 1. In your opinion what makes a great work of art?

___ 2. What would be some ways of reducing the noise in our cafeteria?

___ 3. Which do you think is safer, crossing the ocean by air or by boat?

___ 4. How is 5 related to 25?

___ 5. If the United States had lost in World War II; how might life be different now?

___ 6. How does salt help on driveways in snowy and icy weather?

___ 7. What are some ways this box might be lifted without touching it?

___ 8. What are the three purposes of communication?

___ 9. Was John Dewey a pragmatist?

___10. What is the percent of low socioeconomic children with tuberculosis?

___11. In your opinion should the state cut education from the budget to lower tax rates?

___12. Is multiplication the inverse of division?

___13. Why must a teacher provide for individual differences in his classroom?

___14. In your opinion what was the greatest achievement of the 1960's?

___15. What might our transportation system be like if the wheel had never been invented?

~~~~~~

Answer Key

1. E	6. C	11. E
2. D	7. D	12. C-M
3. E	8. C-M	13. C
4. C	9. C-M	14. E
5. D	10. C-M	15. D

Score

13–15 This is more like it. Very good!

11–12 You're getting much closer to understanding.

9–10 Still room for improvement but don't give up.

0–8 You seem to be having difficulty with this section. Perhaps you ought to take a short break, then begin again, working each section until you feel confident that you understand.

~~~~~~

If you have been working for awhile, you have earned a break. This would be an appropriate spot to take one before you proceed to the section on *phrasing of questions*.

~~~~~~

The Phrasing of Questions

The phrasing of a question refers to the way the question is worded. Wording in this sense relates to the terminology used in the question, the number of words used, and the order in which they occur.

In this part of the chapter you will seek to improve your ability to phrase questions. If the objectives for this part of the chapter are achieved, you will be able to perform the following:

A. Given one or more questions, you will be able to classify these questions on the basis of specified criteria for question-phrasing.
B. Given questions that can be considered poorly phrased, you will be able to rephrase (rewrite) these questions so that they are worded in a more effective way.

In the previous section we considered questions on the basis of their function. When you classified questions you identified their purpose according to the level of thought they required. As you did so, it became clear that the wording of the question set the criteria for the kind and number of responses that could be given. It also became clear that the absence of these criteria deters a functional or thoughtful response. For example, a divergent question, properly phrased, demands a high level of thought and permits several acceptable responses; whereas a cognitive-memory question demands a specific answer at a lower level of thought. Communicating these intents is determined by the wording of the question. The importance of this relationship became apparent in the exercises when you changed the wording of a question. By changing the wording you can change the level of thought required by the question. Therefore, phrasing influences the function of the question.

A good question not only does a good job of conveying its function but also is clearly posed. In other words, the grammatical arrangement of the question influences its clarity; it also reflects on the way its intent is communicated. Questions that are too wordy must be considered poorly phrased, as must questions that have an illogical word order, or use words that do not offer suitable criteria for a response. How well a question conveys its purpose and how well it is phrased will be evident in the type of responses received when the question is asked.

The intent of a question may be very sound, but unless it is stated with a logical word order and an appropriate number of meaningful words, the intent will not be communicated to the person who is to respond. A question may seek to encourage more than one response at a high level of thought, but unless it is specific enough, the respondent will have to guess, ask for clarification or fail to respond. The question, then, fails in its purpose. For example, "What about . . . . ?" kinds of questions, such as "What about the space program?" do not offer any criteria for a meaningful answer.

You also observed in the previous section that certain words often give clues to the type of question asked. These clue words, in part, set the criteria for the kind of answer that is to be given. For example, cognitive-memory questions often begin with the words, *who, what, where, which, when,* and sometimes *how,* and *why.* Because *how* and *why* suggest explaining, they are most often a clue to a convergent-thinking question. The words "what if" would be a clue to a divergent question. Certainly, there is nothing fixed about these clue patterns since the wording of the rest of the question can change the complexion of the question entirely, as will be demonstrated by examples that follow.

The problems related to phrasing are many; they are so numerous that it is difficult to isolate them and clearly identify the source of the problem. Some of these problems approach the ridiculous. For example, one teacher was observed to begin many questions with the word "then," also ending them with the word "then." Therefore, his questions sounded like this, "Then this would be a rock then?" Another unique kind of phrasing problem is observed in a question such as "Did you ever not weigh anything, do you think?"

In view of the amount of time that teachers spend asking questions, how well they communicate with children will be greatly dependent on the way they phrase their questions. The importance of effectively phrased questions cannot be denied. Questions that are not effectively phrased do not communicate their intent; they only confuse the pupils and hinder their learning. A teacher who fails to give careful thought to the way his questions are phrased is cheating his pupils of the opportunity to develop thinking skills.

Four examples of question-phrasing problems follow. After you have completed your study of these four problems you should be able to perform the previously stated objectives. Remember that many examples are worded just as they were used in classrooms.

~~~~~~

PROBLEM TYPE ONE: "YES" OR "NO" QUESTIONS

The questions that create this first problem are those that imply or demand a "yes" or "no" response. These are questions that do not use any of the clue words that were mentioned before (what, why, when, which, who, how, and what if). Instead the question is usually initiated with one of the auxiliary verbs—*are, is, could, would, does, do, can, was* and *have*. Recall that examples of these questions were identified as cognitive-memory questions. This problem is not only one of the quality of the question; it is also a problem of the extent to which these kinds of questions are used in classroom instruction. Studies of instruction and teacher questioning reveal that these questions make up a very large percentage of the questions that teachers ask. Some examples of these poorly phrased questions follow:

A. Does all communication have to be spoken?
B. Can you think of a reason why this man is speaking correctly?
C. Is there more than one force acting here?
D. Could we say that wheat is the chief crop of the plains states?

In each case the child could satisfy the criteria established by the wording of the question by responding with a "yes" or "no." To compensate, the teacher will follow this first question with a fragmented question like "What is it?" "What?" or "Why?" This practice of asking two questions, neither of which is completely clear, is uneconomical. The teacher spends more time talking than necessary. The intent of the question would be clearer if it were rephrased and asked as one question. For example, the questions above could be changed to the following:

A. What are some forms of communication other than spoken communication? *or* How can we communicate in ways other than speaking?
B. What is the reason why this man is speaking correctly? *or* Why do you think this man is speaking correctly?
C. What forces are acting on these objects?
D. What is the chief crop of the plains states? *or* Why is wheat the chief crop of the plains states?

Notice that changing the question by using one of the interrogative terms (what, why, who, and so on) does not necessitate a second question. Although the level of thought required may be no higher than that in the poorly phrased questions, the purpose of the question is clearer and the teacher spends less time asking questions. Notice, however, that in some cases the question can be phrased for different levels of thinking.

From the pupil's point of view, the problem may lie in the fact that he is not sure what kind of an answer he is expected to give. As in the poorer examples above, when the possible responses are narrowed to a 50-50 choice between "yes" and "no" the child needs to do no more than guess. You should also note the difference between this "yes" or "no" response question and an evaluative question which requires the pupil to justify his response with evidence.

The following segment of a dialogue from a science lesson conducted with a third grade class where the children were working with drops of water, wax paper and a candle illustrates this problem:

T: Does the candle go in?
S: Yes.
T: What happens?
S: It bounces off.
T: What else do you notice?
S: It scoots away.
T: Won't it let the candle in?
S: Yes.
T: Look at the candle. Is it wet?
S: Yes.
T: Really wet?
S: No.
T: Have you ever seen insects that walk on water?
S: Yes.

There are times, of course, when this type of question may be feasible. Such is the case when the teacher may ask the pupil to clarify or extend his answer. "Can you tell me more about that idea?" or "Can you explain further?" are examples. However, even in this case the question might be changed to "What else can you tell me about your ideas?"

~~~~~~

Try Your Skill. Below are some examples of questions that are illustrative of this question-phrasing problem. *Read* and *rewrite* (rephrase) each question so the intent of the question is clear. After you have rewritten (rephrased) *each* question, compare your rewritten (rephrased) question with the model provided in the next frame. You might try to rephrase the question for different levels of thought.

A. Can you rephrase questions that start with an auxiliary verb so their intent is clearer?
B. Would you recommend this book to a friend?
C. Do you think you could use percentage here?
D. Did the pioneers use four routes to cross the Appalachians?
E. Can you predict the temperature before a reading is taken?

~~~~~~

Rephrased Models

A. How can you rephrase a question that starts with an auxiliary verb so its intent is clearer? *or* Why is the meaning of a question clearer when you do not start it with an auxiliary verb?

B. Why would you recommend this book to a friend? *or* What are some of the reasons why you would recommend this book to a friend? *or* Suppose your friend was not interested in reading this book; how would you convince him that it is a good book?

C. How could you use percentage in this problem? *or* How could you show your answer to this problem in percentage figures?

D. What were the four routes the pioneers used to travel across the Appalachians? *or* How might the way our country was settled have been different if the four routes the pioneers used to cross the Appalachians had been different?

E. What do you predict the temperature of this liquid will be before we measure it with a thermometer? *or* Suppose you didn't have a thermometer; what are some methods you could use to measure the temperature of this liquid?

~~~~~~

Problem Type Two: Ambiguous Questions

This second type of phrasing problem actually includes a host of related difficulties. For the most part, the error lies in the fact that the question lacks adequate criteria for the pupil to form a meaningful response. If a term can be applied to describe the whole gamut of these poorly phrased questions, it might be the term *ambiguous*.

Ambiguous questions include elliptical or "What about . . ." kinds of questions, statements intoned as questions, commands, and fragmented questions (phrases or one word). Questions that encourage guessing could also be considered ambiguous. The following are some examples of ambiguous questions:

What about the United Nations?
Tell us about lenses.
How long do you think man has been on earth?
It gets bigger?

So it's not too far off?
Here?
Most force?
Just that one?
Discuss racism.

These questions are vague, unclear, purposeless, and unfair to the pupil. They fail to communicate the intent of the question. As ambiguous questions, they neither demand nor imply a complete answer. They provide no guidance for an answer and consequently, contribute to rambling answers. For example, a teacher conducting a discussion with children on green plants suddenly posed the question "And, what about non-green plants?" Even when questions of this type are placed in the context of a subject matter they tend to confuse and lead to misunderstanding. In classrooms where children's language abilities are limited and they lack understanding of the subject matter and related concepts, a teacher will fail to communicate if he uses questions of this sort. A segment of a dialogue from an actual classroom lesson is illustrative:

T: How does gravity affect the balls?
S: Well, it pulls them down.
S: Force
T: Gravity is like a force?
S: I mean push.
T: Is there a difference between a force and push?
S: Yes, force is two things.
T: What about force?
S: Push and pull of the earth.
T: Do you think this is an electromagnet?
S: Could be.
T: Is it?
S: Yes.
S: If that's a battery it probably is.
T: What do you think this tin can is made of?
S: Metal.
T: Metal?
S: Tin.

One study[14] on teacher questioning revealed that 40 percent of the questions teachers ask suffer the ills characteristic of ambiguous questions. A major cause is that teachers assume too much about their pupils' per-

---

[14] John R. Moyer, *An Exploratory Study of Questioning in the Instructional Processes of Selected Elementary Schools* (unpublished doctoral dissertation, Columbia University, 1965), p. 209.

ceptivity and their knowledge of the subject matter. A teacher who uses ambiguous questions has not carefully considered a teaching strategy for accomplishing his instructional objectives or planned suitably phrased questions. In so doing he also demonstrates his lack of a thorough knowledge of the subject matter. Carefully formulated instructional objectives and questions, planned to bring achievement of these objectives, will help to avoid ambiguous questions.

A question that is properly structured will contribute to a clear understanding, serve as a model for pupils, and insure accurate communication of the question's purpose. When properly phrased, a question will employ clear wording, contain vocabulary suited to the group with which it is used, employ wording appropriate to the level of thinking sought in the question, be grammatically correct, and possess content relevant to the purpose of the question.

Some additional examples of ambiguous questions and models for rephrasing follow:

A. "What about shapes Seurat uses in his paintings and his placement of people?" could be changed to "How would you describe the shapes Seurat used in his paintings?" and "What is unique about Seurat's placement of people in the paintings?"
B. "Something happened?" changed to "What happened to the object?" or "What would happen if you changed the objects?"
C. "Discuss mathematical sentences." changed to "Why are mathematical sentences easier to use?"

The lack of a subject matter context makes rephrasing more difficult. Obviously, removing questions from context adds to their vagueness, but it does make the problem more evident. As observed in the previously described dialogue, considering them in context doesn't help a great deal.

~~~~~~

Try Your Skill. In each of the poorly phrased (ambiguous) questions that follow rewrite each question so that it is more suitably phrased. You may have to assume some sort of context to add terms for clarity. After rewriting all the questions, compare your questions with the models provided in the next frame.

A. What about questioning?
B. Phrasing is a problem in questioning?
C. Phrasing is important?
D. What about some synonyms for *blue?*

~~~~~~

REPHRASED MODELS

A. What do you think are the key points a teacher should be concerned with in relation to his questioning? *or* What are some of the more important concerns about questions asked by teachers?

B. Why could poor phrasing of questions be considered a problem? *or* What are some of the results of asking poorly phrased questions that deter learning?

C. Why should a teacher be concerned about the way he phrases his questions? *or* Why do you think effective phrasing of questions is important?

D. What are some synonyms for the word *blue?*

~~~~~~

PROBLEM TYPE THREE: "SPOON-FEEDING" QUESTIONS

Questions characteristic of this problem are questions that give too much guidance for a response. In fact, one gets the impression that sometimes the answer is so obvious that it was hardly worth the time to ask the question. The persistent use of this kind of question is reason enough to consider it a problem. It is a "spoon feeding" approach; as a result, the pupils can become lazy and inexact in their thinking. The source of the problem, again, lies with the teacher's lack of concern for effective phrasing of questions. It appears as though the teacher is seeking some sort of reassurance that the pupils can repeat the "right" answer or that he lacks confidence in the pupils' ability to deal with the subject matter. A teacher who turns a review statement in the textbook into a question, leaving out certain words, creates this kind of problem.

This problem of phrasing includes leading questions such as "So we can say the fulcrum is the place that supports a lever, isn't that right?" or "In other words, you can apply a greater force?" Other examples are questions that include the answer in the question or offer a choice between two answers included in the question such as "Are the things round or square?" or "The light area is broken down into the color it wants to project, so green grass would be in dots of what color?" Some questions that offer a choice are probably best asked as two separate questions.

Although slightly different, questions that are inverted such as "The kinds of word patterns before the blank space in each case are what?" and the verbally fill-in-the-blank type of question such as "The greatest iron and steel manufacturing center in the world is _____?" are similar in their lack of good phrasing. Teachers who consistently use questions phrased like those above are forcing the answer on the children by demanding a predetermined response. Certainly, it reflects poor thinking habits on the part of the teacher.

The questions illustrated above might be rephrased for greater clarity in the following way:

> What is the name of the place that supports a lever? *or* What is the purpose of a fulcrum?
> How would you describe the shape of these objects?
> Why is green the color that we see when light shines on grass?
> What kinds of word patterns do you find before the blank in each case?
> What is the name of the greatest iron and steel manufacturing center in the world?

Obviously, these questions are still narrow questions but remember that this is the nature of the original questions. In their rephrased form they are grammatically correct and are clearer because of their word order.

~~~~~~

Try Your Skill. Try your hand at rephrasing the questions listed below. After you have rewritten each question, compare them with the models provided in the next frame.

A. The kinds of words you have listed for sentence two are what class words?
B. Is the tone of your voice something you've learned or something you just naturally do?
C. Is Canada larger or smaller than the United States?
D. The name of the process where water changes into a gas is called what?
E. The place where General Washington and his army spent the worst winter is called _____?

~~~~~~

REPHRASED MODELS

A. What class words are those that you listed for sentence two?
B. How does the tone of your voice develop?
C. How do Canada and the United States compare in land size?
D. What is the name given to the process by which water becomes a gas?
E. Where did General Washington and his army spend their worst winter?

~~~~~~

PROBLEM TYPE FOUR: CONFUSING QUESTIONS

Questions that include too many factors for the pupil to consider at one time do more harm than good. Teachers who ask these kinds of questions mistakenly assume that the inclusion of a number of factors will help the child form a complete response. However, the result is usually confusion. Because all the factors are difficult to keep in mind, the pupil is confused by the time the question is completed. A question that is phrased in an effective way will present one idea.

Some examples of this type of poorly phrased question follow:

A. Why did boiling the water without the balloon and placing the flask in a cool place make the air pressure in the flask different from the pressure of the first experiment?
B. How can you tell when a word from your list of auxiliaries is being used as an auxiliary and when it is being used as some other kind of word instead?
C. How, when, and why did the War of Independence begin?
D. What causes, or where could it be caused, more or less air to enter and leave the lungs?
E. Do you think from what I told you previously that gravity or gravitational attraction would affect in any way the projectile that got shot or the ball that fell over that way?

The solution to better phrasing in most cases is to ask two or more questions that are clearer and briefer. A practice of asking two questions as one has similar ills. When faced with a "double-barreled" or "dual" question the child must think "Which one do I answer?" The following are examples:

A. What is a predicate and can you tell what kind of sentence this is?
B. Is there air in the bottle and how can we get air in without taking it out of the water?

C. Where are the chief lumbering areas in the North Central States and what are the chief minerals of this area?

D. What is the big difference between American and Athenian democracy and why did this work for them but not work for us?

Obviously, the solution to better phrasing of these questions is to ask them as separate questions with one main idea in each.

A related problem is the use of terms that are beyond the understanding and experience of the children being questioned. This kind of phrasing problem is characteristic of an inexperienced teacher who has done his homework with the subject matter but not with understanding the knowledge level of his pupils. To use words that do not have meaning for the pupils will only lead to frustration and confusion.

It is important to remember that the previously discussed problems of phrasing prevent effective thought and impair the quality of a response. The learning process should not be hampered by questions that fail to communicate.

In the brief self-test which follows you can check to see how proficient you have become at *identifying* and *rephrasing* poorly phrased questions. *Rephrase* those questions you identify as poorly phrased and then check your skill by comparing them with the models that follow.

~~~~~~

Self-Test

Apply the criteria for poorly phrased and effectively phrased questions by using the following symbols:

PP: Poorly Phrased
EP: Effectively Phrased

Rewrite those you identify as poorly phrased questions.

___ 1. What about the pollution problem?

___ 2. Words used in a question that cause it to be phrased so that it implies a "yes" or "no" answer are _____?

___ 3. What disadvantages other than slowness are there to shipping goods by canal and what kinds of transportation are now competing with railroads?

___ 4. What is the relationship between the verb *protest* and the noun *protestant?*

___ 5. Why does the system of castes which worked for hundreds of years in India not work so well today?

___ 6. Which single fraction names the sum $11/36 + 15/36?$

___ 7. The question category that includes questions that require making judgment of value is what?

___ 8. What are some ways you might make these objects float?
___ 9. Does it make a difference how you phrase a question?
___10. What do you think is the best way to solve this problem?
___11. Can you say that all dogs belong to the same family?
___12. How many numerals are inside the circle?
___13. What changes do you think we might find if we had a way to analyze these materials after they burned?
___14. Are these questions convergent or divergent?
___15. What is a question?

~~~~~~

Answer Key

1. PP	6. EP	11. PP
2. PP	7. PP	12. EP
3. PP	8. EP	13. EP
4. EP	9. PP	14. PP
5. EP	10. EP	15. EP

If you missed fewer than 3 out of 15, you have done very well. If you missed 4 or more, examine the rephrased models below; construct some questions and try rephrasing them in different ways.

~~~~~~

REPHRASED MODELS

The following are samples of ways to improve the exercise questions which were poorly phrased.

1. Because of its ambiguity there are any number of possibilities for rephrasing this question.

   A. What are some ways we could solve the problem of air pollution?
   B. What are some of the major factors that contribute to pollution of our rivers?
   C. What is your opinion about the government's right to impose restrictions on industry to control pollution?

2. What name is given to the words used in the phrasing of a question that commonly suggest a "yes" or "no" answer?

3. A. What disadvantages other than slowness are there to shipping goods by canal?
   B. What kinds of transportation are competing with railroads today?

7. What is the name of the category used to describe questions that require making judgments of value?

9. How does phrasing influence the quality of a question?

11. A. Why could all dogs be classified in the same family?

    B. What is the name of the family to which all dogs belong?

    C. Suppose you had an animal you thought was a dog; what evidence would you look for that would tell you it was a dog?

14. What is the category in which you would classify these questions?

This would be an appropriate place for a break in your work with this chapter before going on to the last section on strategies for question-asking.

Strategies for Question-Asking

Your effectiveness as a question-asker will depend not only on your formulating good questions but on the way you use these questions. The ultimate purpose of a question is to stimulate, direct and extend thinking. The true measure of an effective question is the answer it elicits. However, an effectively phrased, thought-provoking question does not assure a well-rounded answer, especially when children have been conditioned to give brief, factual answers. If your question is to realize its full potential and serve the purpose for which it was designed, you must be able to employ certain strategies.

A strategy may be considered a plan or way of using questions, or answers to these questions, that leads to suitable response patterns on the part of the pupils being questioned. An effective strategy for question-asking goes beyond finding out what has been learned; it enhances or changes the pupil's way of answering. This change may be identified by longer and more thoughtful responses as the student moves beyond the factual recall level.

Pupils test and develop their thinking skills through verbal expression. Therefore, the quality of this verbal expression will weigh heavily on the thinking skills that pupils develop. The teacher's way of managing questions and pupils' answers will determine the quality of this verbal expression; thus, the effectiveness of a learning experience is dependent upon the question-asking strategies the teacher uses to facilitate pupil participation in that experience.

The aspects of question-asking studied in the previous parts of this chapter suggest certain strategies for question-asking. The strategies studied in this part of the chapter are primarily concerned with increasing the amount and quality of pupil participation. The objective for this part of the chapter is that you should be able to identify those strategies that create a more effective approach to question-asking.

Ask Fewer Questions

A question-asking strategy that employs a large number of questions deters the development of the ability to think. Studies have shown that teachers ask too many questions. In 1912 Stevens [15] found teachers asking as many as 150 questions in a 40-minute period. Unfortunately, there seems to have been little change since that study; Floyd [16] found primary school teachers asking 3½ to 6½ questions per minute and an average of 348 questions a day. A recent study [17] of student teachers found them asking 70 to 90 questions in several 20-minute science lessons.

The use of a "rapid-fire," question-answer-question-answer pattern of questioning is based on the mistaken idea that this is the way to keep attention on the topic. Teachers who depend on this kind of approach are also misled by the *quantity* of participation; verbal activity does not necessarily reflect thinking. The emphasis on quick, factual recall answers may bring many answers, but it represents a neglect of individual differences, for it is a denial of the opportunity for the pupil to develop skill in verbal expression. It also lessens his time to evolve complete and thoughtful responses necessary to the development of his ability to think.

If you are to help develop the intellectual skills of your students, you will have to ask fewer questions. An effective question-asking strategy would provide for this goal.

~~~~~~

Which of the following suggests the best way of reducing the number of questions asked? Make your selection and move to the next frame to determine the suitability of your answer.

___A. A strategy that primarily uses broad questions
___B. A strategy that uses both broad and narrow questions with appropriate pauses
___C. A strategy that employs the consistent use of a pause after each question

~~~~~~

A. Well-constructed broad questions will help reduce the number of questions asked, but are only a partial solution. Your mistake is under-

[15] Romiett Stevens, *The Question as a Measure of Efficiency in Instruction* (New York: Teachers College, Columbia University, 1912), p. 7.

[16] William Floyd, *An Analysis of the Oral Questioning Activity in Selected Colorado Primary Classrooms* (unpublished doctoral dissertation, Colorado State College, 1960).

[17] Roger T. Cunningham, *A Descriptive Study Determining the Effects of a Method of Instruction Designed to Improve the Question-Phrasing Practices of Prospective Elementary Teachers* (unpublished doctoral dissertation, Indiana University, 1968), p. 156.

standable. Nevertheless, unless time is allowed for the pupil to think about the question, the broad question is no more effective than the rapid-fire technique; in fact, it is probably more likely to cause confusion and misunderstanding. Select another alternative.

B. This is the best alternative. A few well-constructed broad questions, used in conjunction with suitable pauses to allow thinking to take place, can best achieve the purpose of asking the questions. Narrow questions are necessary. They help set the stage for the broad question and help the child clarify and extend his answer for better understanding and more complete thought. Refer to the discussion in the next frame.

C. This cannot be a suitable strategy. To pause after a narrow question is merely wasting time. It also leads to creating undesirable behavior patterns. Select another alternative.

~~~~~~

The skillful use of the pause is not easily mastered. Once you can feel comfortable with the silence, however, it can be an effective means for encouraging thinking. Children can learn to use this time to construct a good response. Remember, when you ask a question you have an answer in mind. The pupil, in contrast, has to interpret the question, recall ideas, associate and evaluate these ideas, form a conclusion, and select the right words with which to respond. This process takes time. It has been suggested that a five-second pause after a thought-provoking question is desirable.[18] However, the five second pause is quite arbitrary.

~~~~~~

Strategy One: Ask fewer questions with more balance between broad and narrow questions and provisions for appropriate pauses.

~~~~~~

DISTRIBUTE QUESTIONS MORE EQUITABLY

A teacher can misjudge the effectiveness of his teaching on the basis of the extent to which pupils participate. Asking several narrow questions at a quick pace may result in a large number of answers. However, the *quality* of the answers and the *number of students* who actually respond to questions should be of concern; for it is not uncommon for a few students to monopolize the answering of questions. The real danger lies in judging

[18] Teacher Education Program Staff, *Minicourse One: Effective Questioning in a Classroom Discussion* (Berkeley, Calif.: Far West Laboratory for Educational Research and Development, 1968), p. 23.

the quality of learning for the entire class on the basis of what is done by a few, since often those who are being questioned the most need it the least.

~~~~~~

Which of the following strategies would best characterize an effective approach to question-asking?

___A. Call on only the willing volunteers since they are more likely to have the correct answer and the non-volunteers may learn from them.
___B. Call primarily on the non-volunteers to encourage them to be active participants.
___C. Call on both willing volunteers and non-volunteers to provide wider distribution of questions.

~~~~~~

A. If you selected *A,* you missed the point. This is the crux of the problem: Only the volunteers benefit from the verbal expression. All too often this strategy materializes into a process of mutual reinforcement between the teacher and these few pupils. The teacher reinforces them for giving the "right" answers and they in turn reinforce the teacher in his attitude about his effectiveness in asking questions. Select another alternative.

B. This method would not solve the problem. Although non-volunteers are much in need of the benefit derived from verbal expression, calling consistently only on them discourages the willing volunteers. In addition, the non-volunteers soon learn that the trick is to raise your hand, and you won't be called on to answer the question. Select another alternative.

C. Very good! If the learning experience is to be beneficial to a large majority, then this strategy offers greater potential. As much as possible, each child should have an opportunity to test his thinking by verbal expression of his thoughts. The opportunity to do so can help to clear misconceptions, develop complete ideas, and lead to a better understanding of concepts that are being emphasized. It is one thing to have a thought, but it is quite another thing to be able to convey that thought to others. If the child can see the worth of his ideas, the quality of his participation is more likely to change.

~~~~~~

Strategy Two: Provide for better balance in participation by calling on both willing volunteers and non-volunteers.

~~~~~~

ENCOURAGE PUPIL PARTICIPATION

If classroom discussions are to be purposeful, allowing well-constructed questions to reach their full potential, pupils must be encouraged to participate. The strategies employed should seek to decrease the amount of teacher talk and increase opportunities for verbal expression on the part of the children. The previously mentioned strategies partially accomplish this goal. Additional strategies for increasing pupil participation are possible.

Which of the following strategies would best encourage an increase in pupil participation?

__A. Repeat or rephrase questions often to be sure that they are clearly understood.

__B. Ask questions that can be directed to more than one individual.

__C. As you ask a question, designate a pupil by name to respond to it, so he can be thinking about his answer.

~~~~~~

A. No! This practice should be discouraged. It only increases the amount of time the teacher spends talking and creates habits of inattentiveness on the part of the pupils. The pupil learns that he doesn't have to pay attention because the question will be repeated. Rephrasing a question on occasions may be necessary to be sure that your initial question was not ambiguous. Sometimes rephrasing the same question different ways before allowing responses helps to match the question to the variety of thinking patterns held by the different members of a class. This strategy is particularly effective when a thought-provoking question is presented, providing that the question is not rephrased so it becomes a narrow question. However, as a general rule, rephrasing and repeating questions should be avoided. This is a common problem for beginning teachers as this segment from an actual classroom dialogue illustrates:

T: Who knows what kind of movement this fish makes?
S: (No response)
T: What kind of movements do these fish make?
S: They move their tails.
T: What else do they use?
S: (No response)
T: Can anybody else see anything else they use?
S: They use their fins.

Return to the previous frame and select another alternative.

B. Good thinking! This is the best alternative. The developers of Minicourse One refer to this as "redirection." [19] This means the strategy involves directing the same question to more than one pupil. The following examples are illustrative:

1. Good idea Matthew! How might you add to or change the answer that he has given?
2. Several observations on these objects are possible. Mary, what might be one? (Others would be encouraged to give additional observations after Mary has given hers.)

Because it permits alternative responses, a broad question is effective in this situation. A narrow question that may include listing or identifying different objects or events will also allow the use of this strategy. "What are some of the many resources that are important to the northern United States?" would be an example. The intent is to develop a teacher question-pupil-pupil-pupil response pattern as opposed to a question-answer-question-answer approach. A verbal prompt that informs students that several answers are possible and that you expect a number of students to respond will help. An example of this kind of prompt is "This question has many answers so I would like many of you to answer." "When you answer give only one idea" is another example. An evaluative question or one that raises points on which there may be conflicting opinions also helps to increase involvement. A pattern of sustained pupil responses and pupil-to-pupil interaction should be your goal.

C. No. Addressing the question to one pupil is an automatic signal for the others to tune you out. If the question is directed to Johnny, the others will think "Let Johnny do it." There may be occasions when this technique can be used to urge a given child to develop a more complete answer or to draw the inattentive student into the discussion ("Bill, what can you add to Linda's answer?"). The more common practice, however, should be to direct a question to the whole group. The gain lies in the fact that all the students form a tentative answer. They will all do some thinking about the question. This fact can be used to advantage as the question is explored further. The teacher should create a feeling of expected participation by everyone.

~~~~~~

Strategy Three: Use questions that both permit and encourage several pupils to respond.

~~~~~~

[19] Teacher Education Program Staff, *Minicourse One,* p. 36.

Improve the Quality of Pupils' Responses

The real challenge for skillful question-asking involves effective use of pupil responses, which is probably the most crucial aspect of question-asking. Few other activities draw as much attention or time on the part of the teacher. Question-asking reflects the quality of teaching ability. The teacher's use of an answer is as important as his asking a good question. The effectiveness of his question-asking approach will depend on the way he accepts, reinforces, or encourages the pupil to build on his initial response. Wholesale acceptance of any answer a child gives deters the development of suitable thinking skills, whereas punishing a child for a wrong or incomplete answer discourages participation. Failure to hold a question long enough to allow a complete thought to develop must be considered an ineffective use of questions.

The answers received for a question may range from no response at all or "I don't know" to a well developed answer that may go beyond the expectations of the teacher. Seldom will a pupil deliberately give a wrong or weak answer. If his thinking is incomplete or based on a misconception, the teacher's strategy should be to help the pupil develop a more complete thought and clear up misconceptions. Correct answers are easily reinforced. The measure of a good question-asker is the way he handles wrong or incomplete answers.

~~~~~~

Which of the following would be the most effective way of handling a weak answer?

___A. Repeat the child's response so that both he and the class can reconsider the answer.

___B. Inform the child of the incorrectness of his answer and direct the question to someone else.

___C. Use verbal prompts or additional questions to help the child correct or clarify his answer.

~~~~~~

A. Repeating answers must be considered an undesirable strategy. It encourages inattentiveness. Pupils develop a habit of listening to the teacher and ignoring what other pupils have to say. This practice also degrades the value of pupils' responses. There may be occasions where the teacher could utilize the child's responses to direct a question to another child or ask the child to repeat his answer to emphasize its value or importance. However, repeating answers should usually be avoided.

The following segment from an actual classroom dialogue illustrates the flaws of this approach:

T: What can you observe about these two liquids?
S: One's red and one's green.
T: All right, you see red in number one and green in number two. Anything else?
S: You can see through them.
T: You can see through them, that's a good observation. Any others?
S: They're in jars.
T: They're in jars, aren't they? Do you think the liquids are the same or different?
S: Different.
T: You think there are two different liquids then?

B. This practice must also be considered less desirable. If a child gives an incorrect answer, he should have an opportunity to correct his error. This may be accomplished by asking another question at a lower level of thought and on information familiar to the pupil. Prodding the child to guess the right answer is not the solution. However, he should realize that he is expected to improve on his answer. When a child is completely wrong he can be tactfully informed of his error. The teacher can allow others to respond to the question and return to this child at a later time to give him a second chance. A verbal prompt such as "Think about your answer and we'll come back to you," might be used.

C. This strategy must be considered the best alternative. It applies to three types of responses. When the child gives a wrong answer the teacher can direct to him additional questions that are narrower in nature and deal with information with which he is familiar. With some prompting he can build a correct response. The teacher might also reinforce him for giving an answer and encourage an alternative or direct the question to others for a response. The student should see that not just any answer will suffice.

If an answer is partially correct, the teacher can tell the child which part is correct and encourage him to correct or clarify the incorrect or incomplete part with requests such as "What else can you tell me about your idea?" "What might be some other reasons?" "How might you say it another way?" "Your answer is about ⅘ right. What do you think is your mistake?" The use of this procedure might also be a way of bringing others into the discussion with something like "Sam's answer is pretty close. How could we improve on it?"

If an answer is correct, the teacher should use verbal cues or questions that will encourage the pupil to broaden his response to other contexts or to raise it to a higher level of thinking.

In any case, the teacher should strive to develop students who give longer and more thoughtful responses and who respond more to each other.

~~~~~~~~~~~~~~~~~~~~~~~~~~~~~~

Strategy Four: Improve student responses by using verbal prompts or questions that cause the pupil to correct, clarify, or extend his answer.

~~~~~~~~~~~~~~~~~~~~~~~~~~~~~~

Summary

The foregoing activities have dealt with some of the dimensions of question-asking. Certainly there are others. You must recognize that question-asking is one of several effective teaching techniques. Skill with this competency is not an end in itself but a means to an end. Question-asking will be effective only if it serves the teacher's purposes and facilitates the learning of his pupils.

If you are genuinely concerned with developing intellectual skills with those you will instruct, proficiency with this competency will be necessary. When these intellectual skills are clearly defined and effective questioning practices are applied to meaningful subject matter, then learning and development of appropriate thought patterns are enhanced.

Hopefully, one of the benefits derived from your work with this chapter is the realization that you can *change* your questioning behavior. Research has shown that questioning behavior can be changed significantly. This research also demonstrates, however, that skill in constructing questions may be different from skill in using questions during the act of teaching. This discovery suggests that teachers must continually analyze their questioning behavior. You will improve your own teaching when you first look at what you do and then try to view it from the vantage point of those you are trying to teach.

Applying the skills you have developed in this chapter will give you the means to analyze your own behavior. Planning for suitable questions and question-asking procedures will enhance your effectiveness. A critical analysis of one's question-asking and its influence on learners, accompanied by appropriate changes based on identified behaviors, is the only way question-asking techniques will emerge as a skill.

~~~~~~~~~~~~~~~~~~~~~~~~~~~~~~

Bibliography

AMIDON, EDMUND, AND ELIZABETH HUNTER, *Improving Teaching: The Analysis of Classroom Verbal Interaction.* New York: Holt, Rinehart & Winston, Inc., 1966.

This paperback seeks to apply research knowledge about verbal interaction in the classroom to practical teaching situations. The Verbal Interaction Category System (VICS), developed by the authors, is applied to the analysis of classroom situations. Several of these situations are described for each of the teaching activities of motivating, planning, informing, leading discussion, disciplining, counseling, and evaluating. Each situation provides an analysis and a skill session for categorizing the nature of the verbal behavior exhibited by teachers and pupils.

BOSSING, NELSON L., *Progressive Methods of Teaching in Secondary Schools.* Boston: Houghton Mifflin Company, 1942, pp. 329–61.

This chapter covers the topic of "The Question in Teaching." Some very useful points about the functions of questions, types of questions, characteristics of good questions, techniques to use in questioning and suggestions for handling students' responses to questions are discussed.

CRUMP, CLAUDIA, *Self-Instruction in the Art of Questioning.* Unpublished booklet, Indiana University, 1969, 65 frames.

An interesting programmed learning activity designed for in-service and pre-service teachers. The program seeks to develop an understanding of levels of questioning which elicit a hierarchy of thinking processes within the context of social studies. By way of a parallel construction, an examination is made of questions typical of textbooks, curriculum guides and oral questions used by teachers.

CUNNINGHAM, ROGER T., *A Descriptive Study Determining the Effects of a Method of Instruction Designed to Improve the Question-Phrasing Practices of Prospective Elementary Teachers.* Unpublished doctoral dissertation, Indiana University, 1968.

An investigation into a method of instruction using video-taped classroom lessons as a basis for the analysis of questioning behavior. The category system described in this chapter was used as a basis for analyzing questions. The study demonstrated that prospective elementary teachers could change their questioning behavior. The change in their ability to construct more thought-provoking questions was found to be highly significant. The reduction in factual recall or rote memory questions asked was found to be equally significant.

FLOYD, WILLIAM D., *An Analysis of the Oral Questioning Activity in Selected Colorado Primary Classrooms.* Unpublished doctoral dissertation, Colorado State College, Greely, Colorado, 1960.

Forty primary school teachers, judged to be the "best" by their principals, were taped during the teaching act. The study demonstrated that teachers dominate classroom verbal activity. More than 1,000 questions were analyzed with less than 100 judged worthy of reflection and only 6 percent stimulating thinking. Nearly 75 percent of the questions demanded factual-recall or rote-memory responses.

GALLAGHER, JAMES J., *Productive Thinking of Gifted Children.* Cooperative Research Project No. 965. Urbana, Illinois: Institute for Research on Exceptional Children, University of Illinois, 1965.

This study includes a description of the Aschner-Gallagher System for Classifying Thought Processes in the Context of Verbal Interaction. The system developed by Gallagher and Mary Jane Aschner includes the four categories, *cognitive-memory, convergent, divergent,* and *evaluative,* used in this chapter for the purpose of classifying questions. In addition to the above four cognitive levels for classifying teacher-pupil interchanges, Aschner and Gallagher included a fifth category called *routine.* This category is used to categorize classroom management type activities. Several subcategories were developed to identify cognitive performances in children. The investigators were concerned with variations in intellectual operations.

MOYER, JOHN R., *An Exploratory Study of Questioning in the Instructional Processes of Selected Elementary Schools.* Unpublished doctoral dissertation, Columbia University, New York, 1965.

A rather involved investigation of question structure and function based on the analysis of a large number of questions asked by teachers. Questions are analyzed both from their grammatical structure and from their functional aspects. The study highlights some of the common problems of question-asking.

SANDERS, NORRIS M., *Classroom Questions: What Kinds?* New York: Harper & Row, Publishers, 1966.

A helpful paperback that presents a scheme for classifying questions based on Bloom's *Taxonomy of Educational Objectives.* The seven categories are applied to questions for social studies. Each chapter deals with examples of questions for each of the seven cognitive levels of the taxonomy. The last chapter gives pertinent ideas on planning for questioning. More attention is given to written or examination questions than to oral questioning.

STEVENS, ROMIETT, *The Question as a Measure of Efficiency in Instruction.* New York: Teachers College, Columbia University, 1912.

An investigation into the number of questions asked by a teacher as an indication of instructional efficiency. By way of transcribed classroom dialogues, analyses are made of both a large and a small number of questions as a measure of effective teaching. A brief examination is made of question quality. Although this study was conducted approximately 60 years ago many of the findings are still common to classrooms today.

TABA, HILDA, SAMUEL LEVIN, AND FREEMAN ELZEY, *Thinking in Elementary School Children,* Cooperative Research Project No. 1574. San Francisco: San Francisco State College, April, 1964.

TEACHER EDUCATION PROGRAM STAFF, *Minicourse One: Effective Questioning in a Classroom Discussion.* Berkeley, Calif.: Far West Laboratory for Educational Research and Development, 1968.

Minicourse One is the first in a package of instructional programs designed to help in-service teachers to improve their teaching competence. This program is a self-instructional device that seeks to improve questioning skills. The program consists of four instructional sequences. These include a set of described strategies designed to serve as models for the teacher. Each instructional sequence seeks to accomplish a behavioral change on the part of the teacher. The objectives are directed to (a) increasing the pupils readiness to respond; (b) decreasing amount of teacher participation and increasing the amount of pupil participation; (c) increasing use of teacher behaviors that change pupils' way of responding; and (d) decreasing teacher behaviors that deter effective questioning. The focus is on ways of employing questions rather than on types of questions. This includes such strategies as pausing, prompting, redirecting, refocusing and seeking clarification. This program would be a good follow-up to the section on strategies in this chapter.

Developing
4 a competency for
sequencing instruction

DORIS A. TROJCAK

University of Missouri-St. Louis

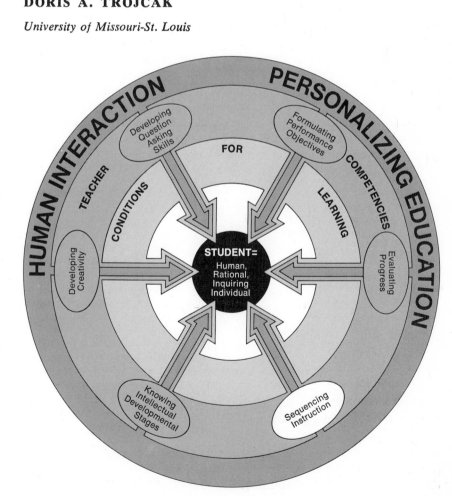

One: What Are Some Important Considerations Prior to Sequencing Instruction?

After completing section One, you should be able to explain the meaning and importance of the following considerations:

   I.   Terminal goal or performance
  II.   The conditions of learning
       A. The learner: his entry behavior
       B. The learning environment: interaction
       C. The teacher: designer of the learning environment
 III.   The factors which influence your instructional role.

~~~~~~

All of us wish we will someday discover that we have enough free time for an unexpected three-week vacation. Let's suppose it has happened to you; you can't afford to fly, so you decide that you'll leave as soon as possible and drive to the West. You can almost feel yourself behind the wheel when you realize that you'd better spend some time planning that trip if you really want to make the most of it. If you were to follow this advice, what plans would you make for your three-week trip?

(Briefly outline your ideas in the space provided below.)

~~~~~~

Examine the ideas you just outlined and check if your planning includes answers to the following important questions.

yes   no

__   __   A. Do you know where you want to go?

__   __   B. Why do you want to go?

— — C. Do you know what you'll need to get there? (Mode of transportation, time, money, food, clothing, other supplies?)
— — D. Do you know the best way to go?

If your plans didn't include answers to these questions, chances are
your traveling efforts will lead you toward ways of frustration rather than
days of vacation.

~~~~~~

Perhaps you've never considered this analogy, but teaching and learning
have much in common with traveling. The traveler has countless places
to go and numerous ways of getting there. The teacher has an almost
endless supply of information to reveal and a wide variety of ways of
presenting it. Both teaching and traveling are highly dependent upon good
planning. Yet both acts are often filled with unexpected events—interesting
side trips, unpredicted sights as well as an occasional "dead battery" or
"flat tire." However, it is often true of both teaching and traveling plans
that the more you put in the more you get out.

If you were planning for several weeks of instruction rather than three
weeks of vacation, how might your questions be similar to those asked
about traveling? (List your questions below.)

~~~~~~

Terminal Goal or Performance

Some of the most important questions you might ask in planning for
teaching are the following:

A. What do you want the students to learn or be able to do?
B. Why do you want the students to learn or be able to do this?
C. What do you need for teaching them?
D. What are the best instructional strategies to meet your goals?

How do your questions correspond to these? You can readily see that both sets of questions for traveling and teaching are concerned with an end product or a *terminal goal* to be achieved. Both inquire about the materials needed as well as the procedures used to reach the desired terminal goal. Both emphasize the necessity for planning. If a bus driver were to take you on a three-week trip to the Grand Canyon, he probably would not suddenly board the bus and immediately say, "Let's go!" Nor should a teacher aimlessly stroll into the classroom Monday morning, glance at the children and wonder, "Hmm, what shall I do with them this week?"

If you are unable to define clearly what you want to accomplish or cause to happen as a result of your traveling or teaching, you will never know if you have reached your terminal goal. On the other hand, if you are able to state explicitly what terminal performance you expect of your learners, you will have a means for evaluating the effectiveness of your instruction and for determining if additional instruction is necessary. If your terminal performance is made known to your learners, they, too, will have a means for evaluating their own performance. Motivation can become self-generating, and learning will probably proceed at a faster rate.

The Conditions of Learning

If you want to plan well for effective teaching, you need to consider the conditions in which learning will occur or the major factors involved in the teaching-learning act. No one can possibly account for all of these conditions, so it might prove more practical to concentrate on just three important ones now; namely, *the learner, the learning environment,* and *the teacher*. Based on your own experience, as student and/or instructor, what do you think you need to know about *the learner* in order to be a better teacher? (Try to list five to ten factors.)

THE LEARNER: HIS ENTRY BEHAVIOR

Here are eleven variables you could consider in "getting to know" each learner. Check the factors you think are similar to your answers.

__A. His ability to recall facts and/or relationships
__B. His physical, emotional, and social maturity
__C. His desire to learn
__D. His ability to concentrate on the task at hand
__E. His ability to work alone and/or with groups
__F. His muscular coordination
__G. His reading and listening abilities
__H. His ability to express himself orally and/or in writing
__I. His need for reinforcement
__J. His reliance on physical or concrete material and/or his ability to abstract and generalize
__K. His learning pace or the rate at which he can progress best

An experienced teacher might quickly add that this list is by no means entirely complete since knowing the learner thoroughly is actually a continuing process. All of these getting-acquainted factors could be combined to define operationally the learner's *entering behavior,* that is, how much he already knows or can do before you try to teach him. Identifying the learner's entry behavior is probably one of the most important yet most frequently ignored tasks of the teacher.

It would be foolish to plan for an instructional goal without considering where to begin and when to conclude your instruction. You can choose the latter (the terminal performance) but not the former (the entry behavior). If you fail to try to identify each learner's entry behavior, you will tend to treat all learners too much alike. Certainly, they are all alike in some ways, but they all differ somewhat in their entering behaviors. You probably already realize that much more planning is necessary to cope with these unique differences.

~~~~~~

THE LEARNING ENVIRONMENT: INTERACTION

One method for coping with individual differences can be found by improving *the learning environment.* But what is meant by the learning environment? Certainly it means more than having a well-ventilated room with proper lighting and clever eye-catching bulletin boards surrounding comfortable desks and chairs. What else would you want to consider in order to provide the most effective learning environment for your students? (Be as creative as you can, but be able to justify your considerations.)

~~~~~~~~~~~~~~~~~~~~~~~~~~~~~~~~~~~~~

The question elicits many possibilities—interest centers, multilevel textbooks and trade books, places for individualized learning or small group discussions, opportunities to move about, to handle and/or observe objects, access to any materials needed to improve learning, and so on.

But have you reached the conclusion that it is difficult to describe an effective learning environment *per se* just as it is difficult to describe a successful vacation without including the people, things, and/or events you encountered?

It is primarily the *teacher's use* of the objects in the classroom, the school, or surrounding area that sets the stage for an effective learning environment as well as the students' receptivity to these objects that produce the successful learning situation. In other words, there must be *interaction* between the teacher and learner with objects and/or ideas if the learning environment is to be alive and dynamic rather than passive and static.

Certainly, there can be different degrees of this threefold interaction as illustrated in Fig. 4–1.

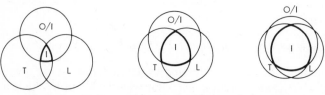

T = teacher, L = learner, O/I = objects and/or ideas, I – interaction

Fig. 4–1

If learning is to occur, then interaction must occur. It is the learner's experiences with the learning environment which bring about changes in behavior, the hallmark of learning.

~~~~~~

THE TEACHER: DESIGNER
OF THE LEARNING ENVIRONMENT

Viewing learning from this perspective might necessitate your re-examining the teacher's role. A teacher should not be merely a disseminator of facts, a "walking encyclopedia," or the star attraction, but rather, a *designer of the learning environment*. A teacher cannot *cause* learning to happen but *can* establish the best conditions in which learning is most likely to occur.[1] If you want to be a competent teacher, you will have to assume several roles in designing the most effective learning environment. Three of your most important roles will be that of *lecturer, listener,* and *"lamplighter."* Depending on the grade or subject you wish to teach, when and why might you function in each capacity?

~~~~~~

You could read in Ecclesiastes (3:1–4) or hear from Judy Collins' rendition of "Turn! Turn! Turn!"[2] that "there is a time for every purpose under heaven . . . a time to plant and a time to reap; a time to laugh and a time to weep. . . ." So, too, there are times for a teacher to talk and times to listen. There are times when students should be allowed to grope unaided toward discovery and times when the teacher must shed some light to guide the way. Your "lamplighting" might occur in varying shades

[1] Harry Kay, Bernard Dodd, and Max Sime, *Teaching Machines and Programmed Instruction* (Baltimore, Maryland: Penguin Books, 1968), p. 30.

[2] "Turn! Turn! Turn! / To Everything There is a Season" (Ecclesiastes-Seeger, Melody Trails, Inc., BMI), *Judy Collins #3,* The Elektra Corporation, New York, 1966.

and intensities to spark interest, keep the learners from going astray, ignite creativity, reveal new avenues, guide inquiries, or provide motivation.

~~~~~~

The Factors Which Influence Your Instructional Role

The amount of effort you spend in lecturing, listening, or "lamplighting" depends on many factors. Included among the most important factors are the newness and complexity of the information being presented or the performances expected of the learner, the amount of time that can be spent or needs to be spent on each specific lesson or topic, your ability to be flexible and vary your roles according to the needs of the students, and the willingness of your students to attend and respond to the learning situation.

At this point, you might well be tempted to succumb to frustration and conclude that it might be far easier to plot a vacation trip than it is to plan an instructional sequence. Perhaps the next section can provide some "lamplighting." But before you continue, try to answer the key question for this section—*What are some important considerations prior to sequencing instruction?*

~~~~~~

Your answer should include a discussion of the meaning and importance of the following factors: (1) the need for planning the achievement of a specified terminal goal, (2) the conditions in which learning will occur (i.e., the learner, the learning environment, and the teacher), and (3) the factors which influence your role in designing the learning environment. If you accounted for these factors, proceed to the next section. If you judge your considerations to be inadequate, you could profit by rereading section One.

~~~~~~

Two: What Are Some of the "Road Maps" or Models That Can Be Used for Sequencing Instruction?

After completing section Two, you should be able to compare five instructional models by filling in a chart which interrelates the components of each strategy.

On many occasions there are numerous routes to choose from in driving from one place to another. The choice of the most appropriate route primarily depends on the type of trip you wish to take, what you have at your disposal, and how you like to travel. Similarly, there are varieties of teaching-learning models or "road maps" you can use in planning your instructional procedures. The choice of an instructional model will depend largely on (1) the type of learning you wish to occur, that is, the terminal behavior expected of the learner, (2) the present status of your learners and the learning environment, and (3) the style or method of teaching by which you are most effective.

This section will serve as an instructional center from which you can obtain information on five possible instructional models for a variety of instructional goals.

The Motor Model

One of the most basic instructional strategies for your consideration is the *motor model.* You might wish to use this strategy if you are interested in helping your learners develop motor skills or capabilities involving muscular coordination. Some terminal performances of this nature might include the ability to print or write legibly, to operate a lathe, a sewing machine, or tape recorder proficiently, to play a musical instrument artistically, to manipulate a balance scale or microscope accurately, to handle athletic equipment skillfully, or to drive a car safely. In what ways are these goals similar and in what ways are they different?

All of the motor skills mentioned require varying degrees of muscular coordination as well as manipulation of equipment. Some learners would have more difficulty in performing them than other learners. All of these skills require mastery of certain basic prerequisites or subordinate skills. Therefore, it would be most helpful to know the learner's entry behavior and what is required of him before planning your sequence of instruction for any of these motor skills.

One possible route you could use in guiding your learners toward the attainment of motor skills appears in Fig. 4–2.

Suppose you want to teach some primary children how to print the word *doll* as ⎯⎯ḋȯⅼⅼ⎯⎯ . Assume their entry behavior to consist of control of movements of the entire body or the most basic gross bodily movements. How would you apply the motor learning model in developing an instructional strategy for helping children achieve this terminal performance of printing the word *doll?* (Sequence the prerequisite skills in the space provided.)

Does your answer include consideration of most of the following prerequisites or subordinate skills?

yes   no

— — 1. development of arm movements (e.g., forming the letter in the air, on the chalkboard, and so on)

— — 2. combining upper and lower limbs to achieve proper writing posture

— — 3. hand-finger coordination for holding the pencil correctly

— — a. ability to make the basic vertical stroke of |

— — b. ability to make the basic circular stroke of ○

— — c. ability to combine the ○ and | strokes to form the letter d

— — 4. eye-hand coordination to print the word *doll* as ⎯ḋȯⅼⅼ⎯

Now choose a terminal performance you might eventually need to teach which requires the development of motor skills. You may select a skill listed previously; other possibilities might include the motor skills of swimming, throwing, hitting, writing, typing, painting, constructing, or measuring.

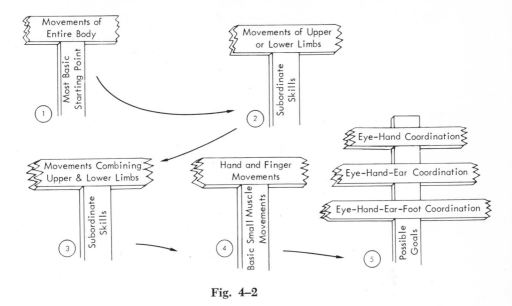

Fig. 4–2

Choose a task which you think is relevant to your prospective learners. Outline your instructional sequence for the motor task of your choice. Begin by stating (1) the terminal performance expected, (2) the assumed entry behavior of your learners, and (3) the sequence of subordinate skills necessary to achieve your stated goal. After you've completed your "road map," compare your sequence to the motor-learning model in Fig. 4–2 to determine if you're leading your learners in the right direction.

S.P.C.P. Model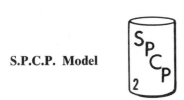

Perhaps one of the simplest cognitive road maps to read but one of the more difficult to follow is the S.P.C.P. version—symbolized here as

SENSATIONS ⟩   PERCEPTIONS ⟩   CONCEPTS ⟩   PRINCIPLES .

(Although the S.P.C.P. model might sound like a new oil or gasoline additive, it can add thrust to your inductive or discovery approach to sequencing instruction.)

Learning begins with *sensations,* the products of stimulation of the sense organs, that is, any responses registered by the senses. The more the learner uses and combines his senses, the more the sensations are improved. Sensations are the "stuff" from which *perceptions* or impressions of experience with objects, events, qualities, or relationships are formed. That is, perceptions result from a synthesis of separate sensory elements. It is important to note that many factors influence a learner's perceptions. Sometimes he perceives only what he has learned to perceive or only when his observations fit into a meaningful pattern. The perceptions of others might also influence his. As the learner gathers more perceptions, he begins to form *concepts* or abstractions of particular impressions organized into categories. Some examples of concepts could include the name of an object (car), an event (vacation), a process (combustion), a property (distance), a class (mammals), or a symbol ( ). When the learner is able to organize or chain relationships among concepts, he can formulate *principles* or generalizations. (The following example of a principle shows the relationship among seven concepts: When *two vowels* occur *together,* the *first* is *long* and the *second* is *silent.*) If the learner has been deprived of sufficient stimuli, that is, if his interaction with the learning environment has been limited so that he has experienced few sensations, his perceptions will be restricted and probably inaccurate. This, in turn, will have detrimental effects on his concept and principle formation.

ROAD
WORK
AHEAD

You've been reading a great deal and can become like a driver in a near-hypnotic trance when he's been staring straight ahead too long. Take a moment to think, then outline your answer to this very important question: What implication does the S.P.C.P. learning model have for your instructional planning and/or teaching?

Have you come up with four or five implications? If not, think a little longer.

Which of the following implications correspond to your outline?

1. ___the need for providing direct or first-hand experiences rather than in-direct or vicarious experiences (a "hands on" rather than a "hands off" approach)
2. ___the opportunity for the learner to use as many of his senses as possible
3. ___providing for active involvement in a meaningful learning environment based on individual needs
4. ___adjusting your instructional material to the maturity and background of the learners
5. ___recognizing that all learners do not have the same perceptual skill
6. ___examining the principles the learners encounter in textbooks, films, oral explanations, and so on. (Can they comprehend the concepts involved? Have their perceptions been accurate?)

RESUME
SAFE
SPEED

Teachers often require their students to interpret data, expository writing, fiction, or poetry. How would you use the S.P.C.P. learning model to guide your learners to interpret either of the following poems? (Establish the assumed entry behavior and background of your learners.)

Apartment House

A filing-cabinet of human lives
Where people swarm like bees in tunneled hives,
Each to his own cell in the towered comb,
Identical and cramped—we call it home.[3]

Apartment Houses

Apartment houses on our street
Stand side by side.
Some of them are narrow,
Some are wide.

[3] Gerald Raftery, "Apartment House," *The New York, Sun,* 1965.

Some of them are low,
Some are high,
Some of them have towers
That reach into the sky.

All of them have windows,
Oh, so many!
There is not one house
That doesn't have any.[4]

(Are you considering the first poem, "Apartment House," or the second, "Apartment Houses"? Circle your choice.)

Assumed entry behavior:

Sensations to be provided:

Perceptions to be formed:

Concepts to be developed:

Principles to be formulated:

It should be quite obvious that there is no "one right answer" to be developed according to the S.P.C.P. model for either poem. However, de-

[4] James S. Tippett, "Apartment Houses," from James S. Tippett, *I Live in a City* (New York: Harper & Brothers, 1927). Copyright © 1927 by Harper & Brothers; renewed 1955 by James S. Tippett. Reprinted by permission of Harper & Row, Publishers.

pending on the background and entry behavior you assumed for your learners, your answer might include the following:

First Poem, "Apartment House"	Second Poem, "Apartment Houses"
Sensations	*Sensations*
1. see various apartments	1. same as first poem
2. feel what it's like on the top story	2. same as first poem
3. see how much room is available	3. same as first poem
4. observe a filing cabinet, a swarm of bees, a bee hive	4. see the many windows
5. feel the tunnels of a hive	
6. feel how close each cell is	
Perceptions	*Perceptions*
1. crowded living conditions in identical cell-like quarters	1. different sizes of apartments
2. rushing from place to place	2. multitude of windows
Concepts	*Concepts*
1. filing cabinet	1. apartment houses
2. human lives	2. street
3. people	3. side by side
4. swarm	4. narrow
5. bees	5. wide
6. tunneled hives	6. low
7. cell	7. high
8. towered	8. towers
9. comb	9. sky
10. identical	10. windows
11. cramped	11. house
12. home	
Principles	*Principles*
1. Men sometimes must live very regimented lives.	1. There are many kinds of apartment houses.
2. Apartments serve as homes.	2. Apartments have many windows.
3. Analogies make poetry more meaningful.	

By now you should be able to analyze the various components of the S.P.C.P. model, but how would you go about teaching them? *How,* for example, would you teach a concept? The following nine steps could be used in teaching a concept:

Step 1: Specify the terminal performance you expect of the learner after he has learned the concept.

Step 2: Decide on the number of important attributes or characteristics of the concept to be learned.

Step 3: Establish the vocabulary necessary for learning the concept.

Step 4: Present examples and non-examples of the concept. (Keep a specific example before the students at all times as a basis for comparison.)

Step 5: Present the examples simultaneously or in close succession.

Step 6: Allow the learner to generalize—present a new example (perhaps a more difficult one) and ask the learner to identify it as an example or non-example of the concept. (He has learned the concept if he can identify it as a new positive example.)

Step 7: Verify the learning of the concept by presenting additional examples and non-examples.

Step 8: Have the learner define the concept if this is required by your terminal performance.

Step 9: Provide opportunities for student responses and reinforce these responses during Steps 4–8.[5]

~~~~~~

How well can you apply the preceding steps? Identify the following components from a lesson on teaching the concept *vacation* according to the previous nine steps listed. (Include Step 9 with the appropriate five final steps.)

__A. So that the student can always have the example in view *as a basis for comparison,* the teacher staples on the bulletin board a large picturesque poster from the travel bureau entitled, "Sun and Fun in the Bahamas!" Pictures of men playing golf and men entering a steel mill are also shown.

__B. The learners should be able to *pronounce* the word vacation.

__C. The learners are able to *state a definition* of vacation.

__D. The four *main characteristics* of *vacation* are suspension of work, rest, recreation, traveling for pleasure.

__E. A series of pictured *examples* is presented and discussed *in succession*— a surfer, a family having a picnic, a cab driver, a coal miner, a construction crew, boys putting up a tent, and so on.

__F. The learners are required to categorize eight new *additional examples and non-examples* of pictures under two headings: *Examples of Vacation* and *Not Examples of Vacation,* and explain their choices.

__G. *At the end of the lesson,* the *learners are expected* to be able to define and identify an example of the concept vacation.

[5] John P. De Cecco, *The Psychology of Learning and Instruction: Educational Psychology* (Englewood Cliffs, New Jersey: Prentice-Hall, Inc., 1968), pp. 402–18.

___H. The learners are asked *to generalize* if a picture showing hikers in the mountains is similar to the Bahamas poster.

Your arrangement of the steps for teaching the concept of vacation should be A = Steps 4 and 9, B = Step 3, C = Steps 8 and 9, D = Step 2, E = Steps 5 and 9, F = Steps 7 and 9, G = Step 1, and H = Steps 6 and 9. If you missed more than three of four, reread the nine steps for teaching a concept and try again, arranging the appropriate step for A through H.

~~~~~~

As you might surmise, there is also a series of steps you might follow for teaching principles. (Look for similarities between this list and the list of steps for teaching concepts.)

Step 1: Specify the terminal performance expected of the learner after he has learned the principle.

Step 2: Analyze the learner's entry behavior to determine which component concepts or subprinciples the learner must comprehend in learning the new principle.

Step 3: Develop the component concepts if necessary.

Step 4: Guide the students in establishing the proper relationships of the component concepts.

Step 5: Provide opportunities for the learner to use the principles.

Step 6: Have the learner define the principle.

Step 7: Verify the learning of the principles by presenting additional opportunities for application.

Step 8: Provide opportunities for reinforcement of student responses as well as additional practice of the principle if necessary.[6]

Suppose you wanted to teach this principle: When two vowels occur together, the first is long and the second is silent. Which of De Cecco's steps in teaching principles are stated in the following tasks?

Step ___ The learner should give an example of a vowel.

Step ___ Given the words *boat, pail, train,* and *please,* the learner should demonstrate how to pronounce them.

(The first task exemplifies step three and the second, step five or seven. By the way, you just experienced step eight.)

~~~~~~

[6] *Ibid.,* pp. 418–27.

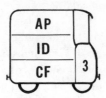

Taba Tri Tram

Let's now examine a third instructional "road map." This model has been dubbed the Taba Tri Tram and consists of three cognitive tasks or clusters of intellectual processes:

Level I. *Concept Formation.* This involves organizing unorganized information by
   1. Enumerating and listing
   2. Identifying common properties, abstracting
   3. Labeling and categorizing, determining the hierarchical order of items.
Level II. *Interpretation of Data.* This involves forming generalizations or using inductive reasoning by
   1. Identifying points, examining similar aspects of selected topics
   2. Explaining items of identified information, comparing and contrasting, identifying cause and effect relationships
   3. Forming inferences, implications, or extrapolations.
Level III. *Application of Principles and Facts.* This involves the process of deductive reasoning by
   1. Predicting consequences, hypothesizing
   2. Explaining and/or supporting the predictions or hypotheses
   3. Verifying the prediction or hypotheses.[7]

Your attempts at implementing the Taba model will become more successful if you carefully predesign or at least selectively ask appropriate lead questions of your learners. The appropriate choice of questions can be a prime means for guiding your learners in forming concepts, interpreting data, and applying principles.

~~~~~~

Consider the following terminal performance: Given the picture illustrated in Fig. 4–3, the learners will name several principles that could be applied in improving damaged land.

---

[7] Hilda Taba, *Teachers' Handbook for Elementary Social Studies* (Palo Alto, California: Addison-Wesley Publishing Co., 1967), pp. 91–117.

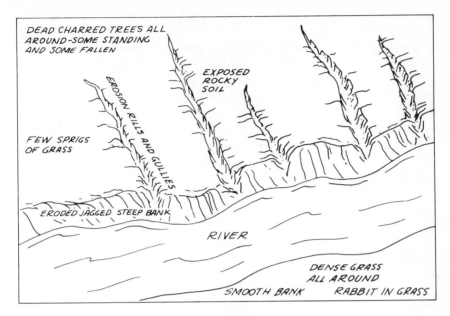

DEAD CHARRED TREES ALL AROUND—SOME STANDING AND SOME FALLEN

EROSION RILLS AND GULLIES

EXPOSED ROCKY SOIL

FEW SPRIGS OF GRASS

ERODED JAGGED STEEP BANK

RIVER

DENSE GRASS ALL AROUND

SMOOTH BANK   RABBIT IN GRASS

Fig. 4–3

Try to identify the major cognitive levels to which the following questions allude. (You can use the abbreviations *CF* for concept formation, *ID* for interpretation of data, and *AP* for application of principles.)

___1. What do you *infer* caused the two sides of the stream to be different?
___2. What do you *see* in the picture?
___3. Which of the objects pictured are *most alike*?
___4. What do you *predict* might eventually happen to the stream?
___5. How does the upper left part of the picture *differ* from the lower right portion?
___6. What would be necessary to improve the area pictured?
___7. How would you *categorize* the objects pictured?

(If you feel as if you're being "washed away," refer to the model on page 148.)

The questions which would help the learners toward concept formation are *2* (enumerating and listing), *3* (identifying common properties), and *7* (determining the hierarchical order of items). The questions requiring interpretation of data are *1* (form inferences) and *5* (compare and contrast). Two questions call for the application of principles—*4* (predicting consequences) and *6* (explaining predictions).

~~~~~~

Suppose another terminal performance requires the learners to be able to describe how people's lives would be different if they moved to large flat land areas located at 80° to 85° south latitude after having lived on similar land along 15° to 20° north latitude. How would you categorize your questions according to Taba's model to guide the learners toward this terminal performance? (You might find it helpful to discuss this task with three or four people who are also reading this chapter.)

Concept Formation:

Interpretation of Data:

Application of Principles:

~~~~~~

Again, there is no one right answer or foolproof set of questions for this problem. However, the following points can be used for comparison.

 I. Your questions should help the learners form concepts about parallel lines of latitude, degrees of latitude, sea level, what one would see and/or feel at the specified locations, how the people's lives can be categorized, and so on.
 II. Your questions could cause the learners to interpret and compare data from annual temperature graphs and amount of precipitation graphs, make inferences based on these data, explain what natural resources are present in both areas, imply occupations, and so on.
 III. Your final questions should guide the learners in predicting consequences based on principles previously developed, in supporting the differences suggested, then verifying the predictions with new factual information.

Notice that in using the Taba model the teacher does far less lecturing, much more listening, and a great deal of "lamplighting."

Bloom's Taxi

Suppose you prefer a taxi to a tram. Then you might be interested in Bloom's Taxi, a model based on the *Taxonomy of Educational Objectives* [8] for the cognitive domain. A taxonomy is a system of organizing according to their natural relationships not only plants and animals, but also types of behavior and levels of understanding. Bloom and his associates have arranged intellectual behavior into a hierarchy consisting of six major categories. Each category or level is progressively more complex and is therefore dependent on the preceding. A stairway can be used to represent this model. (See Fig. 4–4.)

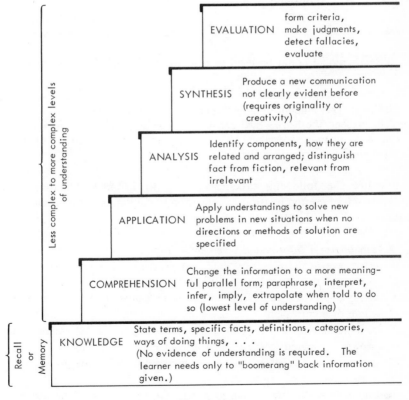

Fig. 4—4

[8] Benjamin S. Bloom, ed., *Taxonomy of Educational Objectives. Handbook I: Cognitive Domain* (New York: David McKay, 1967).

~~~~~~

Which of Bloom's cognitive behaviors would you elicit from the learner if you asked him to

___1. *state an inference* which has some degree of probability
___2. *solve a new problem* without seeking help
___3. *name* the three main branches of government
___4. *design* an *original* floor plan for a new school
___5. explain which of two courses of action produced *better* results
___6. *determine the main points* from a state-of-the-union address

~~~~~~

Task *1* requires comprehension; *2,* application; *3,* knowledge; *4,* synthesis; *5,* evaluation; and *6,* analysis.

~~~~~~

Bloom's model could be used in teaching this terminal performance.

Given unorganized data on a corn plant consisting of water given per day, soil type, amount of growth per day over three weeks, and amount of light present, the learner will construct a bar graph showing the growth of the corn plant and evaluate the accuracy of the graph according to the normal growth curve for plants.

Identify the following tasks according to Bloom's cognitive levels of knowledge, comprehension, application, analysis, synthesis, and evaluation.

___A. can *interpret information* given in a graph
___B. can organize the necessary data and *produce* a bar graph showing the growth of the corn plant
___C. can *use* previous knowledge of growing plants to predict the growth curve of a corn plant
___D. can *examine agreement* among data presented in the bar graph of corn growth compared to the normal growth curve for plants
___E. can *determine relevant data* to be used in graphing the growth of the corn plant
___F. can *state* which data pertain to water, soil, growth, and light, can recognize a bar graph and the normal growth curve for plants

~~~~~~

The cognitive levels for these tasks may not seem unquestionably clear-cut, but the following classification is highly reasonable: A = comprehension, B = synthesis, C = application, D = evaluation, E = analysis, and F = knowledge.

~~~~~~

Now, try to develop your own sequence of prerequisite skills based on Bloom's model for this similar (yet less specific) terminal performance:

> Given an incomplete story describing an episode in the lives of three individuals, the learner will write two endings for the story and evaluate the endings according to what would most likely happen.

Or, if you prefer, compose your own original terminal performance. But, in either case, establish the assumed entry behavior of your learners and compare your instructional sequence with Fig. 4–4.

Assumed entry behavior:

Terminal performance:

Knowledge prerequisites:

Comprehension prerequisites:

Application prerequisites:

Analysis prerequisites:

Synthesis prerequisites:

Evaluation prerequisites:

~~~~~~

Perhaps you've become aware or were already aware that it is far easier to ask the learner questions or require tasks at the knowledge or recall level than at any of the five higher levels. This is another reason why pre-designing your instruction sequentially is so necessary. Students will not develop the intellectual skills of comprehension, application, analysis, synthesis, or evaluation automatically. It is your job to "lamplight" the proper learning environment so that these cognitive levels can be reached. You might try asking yourself each day you teach: What opportunities am I giving my students to demonstrate their comprehension, to apply what they comprehend, to analyze and synthesize, and to evaluate?

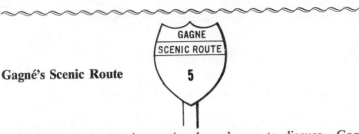

Gagné's Scenic Route

We have one more instructional road map to discuss—Gagné's cumulative learning model, which will enable you to take a more comprehensive or "scenic" route. Gagné's model begins with one of the simplest types of learning, specific responding, and terminates in one of the most difficult types, problem solving. Examine the "road map" of Gagné shown in Fig. 4–5.

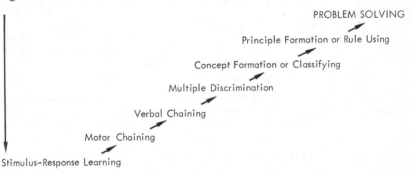

Fig. 4–5

Study Table 4–1 (p. 156) carefully; begin at the bottom of the table with the simplest type of learning, stimulus-response learning.

Analyze the following performances, and sequence them according to Gagné's learning model by numbering them one through seven. (You might wish to cut out and separate these tasks if it will facilitate your sequencing them.)

A. focusing a magnifying glass to examine a seashell

B. placing all of the seashells in one group and all of the non-seashells in another group

C. stating a descriptive sentence about seashells (e.g., "This looks like the Shell gas sign.")

D. saying "seashell" after the teacher has said "seashell"

E. giving an operational definition of seashell

F. finding three similarities between a seashell and a house

G. naming the basic shapes, colors, and textures of ten seashells

~~~~~~

Table 4-1 Performances Typical of Various Types of Learning

Type of Learning	*Performances*	*Examples*
Problem Solving	Solving a novel problem to achieve a goal by applying one or more rules	e.g., determining the weight of two objects when no scale is available
Rule Using (Principle Formation)	Relating two or more concepts; performing an action based on a rule or chain of concepts	e.g., placing a question mark at the end of an interrogative statement.
Classifying (Concept Formation)	Responding to things or events in terms of some common abstract properties to form a class; ability to generalize	e.g., assigning all of the nouns to one group and the verbs to another
Multiple Discrimination	Recognizing physical differences among stimuli and making different responses accordingly to them	e.g., identifying all the trees in a park or remembering the names of your students
Verbal Chaining	Combining words to form verbal responses	e.g., saying the pledge of allegiance or naming an object
Motor Chaining	Demonstrating a series of related actions; learning motor skills	e.g., tying a square knot or writing with a pen
Stimulus-Response Learning	Giving a certain specific response to a specified stimulus	e.g., raising the right hand when asked to do so

Your final product should look like this:

1st: *D* (stimulus-response learning)
2nd: *A* (motor chaining)
3rd: *C* (verbal chaining)
4th: *G* (multiple discrimination)
5th: *B* (concept formation or classifying)
6th: *E* (principle formation or rule using)
7th: *F* (problem solving)

~~~~~~

One of the more important changes in behavior which can readily be used as a terminal goal of instruction is problem-solving ability as specifically described by Gagné or in the broader sense of reaching the top levels of the other four strategies previously discussed. This type of ability requires the learner to *use* the skills and/or principles already mastered to achieve a new goal. Too often students are required merely to memorize terms, or lists, or formulae just for the sake of memorizing, and the terminal goal measures only their "boomeranging ability." In providing for problem-solving ability, the teacher gives the students opportunity to *apply* what they have learned. Such behavior can be observed best when the students are confronted with a novel problem, one not previously presented or discussed in class, but one which the learners can solve if they apply their skills and/or understandings.

~~~~~~

Which of the following objectives do you think require(s) the learner to demonstrate problem-solving ability? (Put a check before your choice or choices.)

___1. Given the vocabulary words, *dolichocephalism, Czechoslovakian, Stradivarius,* and *jollification,* the learner should be able to use his dictionary and syllabicate them.
___2. Having mastered addition problems involving the Arabic numerals 1–10, the children should be able to design their own original symbols for 1–10 and construct five addition problems using their new numerals.
___3. Having previously studied an account of the early attempts at colonizing America, the students should be able to name and give the founding dates of the thirteen original colonies.

Justify your choice or choices in the space below.

~~~~~~

How's your own problem-solving ability? You've just demonstrated it correctly if you chose the second statement. This is the type of task which requires the learners to evidence some original thinking. They have to apply what they already know to a new situation. The first statement is little more than a reinforcement activity. It provides the learners additional practice in using the dictionary but does not require them to do original thinking. If the students had studied the rules of syllabication and were then asked to apply these rules without using the dictionary, they would be demonstrating problem-solving ability. Task three requires the students to recall specific facts and dates; it does not require them to apply their understanding in a new situation, to do something with it and produce something uniquely their own.

Choosing the various goals to be achieved during the daily, weekly, and monthly teaching-learning interactions is never an easy task. One way to judge the value of the terminal performance expected of the learners is to view the end result honestly in terms of two questions: Am I training (<L. *trahere,* to pull) my students to be loquacious parrots and proficient "boomerangers"? or am I educating (<L. *e-,* out + *ducere,* to lead) them to be creative thinkers and capable doers? Often your students' interests, needs, or concerns can supply the most relevant guidance in answering these important questions.

Once you have decided on the terminal behavior you expect of your learners, you need to consider the prerequisites necessary for their reaching that goal. As a designer of instruction you need to ask again and again, "What must the learner already know or be able to do to achieve the desired new knowledge or understanding?" The results of the sequential answering of this question become a learning hierarchy. This learning hierarchy then becomes your instructional road map designating where you begin, how you progress with the instruction, and where you terminate the teaching-learning act. The learning hierarchy is also analogous to a learning ladder with the size of the learning steps or the requirements of each subsequent objective dependent upon the ability of the learner to climb. For example, you cannot usually expect a learner to leap to problem-solving ability before he has mastered the prerequisite steps of principle formation, concept formation, multiple discrimination, as well as those levels farther down the learning ladder.

It has probably become more evident that the choice of any terminal performance for any level of learning is seldom an easy decision. But the choice becomes less perplexing if the goal is defined as an observable and therefore measurable *change in behavior.* By achieving a clearly defined terminal performance, you should be able to answer the question, "As a result of your instruction, what can the learner now do that he was previously unable to do?"

Consider these two proposed terminal goals of instruction: (1) I want my learners to appreciate the freedom of expression provided by poetry; (2) my students should have a clearer understanding of the complexities of a single living cell. Explain why these statements are or are not suitable terminal goals of instruction.

Certainly the previous goals are worthwhile objectives for any teachers of literature or biology, but how will the teachers know that the goals have been achieved? They are neither observable nor measurable. If your terminal goal in traveling is to see the Grand Canyon or spend several days in Las Vegas, your senses (or lack of cents) will let you know you have achieved your goal. However, you'll have a far more difficult time judging the attainment of your instructional goals unless they are directed toward changes in behavior which are observable and therefore measurable. The five instructional road maps previously discussed can give you some guidance as you strive to lead your learners toward observable, measurable, and, hopefully, meaningful goals.

Two: Final Check Point

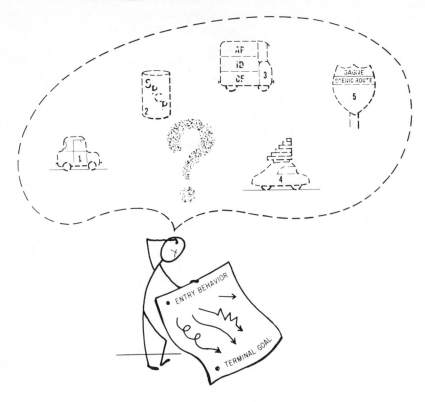

Here's the final checkup on your understanding of section Two. Compare the five sequencing strategies by placing an "X" in the appropriate box in Fig. 4–6. Some of the descriptions are applicable to more than one instructional model.

Have you just experienced duress or success? Compare your answers with those in Fig. 4–7; then administer the appropriate fine.

～～～～～～～～～～～～～～～～～～～～～～～～～～～～～～

  0 violations: The judge awards you a certificate of excellence.
1– 4 violations: You win permission to proceed to section Three.
5– 8 violations: You receive a warning ticket. Review before proceeding.
9–12 violations: You are issued a court order to reread each instrumental model.
13–16 violations: You receive a double court order to reread each model and rework each example.
17–20 violations: You need driver's training. Go back and reread this entire section.

～～～～～～～～～～～～～～～～～～～～～～～～～～～～～～

	Motor Model	SPCP Model	Taba Tri Tram	Bloom's Taxi	Gagne's Scenic Route
1. Has concept formation as a specific level					
2. Most applicable for teaching only manipulatory skills					
3. Begins with concept formation					
4. Requires intellectual synthesis at the highest level					
5. Emphasizes sensory experiences prior to concept formation					
6. Illustrates a taxonomy of cognition					
7. Incorporates principle formation at highest level					
8. Has seven distinct levels of learning					
9. Terminates with the use of a criterion					
10. Can be used to individualize instruction					

Fig. 4–6

	Motor Model	SPCP Model	Taba Tri Tram	Bloom's Taxi	Gagne's Scenic Route
1.		X	X		X
2.	X				
3.			X		
4.		X	X	X	X
5.		X			
6.				X	
7.		X	X	X	X
8.					X
9.				X	
10.	X	X	X	X	X

Fig. 4–7

Three: What Are the Disadvantages and Advantages of Sequencing Instruction?

After completing this section, you should be able to state and defend what you believe are the most important disadvantages and advantages of sequencing instruction.

Hopefully, you've now reached a point in your reading and thinking where you are able to look more critically at various strategies for sequencing instruction. You should be able to recognize more realistically some of the advantages and disadvantages of attempting to sequence the teaching-learning act. What do you think are the main *disadvantages* you might encounter or have already experienced? (Think about this carefully and honestly before you list your ideas.)

~~~~~~

Have you considered the following five problems associated with sequencing instructions?

1. There is presently no "best" method, (nor will there probably ever be) by which learning should be sequenced. There is no proven formula that can be revealed to you before you enter the teaching profession or one that you will surely discover after you've been teaching for several years. Learning is far too unpredictable since human behavior is still so incompletely understood.

2. No single strategy of sequence will be appropriate for every learner. It must be understood that just as a teacher cannot cause learning to occur, neither can the most logically designed sequence of instruction. A sequence of instruction is simply a means for presenting material and/or providing tasks with which the learners can interact. Such a presentation may not be optimally effective for all members of your class. An "ideal" sequence of items for one student may be dramatically ineffective for another.

3. There are presently few validly tested models or strategies which can

be used as reliable guides for presenting learning sequentially. For too many textbooks, teachers' manuals, and resource books have been written by individuals who have never (or at least not recently) encountered the learners for which the material was prepared. Learning cannot be sequenced in a void; there must be interaction, assessment, revamping, and more interaction.

4. The "ideal" sequence of instruction, either on paper or in the mind of the designer, will be only as effective or as ineffective as the uses to which it is put. It must always be a means rather than an end in itself. Again, recall the initial task of planning a three-week vacation trip. You need to have some final destination in mind and direct your efforts toward it. But it would be a sad and sterile trip, indeed, if you never took advantage of the numerous opportunities for side trips. Sometimes it is the side trips or series of side trips which might become more meaningful, more stimulating and fulfilling than that originally planned final destination. This phenomenon is also true of teaching. you would teach only sad and sterile lessons if you never capitalized on those unanticipated questions and interests of your students. Sometimes these "side trips" can become more effective routes to follow toward the terminal performance expected than your own plans. It requires a great deal of flexibility and judgment to determine which way is "best"—sometimes on the spur of the moment— but this is one of the reasons why teaching is not only so frustrating but also so challenging.

5. It is quite obvious that good planning requires a great deal of time and thought. Ultimately, only you can decide if the results of this time expenditure are worth the effort. In the final analysis, it will be your decision, to a great extent, which will determine your effectiveness in all phases of teaching.

~~~~~~

Briefly state and defend what you consider to be the most important disadvantages of sequencing instruction.

~~~~~~

But what about the positive side of sequencing instruction? What values or *advantages* can be derived from your attempts to sequence the learning events to be encountered by your students?

~~~~~~

Here are four fundamental values or advantages which can be derived from sequencing instruction.

1. One of the most valuable results of your attempting to sequence learning is the avoidance of a haphazard, hit-or-miss style of teaching. The more you plan your instruction the more confident you'll become in your own effectiveness. You'll be much more capable of having an answer for that fearful and oftentimes panic-producing question, "What shall I do next?" In other words, your sequencing instruction will help you become a more goal-oriented teacher.

2. Sequenced instruction as opposed to haphazard teaching will enable the learner to progress according to his own capabilities. Ideally, your sequenced instruction should require the learner to take only that step which he is at the moment best equipped and most likely to take. As you become more proficient at sequencing your instruction so will you become more competent in meeting the individual needs of your students.

3. Broad areas of content or complex skills become more manageable if they are broken down into smaller, subordinate parts. These lower-level skills or understandings can be predicted to generate a positive transfer to higher level ones. Thus the ability to sequence has diagnostic value as you plan the sequence of learning "down the ladder" or as the learner progresses "up the ladder" of the learning hierarchy.

4. Once you are actually in a position to test your sequence, you will become increasingly aware of some of the most relevant questions to education: How do children learn? What variables or conditions influence learning? In what ways do individuals differ in learning? There are no immediate or complete answers to these questions. However, the implementation of your own strategies for sequencing instruction will at least cause you to realize more directly the existence of these questions and problems. This realization is a necessary prerequisite for any initial attempts at

formulating answers. The progressive answering of these questions will in turn help you toward one of your terminal goals—becoming a more effective designer of instruction.

If you really were concerned about getting the most out of that originally suggested three-week vacation, you could go to a travel agency for advice, read about it in books or magazines, or simply plan the trip on your own. But all of the information you accumulate won't make a trip enjoyable or even real. You have to experience it; you have to take the vacation trip.

The same is true of sequencing instruction. You can talk about it, read about it, or actually reach the point of outlining your strategy for it. But if you really want to determine if your strategy works, you have to try it. Only then can you also determine if the advantages listed here are "for real," and hopefully, be able to state and defend your own list of advantages. You might also see the entire teaching-learning scene in a new and better light.

~~~~~~

Selected References

BLOOM, BENJAMIN S., ed., *Taxonomy of Educational Objectives. Handbook I: Cognitive Domain.* New York: David McKay, 1967. A thorough explanation of six cognitive levels with numerous examples.

DE CECCO, JOHN P., *The Psychology of Learning and Instruction: Educational Psychology.* Englewood Cliffs, New Jersey: Prentice-Hall, Inc., 1968. One of the most excellent treatises on the teaching-learning act. (An almanac rather than a road map!)

GAGNÉ, ROBERT M., *The Conditions of Learning.* Chicago: Holt, Rinehart & Winston, Inc., 1965. An explanation of one of the best learning models for sequencing instruction.

KIBLER, ROBERT J., LARRY L. BARKER, AND DAVID T. MILES, *Behavioral Objectives and Instruction.* Boston: Allyn & Bacon, Inc., 1970. A broad coverage of cognitive, affective, and motor instructional objectives.

TABA, HILDA, *Teachers' Handbook for Elementary Social Studies.* Reading: Mass.: Addison-Wesley Publishing Company, 1967. A model applicable for all areas of curriculum.

TROJCAK, DORIS A., "Five Stages of Instruction for Sequencing Science Activities According to Gagné's Learning Model," Unpublished doctoral thesis, Indiana University, 1969. Good review of the literature and rationale on sequencing instruction.

WALBESSER, HENRY H., *Constructing Behavioral Objectives.* College Park, Maryland: The Bureau of Educational Research and Field Services, 1968. A concise self-instructional program on the components and construction of behavioral objectives and behavioral hierarchies.

Developing
5 a competency for
evaluation in the classroom

RONALD D. ANDERSON

University of Colorado

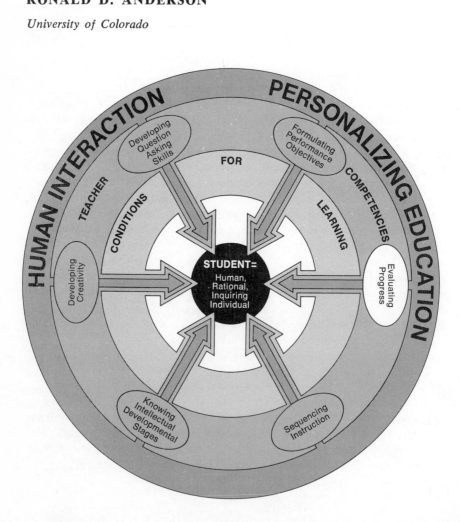

Before You Begin . . .

The chapter which you are about to begin is designed to build your competency in evaluating educational progress. The chapter is easy to use; simply begin with section A of Frame 1 and follow the directions given in that section. In each section you generally will be given a choice of answers to a question followed by the section (e.g., *3A*) to which you should proceed if you have chosen that answer. *3A,* for example, refers to section A of Frame 3. That section will give you directions as to the next section to which you should go, etc., until you have completed the chapter. When you choose a wrong answer you will generally be referred back to the section containing the question, while if you choose the correct answer, you can proceed on without reading some sections.

So, proceed to *1A* and begin. In addition to being an important topic, evaluation is very interesting in itself; enjoy your learning.

~~~~~~

Why Evaluate?

1.

A. If you asked a student whether or not tests and grades served any useful purpose, the off-hand response might be an emphatic "no." This response tells us something about both people and our society, including our educational system. Occasionally, parents may hold out unreasonable expectations of the level of achievement of their children, teachers may use grades as a "club," or students may study for grades rather than for understanding. Like most useful things, grades can be used improperly, a fact which probably explains the many attempts over several decades to eliminate or curtail their use in our educational system. But evaluation, including grades in many forms, is still with us (and probably always will be) because it serves many necessary and valuable purposes.

Which one of the following is a legitimate use of grades?

___a. A teacher uses the threat of a low grade in the course to restrain Johnny from terrorizing his eighth-grade social studies class. (3A)
___b. A teacher uses grades in tenth- and eleventh-grade English as a partial basis for deciding who will be permitted to enroll in a senior honors course in English. (5A)

B. This is an important reason but not as important as one of the others in *5A*.

C. Since no mention was made of any use of the scores, we conclude that this is measurement without evaluation. Return to *4A* and go on to b.

~~~~~~

2.

A. The teacher has evaluated the student's performance as measured on the two tests. Go on to c of *4A*.

B. You have the idea. The student is displaying some degree of understanding of the relative merits of the two historical sources. This does not mean, of course, that informal evaluation should be limited to a single or even to a few objectives. The point is, whatever the objective or objectives, evaluate in terms of the objectives.

Earlier, mention was made of the degree of "trust" that we could put in various measurements. Before proceeding further we need to define two words, *reliability* and *validity,* which are more precise descriptors of this quality of a test or any other source of measures. Reliability is an indicator of the stability or consistency of a measuring device. The extent to which a measuring device is useful for a particular purpose or it measures what it is intended to measure is indicated by its validity.

An example may help. Suppose that a group of students is given a test that consists simply of marking x's on a piece of paper as rapidly as possible for one minute. Each student's score consists of the number of x's that he makes during that time. This is probably a very reliable test; that is, the results would be quite stable or consistent from one time to another if the test were given several times. Although this test is reliable it may or may not be valid, depending on the use to which the scores are put. It is probably a good measure of the speed with which students can mark x's on a piece of paper but not a good measure of the student's intelligence. Thus, this test could probably be described as both a reliable and a valid test of speed of writing x's and a reliable, but not valid, test of intelligence.

Decide whether each of the following statements is true or false and turn to the indicated sections to check your response.

___a. A mathematics test would be described as valid if it were found that the persons taking it tended to receive a comparable score each time they took it, i.e., each time their scores would tend to be among the highest, the lowest or about average, whatever was typical for them. (6B)

___b. A history test would be described as valid if it were reliable and the content of the test were a representative sample of the information the test was designed to measure. (8A)

C. We have been through this question before. Return to *5A* and choose a different answer.

3.

A. Can you really expect a grade that is supposed to represent the degree of achievement in a class to truly do so, if it is altered in accordance with Johnny's social behavior? This is an example of the abuses of grades referred to above. Return to *1A* and choose the other answer.

B. A person's response to this question is very much a matter of opinion but the response of "false" will be defended here. The usefulness of a given type depends upon the situation and it would be foolish to claim that formal evaluation is more useful than informal. More "trust" can usually be placed in a measure acquired through a carefully developed formal procedure but there are countless situations in which such measures are not available and you must make decisions on the basis of information acquired by informal means.

To insure that the information acquired through your informal evaluation is of value it is crucial that you evaluate this information initially with respect to your objectives. This is true of formal evaluation as well, but in practice such a comparison probably is disregarded most often in the case of informal evaluation. There is no intention at this point of entering into a philosophical discussion of the degree to which objectives originate with the teacher, other sectors of the school, society, or the students. Suffice it to say that, regardless of the source of the objectives, there are objectives or a *raison d'être,* and any evaluation is meaningless unless it is based upon these objectives.

In a class where the objectives are determined largely by the students themselves, evaluation would not be based on the objectives.

___a. True (4B)
___b. False (7A)

C. This was not stated, and this writer is of the opinion that it is not the case. Go back to *6A* and try b.

~~~~~~

4.

A. Good! Of more importance than being a basis for reporting progress, is the usefulness of evaluation to the teacher for locating the difficulties encountered by individual students and for deciding how his teaching practices should be altered.

At this point we should distinguish more carefully between evaluation and measurement. A test score by itself does not represent evaluation, even though value judgments are certainly employed whenever a test is constructed. The score is a "measure" and evaluation occurs when judgments are made about the meaning or significance of the score. For example, a score of 43 out of a possible score of 57 on a test represents measurement, while assigning a grade such as A, B, C, D, or F to this score is evaluation. Although the two are sometimes conducted concurrently, we label the construction, administration, and scoring of tests as measurement and use evaluation as the label for the interpretation of scores and the making of value judgments about test scores or any other measure of educational progress.

Decide whether each of the following is measurement or evaluation and turn to the indicated section to check your response.

__a. A fifth grade teacher constructs a mathematics test, gives it to her class and determines the number of correct responses of each student. (1C)

__b. In view of a student's score on the mathematics test and his score on an academic aptitude test reported in the permanent record file, the fifth grade teacher decides that the student's achievement is considerably below his potential. (2A)

__c. Based on her observations of their work with balances, a fourth grade teacher concludes that the majority of the children in her class have learned to determine satisfactorily the mass of an object. (8B)

__d. A first grade teacher reports to a parent that during the first three months of the school year his child has become more willing to express his judgments freely with less fear of his peers' possible disapproval. (6A)

B. Not so; go back to *3B* and try the other choice.

C. In spite of their weaknesses, informal evaluation procedures do have some merits, go back to *8A* and try b.

~~~~~~

5.

A. Correct—if enrollment in the honors course is limited to the students for whom higher than average performance can be expected, it only makes sense to select on the basis of something that has been proven to be a good predictor of performance—previous grades in a similar activity.

There are several important uses or purposes for evaluation; one of them is to be able to report to other persons the level of achievement of a student in a given segment of his educational experience. This information is generally reported to parents and is available in the school records for the use of other members of the school faculty and administration as well as for possible future use by others such as prospective employers or educational personnel at other levels of education.

But records and reports are not the most important reason for a teacher to evaluate the educational progress of students in his class. Most important, a teacher needs to locate the difficulties that students (whether kindergarteners or college students) are encountering, and to aid them in overcoming these difficulties. Realistically, this means that evaluation must be viewed in much broader terms than simply giving tests periodically and recording the scores. To serve this purpose, evaluation must be a continuous activity used as a basis for making decisions in the classroom.

Another important reason for evaluation is to enable you to alter your teaching practices to produce the best learning situation. Not everything you try turns out to be as effective as it appeared when you planned it. Continuous evaluation can provide a basis for deciding which practices you will use in the future, which you will modify, and which you will disregard.

Which of the following is the most important purpose of evaluation?

___a. To provide reports of progress for parents and other interested persons. (1B)
___b. To provide the teacher with the basis for a grading system which can be used to force students to conform to the desired standards of behavior. (2C)
___c. To provide the teacher with a basis for making educational decisions. (4A)

B. This is certainly a commendable contribution to the class, but by itself it gives no indication of attainment of the objective. Return to *7A* and consider this again.

C. This is at the comprehension level since the student must comprehend the meaning of the symbolic language in order to translate it into literal statements. Now try b of *9A*.

~~~~~~

6.

A. The teacher has compared her observations ("measures") of the child's expressiveness and judged (evaluation) that the child is now more expressive and less fearful of disapproval.

It should be evident from the above examples that a teacher's evaluation is not limited to judgments about test scores but is based upon information that is acquired in many different ways. A useful distinction can be made between two kinds of evaluation: *formal* and *informal*. Formal evaluation refers to interpretations based upon paper-and-pencil tests or other activities which are administered uniformly to the students in a class for the purpose of evaluation. A more common type is the informal evaluation which is based upon a teacher's interpretation of his observation of the routine classroom activities. The perceptive teacher carefully notes the kinds of questions that students ask and their responses to his comments and questions and those of other students. Important information is gathered as well through observations of the students' work with equipment and materials. Both types of evaluation—formal and informal—are valuable and complement each other.

Although it is more common, informal evaluation is not as useful as formal evaluation.

___a. True (3C)
___b. False (3B)

B. False. The test should be described as reliable but if it is to be described as valid also, we need some assurance that what it is measuring is knowledge of mathematics rather than one of 1,001 other possibilities. Note that without reliability the test could not be valid, but just because it is reliable, it is not necessarily valid for a given purpose. Return to *2B*.

C. This is in the affective domain, since it deals not with gain of knowledge but development of a desire or value. Go on to b of *10A*.

~~~~~~

7.

A. Right. Of course, if the objectives are unique to each individual in the class, it will be difficult to use a formal evaluation procedure, but this possibility does not negate the fact that any meaningful evaluation must be closely related to the objectives.

Let's consider an example of this relationship in an informal evaluation situation. A second-grade teacher is conducting a class in which the principal objective is for the students to learn to make careful observations. In this case the items being studied are certain plants in the classroom and the children are orally expressing their observations to the entire class and the teacher. In her attempts to evaluate the children's degree of attainment of the objective, the teacher should disregard the children's degree of verbal fluency. The acquisition of verbal fluency may be an important objective for some class sessions, and possibly this session also, but this should not be confused with the substance of what is being verbalized— the observations themselves. Of even greater concern is the tendency of many teachers to confuse behaviors which are indicative of attainment of instructional objectives with social behaviors which are pleasing to the teacher.

A junior high school social studies teacher is teaching a unit on nine-teenth-century American history in which a major objective for the day is for the students to demonstrate an understanding of the greater value of primary historical sources (e.g., official records) as compared to secondary sources (e.g., newspapers).

Which of the following student behaviors would be indicative of some degree of attainment of this objective?

___a. A boy brought to class a copy of an 1858 newspaper that belonged to his family. (5B)

___b. A girl commented that a newspaper account of a court case would not be as reliable a source as the actual court records. (2B)

___c. One student presented an accurate, well organized, and clear oral report on the characteristics of nineteenth-century newspapers based on two reference books he had read in the library. (10B)

B. Multiple choice questions are among the very best of all types, but this particular one is not a direct test of the given objective. Return to *11A*.

C. This requires only memory; thus it is at the knowledge level. How about c in *9A?*

~~~~~~

8.

A. True. The test is reliable and, in addition, it measures what it is intended to measure. This relationship between reliability and validity is sometimes expressed in the following way: *Reliability is a necessary but not sufficient condition for validity.*

Using the terms reliability and validity, a general comparison now can be made between the informal evaluation procedures which have been examined in earlier sections of this chapter and formal procedures which will be examined in detail in the pages ahead. Generally the reliability of informal procedures is considerably less than the reliability of formal pro-cedures; since reliability is necessary for validity this lesser reliability re-sults in lesser validity. In addition, the failure to base the informal evalua-tion initially upon the educational objectives can also reduce the validity. Informal evaluation, however, is an important part of the overall evaluation picture because of the continuous and immediate nature of this feedback and its applicability to a great variety of educational objectives such as changes in attitudes and the ability to analyze, synthesize, and evaluate ideas.

Because of their lower reliability and validity, informal evaluation procedures should rarely be used.

___a. True (4C)
___b. False (10A)

B. Evaluation. In addition to her observations, the teacher has made judgments about the adequacy of the children's work. Return to d in *4A*.

C. Well, it looks like a respectable question for assessing *some* objective, but it is not the most appropriate for this particular objective. Try again in *11A*.

~~~~~~

9.

A. Cognitive, because it is directed toward the ability to distinguish between them with no attention to an interest in, or desire for either type of music.

A more detailed examination of the cognitive domain should give you some insight into the adequacy of measurement and evaluation procedures you might develop in an area, and provide you with additional vocabulary that we will use later in this chapter. This domain contains six levels as given below.

Knowledge. The recall of specifics (e.g., water is composed of hydrogen and oxygen, *or* primary historical sources are more reliable than secondary sources) is mainly a matter of memory and constitutes the first level of the *Taxonomy*. The above examples are classified at this level because of the emphasis upon memory rather than understanding, even though it is possible to pursue these objectives at a higher level also.

Comprehension. This level requires a greater depth of understanding, i.e., the student must understand as well as remember. For example, a student might be expected to translate a sentence from one language to another or translate a statement from mathematical symbols to verbal form.

Application. The third level includes the application of abstractions in concrete situations. An example would be the calculation of the area of a triangle, given its dimensions.

Analysis. This level requires the separation of the parts of a whole and the determination of the relationships among the parts, e.g., identifying the motives of a character in a play from ideas stated and implied, or the determination of the purpose of an event in a novel in relation to the whole book.

Synthesis. The fifth level involves putting ideas together to form a new whole such as the composition of a poem or formulation of a hypothesis to explain why warm air rises.

Evaluation. The highest of the six levels includes making judgments. Examples are the location of the fallacies in an interpretation of historical events and evaluation of a novel in terms of its internal consistency.

Determine the level of the cognitive domain into which each of the following objectives would be classified.

___a. The student will be able to communicate the theme of a poem by changing symbolic language into literal statements. (5C)
___b. The student will be able to list the major musical composers belonging to the romantic period. (7C)
___c. The student will be able to determine which statements about an experiment are hypotheses and which are observations. (11A)

10.

A. Of course! The good teacher will make use of both informal and formal procedures. In spite of the relative lack of reliability and validity, informal procedures give immediate and continuous information on a wide range of objectives.

Of fundamental importance for any meaningful evaluation, either formal or informal, is consistency of the educational objectives with the evaluation. Too often, tests are focused upon only a portion of the educational objectives, namely the acquisition of specific facts and details, while broader and more basic objectives are ignored. A system of classifying educational objectives which may be useful for obtaining a broader picture of the objectives to be evaluated is the *Taxonomy of Educational Objectives*.[1] A brief examination of it should prove useful.

In this system, all objectives are included in one of three categories: the cognitive, affective and psychomotor domains. The educational objectives generally given most attention are those in the cognitive domain, including the acquisition of facts and concepts and the development of intellectual skills. The affective domain includes the development of attitudes, interests, appreciation, and values, while the psychomotor domain pertains to the development of motor, physical, and manipulative abilities.

[1] Benjamin S. Bloom et al., *Taxonomy of Educational Objectives* (New York: David McKay, 1956).

Decide whether each of the following educational objectives falls in the cognitive, affective, or psychomotor domain and then turn to the indicated page to check your answer.

___a. When visiting the library to select books for his personal pleasure, the student will choose books on historical topics. (6C)
___b. The student will be able to distinguish between the musical styles of the Baroque and classical periods. (9A)

B. This activity may be indicative of the attainment of certain other objectives for the class but without some comparison of these newspapers with other sources in terms of their historical accuracy, there is no evidence of attainment of the given objective. Return to 7A and consider this again.

11.

A. This is at least at the analysis level since the student must ascertain the relationships between the various components of the experiment to determine what has been observed and what has been hypothesized. Depending on the nature of the experiment and the student's previous background, it might be at the evaluation level. Exactly how a particular objective might be classified is not of major importance, but the *Taxonomy* will be useful to us in our study of measurement and evaluation.

Before looking at specific guidelines for the construction and use of each of the several kinds of test items, we should consider some general guidelines for the use of formal evaluation procedures. (1) Begin with the objectives. Remember that teaching is a dynamic and flexible activity in which objectives are modified continually. Decide which goals actually have been pursued. (2) Weight the objectives according to their relative importance to determine the proportion of items that should be allotted to various topics. A good index of this importance might be the amount of class time devoted to each. For example, if two days of a history class were devoted to a study of the validity of various sources of historical data and one day to an interpretation of the events preceding the War of 1812, twice as much emphasis might be given to the former in the evaluation. After the objectives have been identified and weighted according to emphasis, the appropriate measurement techniques must be selected. Too often teachers restrict themselves to a certain technique, such as essay tests or true-false tests, instead of initially examining all possibilities and choosing the ones most appropriate to the objectives involved.

A teacher is attempting to assess the degree of attainment of this objective:

Given the average temperature for each day over a period of 3 weeks, the student should be able to plot a graph showing the relationship between time and temperature.

Which one of the following evaluation techniques would be most appropriate?

___a. A true-false question refers to a graph of time *vs.* temperature displayed above the question. The question reads "The graph above shows the relationship between time and temperature." (8C)

___b. A set of temperature data is displayed and the student is asked to draw a graph of the data. (12A)

___c. A multiple choice question designed to determine if the student understands the cause of daily fluctuations in temperature. (7B)

~~~~~~

12.

A. Good! This is a direct test of the performance specified in the stated objective. The other two options are related to temperature fluctuations but are not a direct test of the given objective.

The following are additional guidelines that apply to measurement procedures used in formal evaluation.

1. Every effort should be made to reduce the influence of the student's reading ability on his score. Reading ability affects test scores far more than most teachers realize. Restrict the amount of reading as much as possible and make sentences of minimum difficulty with a vocabulary at the simplest level which still communicates the intended ideas.

2. Give clear and complete directions. Especially with elementary school children, it is important to be sure that all directions are carefully worded and that the children thoroughly understand them.

3. All possible measures should be taken to prevent cheating. Close supervision and wide spacing of seats are among the most important precautions.

4. Allow plenty of time. All or nearly all of the students should be able to finish the test in the allotted time.

5. Avoid the use of direct quotes from textbooks and lectures as the basis for such questions as those of the true-false or completion type. The practice may lead to students attempting to memorize key statements rather than studying for understanding.

The next section of this chapter deals specifically with each of several types of formal measurement techniques. Begin at *13A*.

~~~~~~

Constructing Test Items

Essay Items

13.

A. We will now begin to look systematically at the advantages and limitations of various types of formal evaluation techniques and examine some hints on their construction and use. The first of these is the essay test, which by definition is distinguished from the short answer or completion type. The latter is written with a specific one word or phrase response as the expected answer, whereas an essay question gives the student the freedom to provide a detailed elaboration of his response to a question which requires more analysis, synthesis and evaluation than is normally required from most objective items such as the completion type.

A major limitation of essay tests is low reliability. Lack of consistency and stability has been shown through a large number of research studies. Studies which compare the results of two graders working independently generally show quite low correlations between the two. Low correlation has also been found between the grades given to the same essay graded by the same teacher on two different occasions. In addition, studies have shown low correlation between two forms of an essay test which were designed to be equivalent, thus indicating low reliability. Generally, the reliability of the test itself is lower than the reliability of the grading.[2] The validity of essay tests is open to question because of the low reliability as well as the fact that the person grading the essay may be unduly influenced by *how* well the ideas are presented rather than *what* the ideas are.

> Essay tests have relatively low validity because: (select the one best answer)

___a. Their reliability is low. (17C)
___b. they may unduly measure how an idea is stated rather than the idea itself. (16A)
___c. both a and b. (14A)

B. Not a bad question. The student is clearly expected to do more than list three or four phrases yet he is somewhat limited by the adjective "major" and the restriction of two composers rather than all the composers of a given musical period. Go back to b on *16B*.

---

[2] Julian C. Stanley, *Measurement in Today's Schools,* 4th edition (Englewood Cliffs, N.J.: Prentice-Hall, 1964), pp. 258–60.

C. Under the circumstances, an essay test has few advantages. Go back to *14A* and try the other choice.

~~~~~~

14.

A. Correct! Both a and b are factors that result in low validity for essay tests.

In spite of its low reliability and validity, the essay test does have a useful role in evaluation because of its appropriateness for measuring objectives that would be classified in the higher levels of Bloom's *Taxonomy.* There is no point in using essay tests to measure knowledge and comprehension since this can be done more effectively and efficiently with objective tests. The use of essay items should be reserved for objectives that are in the higher levels of the *Taxonomy,* namely analysis, synthesis, and evaluation. This use of the essay question may also encourage students to focus their studying on a deeper understanding of ideas rather than on simple recall or comprehension. Objective tests can also be used to measure the higher objectives, so in selecting the type of test that will be used, we must consider another characteristic of tests: usability. The comparative usability of objective and essay tests varies with the situation. Although *good* essay tests can not be constructed as quickly as many people believe, essay tests are generally less time consuming to construct than objective tests but more time consuming to grade. Thus, if the number of students involved is small, an essay test may be less time consuming whereas with a large number of students an objective test will be most efficient. This comparison must take account of the fact, however, that any objective items can generally be retained for use with future classes.

An essay test might be a good choice; if the content were the application of biological science ideas, if it were to be given to 90 students, and if there were no plans to use the same test again.

__a. True (13C)
__b. False (16B)

B. This is a bad essay question since it encourages the student to simply list three phrases or brief sentences. Now try c on *16B*.

C. This is a good practice. Return to *17B* and try another choice.

~~~~~~

15.

A. Since this is a matter of opinion, it would be very difficult to grade. It might have possibilities if the vagueness were eliminated by asking the students to explain some of the arguments for or against the practice.

An additional guideline to aid you in constructing an essay test, is to employ several fairly specific and brief questions rather than a few lengthy ones. This provides a broader sampling of the objectives and results in greater reliability and validity for the test. As described above, however, questions can not be so brief that they encourage one sentence responses. The net result of these guidelines is that the teacher must find a reasonable compromise between specificity and generality.

Optional questions should be avoided when constructing an essay test. Students prefer them since it tends to give them some feeling of assurance that they will have some questions which they can answer, but it is a poor practice since the students are not all taking the same test. This lack of comparability reduces reliability and, as a result, validity as well.

Finally, in addition to constructing good essay examinations, the teacher needs to teach students how to take them. Since we know that essay examinations put a premium on how ideas are expressed, we should give everyone the benefit of instruction on how to write good essay examinations. When examinations are returned to the students, the weak points of answers should be explained to enable students to better present their answers on future tests.

The teacher of a twelfth-grade English literature class decides to give her class a one hour essay test containing three questions from which the students are to select two to answer. What improvements should be made in this approach?

___a. The test should be composed of more than three questions. (16C)
___b. All students should be required to answer all questions. (17A)
___c. both a and b (18C)

B. No! Return to *18C,* read this section again, and then try the other choice.

C. This is a good practice. Return to *17B* and try another choice.

~~~~~~

16.

A. Yes, but this is not the only reason. Return to *13A* and try a different answer.

B. Fine! This content can be handled very readily with an objective test and in spite of the fact that it will not be reused, an essay test would be more time consuming than an objective test with this number of students. The greater reliability and validity of an objective test make it the choice, hands down.

The first of several guidelines for the construction of essay items that we will examine is to focus on the higher objectives—the analysis level and higher. This will tend to be the case if you begin with words or phrases like *compare, explain why, tell how,* or *describe.* Words such as *list, what, where, who, which,* and *when* should be avoided since they are likely to lead to short answers of a sentence or less.

Second, although questions should encourage the students to do more than give one-word or phrase responses, the questions should not be so vague and general that the student cannot tell what you are asking. Examples of such poor questions are "How is the sun important?" or "Tell all you know about Napoleon."

Examine each of the following examples of essay questions, decide why it is a good, mediocre or bad question and then turn to the indicated page to check your decision.

___a. Explain the major ways in which Mozart's music differs from Bach's. (13B)
___b. List three causes of the War of 1812. (14B)
___c. Explain what John Steinbeck was trying to say in *The Grapes of Wrath.* (18B)
___d. Should the Federal Reserve Board regulate the money supply as a means of controlling the growth of the economy? (15A)

C. This would be an improvement but more should be done. Try again in *15A*.

~~~~~~

17.

A. This would be an improvement but more should be done. Try again in *15A*.

B. Good! The potential for bias is great; the grader will probably see what he expects to see rather than what is there.

There are several guidelines that should help the teacher in making the subjective judgments which are the basis for the grading of essay exams. First of all, the grading must be done in terms of the instructional objectives. If the test is designed to measure achievement in an area such as art, science or social studies, the grades should not be based on grammar or spelling. This is not to say that writing ability is unimportant; mistakes can be pointed out to students, but their grades should not be based on this factor unless it is one of the specific objectives of this particular portion of the educational program. This does not eliminate the possibility that an elementary school teacher, for example, might use an essay test in social studies for the assessment of achievement in both writing and social studies. The important point is to establish clearly what the educational objectives are, and then grade the examination in terms of those objectives without letting other considerations invalidate the grades.

Grading is usually aided by writing out an ideal answer to the question prior to grading any of the papers. Reliability can usually be increased by weighting the several parts of this ideal answer and assigning a certain number of points to each part. Some people like to reserve a certain limited number of points for the grader to use in terms of his overall impression of the answer in addition to those assigned to the specific parts of the answer. This may facilitate achieving the desired compromise between specificity and evaluation of the students' ability to analyze, synthesize and evaluate.

Which of the following is *not* a good practice in grading essay examinations?

___a. grading in terms of the objectives of the portion of the educational program being evaluated. (15C)
___b. giving credit only for answers in which the English is acceptable. (18A)
___c. constructing an ideal answer and assigning a certain number of points to each part. (14C)

C. Yes, but this is not the only reason. Return to *13A* and try a different answer.

～～～～～～～～～～～～～～～～～～～～～～～～～～～～

18.

A. Right! Unless it is a test of writing ability, the students' usage of English should be disregarded for purposes of determining the grade. Beginning by constructing an ideal answer is an aid to good grading.

Now that guidelines for the construction and use of essay tests have been presented, attention can be given to the various types of objective test items, such as multiple-choice, true-false and matching. This section begins at *19A*.

B. This question is hopelessly vague and general. Steinbeck was probably trying to say quite a lot and the student has to guess what part of it the teacher wants to hear about. Back to *16B* again.

C. Right! The test should contain more questions and everyone should answer all of them. Everyone will then be responding to the same test, it will have more but briefer questions, and this improvement will probably result in an increase in reliability and validity.

The grading of essay tests is a big task and much can be done at this stage to improve the test's reliability and validity. All of the students' answers to a given question should be graded at the same time. Grade all of the responses to number one before doing any of the responses to number two, and so on. All of the responses will then more likely be graded on the same basis. Reading the papers in a different order for each question should help to reduce bias due to a possible tendency to grade papers at a particular point (e.g., beginning or end) more leniently or rigorously than those graded at another time.

It is also important that the identity of the student be unknown to the grader. Bias in grading due to the teacher's expectations for particular students is greater than most teachers realize. One way to avoid this bias is to have the students place their names on the back of the last page rather than on the first page.

> The following statement by a high school English teacher describes a good grading procedure: "Before grading an essay question I always first look to see whose paper it is, so I can more intelligently interpret what the student is saying."

___a. True (15B)
___b. False (17B)

~~~~~~

SHORT-ANSWER ITEMS

19.

A. There are several widely used versions of a general class of items commonly referred to as "objective" items. The word objective refers only to the method of scoring; in contrast to essay questions, scoring is a simple clerical task in which essentially no judgment is required. Obviously, a great deal of subjective judgment is required in the construction of objective test items.

Short-answer, or free-response items are the first of the several types of objective items to be considered here. Because the student is free to respond with the word or phrase of his choice, short-answer items are more similar to essay items than any other type of objective item. The length of the response is the main distinction between the short-answer and essay item.

Essay and short-answer items are used to measure different kinds of objectives.

___a. True (20A)
___b. False (22A)

B. This item still has clues which need not be there. The question clearly indicates a plural answer which eliminates many of the answers which the uninformed student might give. It might better be stated as follows:

The first exploration of the Louisiana Territory was conducted by

_____.

The answer is now more than one word which may increase the scoring task, but this is a less serious matter than giving away the answer.

This completes our examination of the short-answer type of item; study of another type begins at *23A*.

C. We have already seen that the answer is not limited to one word. Even adding a preposition such as "in" after the word "won" would not solve this problem, however, as we have already seen. Return to *22B* and d.

~~~~~~

20.

A. You are correct! This fundamental difference in the types of objectives which can be measured with short-answer items is the most important characteristic of short-answer items. The limitation of a one-word or one-phrase response makes it almost impossible to assess the attainment of objectives at the analysis, synthesis or evaluation levels. Keep this in mind as you decide when you will make use of short-answer items.

A characteristic that distinguishes short-answer from most other varieties of objective items is the time that is sometimes required for scoring. Unless the question is specific enough to limit the correct answer to a specific single word, the person scoring the test must spend time deciding whether the answer found on a test paper is equivalent to the keyed answer.

Which of the following is the major limitation of short-answer items?

___a. the great difficulty of measuring objectives at the higher levels of Bloom's *Taxonomy*. (22B)

___b. the time consuming scoring required (21B)

B. The spacings in the blanks indicating the number of letters in each choice are clues which eliminate many of the incorrect responses which might otherwise be given. Now consider still another version of this question in *21A*.

C. Of course, we do not know since we do not know what curricular materials are in use where the test item is being used. It is, however, a practice that should be avoided. Go back to b in *22B*.

~~~~~~

21.

A. Yes, this item illustrates why the direct question form is usually preferable. To put this item in that form, the test writer would need to be much more specific and ask something like, "In what year was the Battle of Gettysburg won?" or "Which side won the Battle of Gettysburg?" Short-answer items should not be vague, but should indicate clearly the answer that is expected of the knowledgeable student.

There are additional guidelines for short-answer items. (5) Avoid too many blanks in one sentence. Occasionally, an item will be found which is so badly mutilated that it is almost impossible to determine what the question is. (6) Be especially careful not to give the answer away with grammatical cues. For example, the item:

> Voltage is measured with an instrument called a _____ *would better be written as follows:*
> Voltage is measured with an instrument called a(n) _____.

In its original form, the item eliminates ammeter as a possible answer, yet this is the most likely incorrect answer that would be expected of the student who is not completely informed. Wordings such as *is/are* and *was/were* are sometimes helpful. (7) Another clue that is sometimes found is the length of the blanks in the questions. To avoid this, simply make all blanks in the test the same length.

Consider each of the following short-answer items and decide what is wrong with each.

a. _____ was first explored by _____ and _____
   (22C)
b. The Louisiana Territory was first explored by _____ and
   _____. (20B)
c. The first explorers of the Louisiana Territory were _____. (19B)

B. No, the time required for scoring is not nearly as great a problem as the level of objectives which can be handled. Try the other choice in *20A*.

C. There are endless possibilities. How about these for answers: "in three days," "in a rainstorm," "by the North," "in 1863," "at the expense of extensive losses," or "in Pennsylvania." In other words, it is a poor item. Go back to c on *22B*.

~~~~~~

22.

A. The length of response makes it impossible to measure all of the same kinds of objectives with short-answer items as can be measured with essay items. Try the other choice in *19A*.

B. Right! This is a major limitation and restricts the use of short-answer items to those objectives which are generally of less importance.

There are several guidelines which, if followed, should assist you in making wise use of this form of test item. (1) There are two forms in which the short answer item is often found: a sentence with an omitted word replaced by a blank and the direct question. The following are examples of the two forms:

The _____ is used to measure voltage.
What device is used to measure voltage? _____

In most cases the direct question form is preferable because it is easier to construct, is less confusing to students, and is less likely to contain clues to the answer. (2) Whichever form you use, avoid taking statements directly from the textbook because of the possible tendency to cause students to memorize key statements. (3) The task of scoring items is facilitated if there is only one correct answer to an item and it is a one-word or one-number response. (4) An additional aid to scoring is to prepare a scoring key including all acceptable answers in those cases where more than one are acceptable.

Consider this item and decide how many of the following four statements apply to it, and check your response to each in the indicated frame.

The Battle of Gettysburg was won _____.

__a. The statement is taken directly from a textbook. (20C)
__b. This item has only one correct answer. (21C)
__c. The answer is a one word response. (19C)
__d. It is stated in the least preferable form. (21A)

C. There are an apparently endless number of possible answers to this one. It was constructed with "the Louisiana Territory," "Lewis" and "Clark" in mind, but it is hard to argue with the correctness of "Kentucky," "brute force" and "stubbornness." Return to b of *21A*.

~~~~~~

TRUE-FALSE ITEMS

23.

A. There is a second type of objective test item which is generally superior to the short-answer type because it is more readily usable for testing objectives at a somewhat higher level. This form is the true-false item. This form of test item is quite popular because it is relatively easy to construct and score, it is applicable to most subject areas, and a relatively large sampling can be acquired in a given length of time. In short, it is widely applicable and is economical in its use of both teacher and student time.

The true-false form, however, must be used very carefully to avoid its many limitations and, as a result, is probably the most abused of all item forms. Unless carefully constructed it is prone to ambiguity and the testing of trivial matters. Both of these problems can be overcome if the test constructor is skillful and exercises the necessary care, but unfortunately, this skill and care do not seem to be particularly widespread.

The true-false item is the poorest of all forms of objective test items.

__a. True (26C)
__b. False (24B)

B. No! Go back to *24B*, read this section again, and try the other choice.

C. "Usually" is a specific determiner; it can be eliminated. Return to *26A* and item d.

~~~~~~

24.

A. There would be less chance of confusion if "not" were eliminated or if a false statement were constructed like the following:

Thomas Edison was a famous American poet.

Go on to b of *26A*.

B. Right! Generally, the true-false form is superior to the short-answer form because it is possible to use it to test higher level objectives. As used by most teachers, however, it probably is not much better, in spite of its considerably greater potential. In most cases, neither is as good as the multiple-choice form because of their relative potential for measuring objectives at the higher levels of the *Taxonomy*.

Another limitation of true-false tests which is much discussed is the possibility of large chance fluctuations in scores due to guessing. In actual practice, this is not much of a problem if the test contains a relatively large number of items. The chance variations tend to balance out. Correction-for-guessing formulas are sometimes recommended but for most applications they are a waste of time because they only lower all scores and do not change the ranking of scores. Another mythical fault of true-false items is the supposed detrimental effect of students reading false statements and learning false information. Research seems to show these fears to be groundless.

Increased scores due to guessing and the learning of false information through reading false statements are insignificant limitations of true-false items.

__a. True (26A)
__b. False (23B)

C. This is a ridiculous item to find in a true-false test. Neither commands nor statements of opinion are appropriate. Go on to c of *26A*.

~~~~~~

25.

A. There is no basis for this statement so try the other choice in *27A*.

B. Possibly, but this statement is too ambiguous. The flag does contain red and blue but it also contains white. Either of the following versions would be better.

Red and blue are two of the colors in the United States flag.
or
The United States flag is red, white and blue.

Consider some additional guidelines. (5) Try not to use long sentences since they raise the reading level of the test, and more often than not, they are true statements. Probably this results from the attempt of the writer to eliminate all exceptions to a statement in order to ensure that it is true. (6) Express only a single idea in each statement. Items with several parts are often confusing to students. (7) The most important guideline of all is to base items on the key ideas and higher objectives. This goal should receive considerable attention since it is known that true-false items tend to be based on matters of lesser importance.

Evaluate each of the following true-false items and consult the indicated section.

a. Four guidelines should be followed in making pottery. (26B)
b. Carelessness can result in producing welds that are weak and subject to breaking. (27B)
c. T. S. Eliot's poetry displays a revolt against the optimism and cheerfulness of the eighteenth century and his technique is a mixture of subtle suggestions and direct statements. (27A)

C. Fine! The previous section said nothing about this matter, and there is no basis for the statement.

Now that you have completed this section on true-false items, you may proceed to the next type of item in *28A*.

~~~~~~

26.

A. Fine! They are largely imaginary limitations of true-false tests.

As pointed out earlier, true-false items are particularly susceptible to abuse, so observe the following guidelines carefully. (1) Trick questions such as the following should be avoided:

Plants produce food through fotosynthesis.

Note the spelling of photosynthesis. (2) Take great pains to avoid ambiguity; make sentences simple and clear. Carefully consider all possible ways that the sentence might be interpreted. (3) Be diligent in eliminating specific determiners that give away the answer. Dogmatic statements using words like "no," "never," "always," or "in all cases," are usually false while questions with "weasel words" like "mostly," "frequently," "generally," "usually," "sometimes," or "often" are almost always true. Either eliminate such words or else use them equally often in both true and false items. (4) Avoid negative statements; in particular, avoid making false statements out of true statements by merely adding "not."

Carefully evaluate each of the following items, and turn to the indicated page to check your evaluation.

a. Thomas Edison was not a famous American inventor. (24A)
b. Do not play with matches. (24C)
c. Economic policies that tend to combat inflation also usually tend to increase unemployment. (23C)
d. The United States flag is red and blue. (25B)

B. This item is trivial and of little merit. The fact that someone did not group into four categories his suggestions for making pottery is of little consequence. The content of the guidelines should be the subject of testing. Return to *25B* and go on to b.

C. Not so. Try the other choice in *23A*.

~~~~~~

27.

A. This item violates many of the given guidelines. It is unnecessarily long, and more important, it contains more than one key idea—a fact which makes it potentially confusing. The content of Eliot's poetry and his technique would each be alone sufficient material for an item. Another fault is that what would otherwise be a true statement has been made false by changing "nineteenth century" to "eighteenth century." If an item is false, it should be so because of the incorrectness of the key idea being tested. One possible advantage of the item is that, in contrast to most long items, it is not a true item. That evaluation, however, would need to be examined in light of the entire test of which the item is a part.

A final guideline for true-false tests is that the entire test should contain approximately as many true items as false items. Occasionally a teacher has a pattern of using a much higher proportion of one than the other. Some students usually notice such situations and when in doubt choose the favored response with a resultant modest increase in score.

A test should be composed of only one type of item such as true-false, essay, or short-answer.

___a. True (25A)
___b. False (25C)

B. This is another example of triviality. In addition it is the kind of common sense question that most students would answer correctly without any contact with the given portion of the curriculum. Return to *25B*.

~~~~~~

MATCHING ITEMS

28.

A. Another type of objective item which is useful for some purposes is the matching item, i.e., an item requiring that the student match two parallel, equivalent, or contrasting things. Generally a set of statements is given on the left-hand side of the page and a set of words or phrases on the right-hand side; these statements and words are to be matched with each other. Matching items are useful for measuring a student's understanding of the association between pairs such as objects and their functions, items and their locations, events and their dates, or terms and their definitions; they are not, however, very suitable for measuring depth of understanding.

A matching item would be useful for measuring a student's ability to analyze the style of literary writing.

___a. True (29B)
___b. False (29A)

B. This item obviously has many flaws, the most basic of which is the lack of homogeneity. For example, in number 6, a color is specified and there is only one color on the right-hand side, so the answer is given away. Number 1 suffers from the same problem. A homogeneous item that would have some potential could be formed from numbers 2, 3, 4, and 7 of this test. Another clue is given in number 5, which specifies a plural answer, severely limiting the possible choices on the right side. Number 5 could have been written in singular form. An additional problem is that 2, 3, 5, and 7 are so general that the student can not tell what the answer is until he searches through the right hand side to see what might fit. In contrast, the informed student knows the answer to 1 as soon as he reads it. The fact that there are as many responses on the right side as there are statements on the left provides another clue. The student who knows six out of seven answers automatically gets seven correct along with the student who knows all of them.

If you have been concerned that the matching form did not seem to lend itself well to measuring objectives at the higher levels of the *Taxonomy,* you will probably be interested in the next type that we will examine—the multiple choice item. (*30A*)

~~~~~~

29.

A. Good! The matching form is quite limited, although useful for some tasks.

Care in construction of matching items is required to avoid two particular limitations: the possibility of being quite time consuming for the student and the possibility of containing clues that give away the correct answer. Consider the following guidelines. (1) Directions that clearly show the basis for association are necessary to avoid confusion. Whether an answer can be used more than once or whether more than one answer is to be given for any of the questions should be clearly indicated. (2) Each item should be based on homogeneous associations, i.e., the basis for matching, such as events with dates, should be the same for the entire item. (3) Limit the length of matching items to about 12 associations, and in the case of elementary school children, four to eight would be a maximum, depending on their age. Longer items are too time consuming for the students, too dependent upon reading ability, and too prone to lack of homogeneity. (4) The left-hand column should be specific enough that the informed student knows what answer he is searching for on the right, rather than giving an answer and having the student search for a "question" that it fits.

Evaluate the following matching item. (*28B*)

___1. The organ where oxygen passes into the blood   A. Oxygen
___2. A compound formed when wood burns   B. Hydrogen
___3. A gas that is a mixture   C. White
___4. The gas that combines with iron when iron rusts   D. Lungs
___5. They revolve around the sun   E. Air
___6. The color that contains all other colors   F. Planets
___7. A gas composed of one kind of atom   G. Carbon Dioxide

B. Hardly; try the other choice in *28A*.

~~~~~~

MULTIPLE-CHOICE ITEMS

30.

A. The multiple-choice form is probably more widely applicable and useful than any other item form. With this format, the question is presented to the student in the form of either an incomplete sentence or a question, and he must then select the answer from the two or more (usually three to five) choices that follow. This kind of question has many advantages. In contrast to the true-false item where a chance score would be 50 percent, it is only 20 to 25 percent for the typical multiple-choice item. Also any systematic tendency for the student to select any particular choice from among those given is generally absent from this form. A very large sampling of a body of knowledge can be achieved with this item form if there is no repetition among the choices (both correct and incorrect). The most important advantage of all, however, is that this form can be used to test objectives at the higher levels of the *Taxonomy* more readily than any other objective form. Although they are time consuming to construct, multiple-choice items that test the analysis, synthesis, and evaluation levels can be written. Because of their higher reliability and validity such items are generally preferable to essay questions, when they are available for the objectives being tested.

Which of the following is *not* an advantage of multiple choice items?

___a. They can be used to test higher level objectives. (33C)
___b. They can be constructed relatively quickly. (32A)
___c. They provide a large sampling of material. (31A)
___d. Chance scores are relatively low. (33A)

B. The decoys are poor. The following would be more appropriate:
    A. 1
    B. 4
    C. 100
    D. 400
4, 100, and 400 are answers that would likely be acquired by a student who multiplied and/or divided the given numbers in the wrong way. In addition they are now placed in order of increasing size. Of course, in determining the order, do not forget that the correct answer should be placed in each of the positions (i.e., (A), (B), (C), and (D) approximately the same number of times throughout the test as a whole. Go on to b of *31B*.

C. Several of the words in the item are plural, indicating that the answer is plural; thus, only B and C are possible answers. The item could be improved by adding a name such as Bartok to choice A and a composer like Haydn to choice D. Another possibility would be to ask to which period Bach and Handel belonged and use classical, romantic, baroque, and modern as the choices. Go on to b of *33B*.

~~~~~~

31.

A. Since they do provide a large sampling you should return to *30A* and try another choice.

B. This set of items, which is classified at the analysis level is illustrative of what can be done with multiple choice items at this level, if sufficient time and effort are expended.

There are several guidelines which are helpful to the constructor of multiple-choice items. (1) The decoys (incorrect choices) should be definitely wrong but still attractive to the uninformed student. *The writing of the decoys is the most important aspect of writing multiple-choice items,* but also the most difficult part, and it requires the most creativity. In a good item all of the decoys will be attractive to some of the students who are not completely informed. (2) Whenever there is a logical order to the choices, e.g., chronological, they should be so arranged. (3) The stem (the question or incomplete statement) should state fully the central question which is being presented. The student then does not need to read the choices to figure out what the question is and also the reading level of the test is reduced. Evaluate the following items and turn to the indicated sections.

a. Given that $r = 20x/s$, $r = 10$, and $s = 2$, what is x?
 A. 4
 B. 1
 C. 3
 D. 2   (30B)
b. John Steinbeck is
 A. best known as a writer of poetry.
 B. best known as a writer of novels.
 C. best known as a writer of short stories.
 D. best known as a writer of non-fiction.   (33B)

C. The correct item is uniquely different from all the rest. Either D should read "called romantic" ("called" should then be placed in the stem of the item) or choices A, B and C should be descriptions of the given musical period.

Further consideration of the construction of test items is found in the next section beginning at *34A*.

~~~~~~

32.

A. You are right! They are not quick to construct, but their advantages make them the favored form. Since they are time-consuming to construct, you should retain good items for use in future years (an efficient practice for any type of objective item). Tests can be returned to students in class long enough for them to learn what they missed and then collected again without creating a test security problem.

Several illustrations of what can be done with this type of item to test objectives at the higher levels of the *Taxonomy* are given below. The items are three of many that were preceded by the following passage from the play *Major Barbara* by George Bernard Shaw. These three were designed to measure a student's ability to analyze and evaluate an unfamiliar passage and (1) ascertain the importance of the play's theme, (2) ascertain the theme of a passage, and (3) evaluate the validity of generalizations based on a passage. The keyed answer is indicated by an asterisk. What do you think of the items?

> *Barbara:* . . . Yes, you and all the other naughty mischievous children of men. But I can't [leave]. I was happy in the Salvation Army for a moment. I escaped from the world into a paradise of enthusiasm and prayer and soul saving; but the moment our money ran short, it all came back to Bodger: it was he who saved our people: He, and the Prince of Darkness, my papa. Undershaft and Bodger: with their bread, because there is no other bread; when we tend the sick, it is in the hospitals they endow; if we turn from the churches they build, we must kneel on the stones of the streets they pave. As long as that lasts, there is no getting away from them. Turning our backs on Bodger and Undershaft is turning our backs on life.

1. From the above passage it would appear that in this play the theme is
   ___ A. of little importance
   ___ *B. the dominant element
   ___ C. more important than character, but secondary to setting
   ___ D. more important than setting, but secondary to the plot.
2. An analysis of this passage shows its theme to be
   ___ A. money isn't everything but it certainly helps.
   ___ *B. idealistic pursuits are not practical without materialistic support.
   ___ C. the forces of materialism are bitter enemies of those whose main concern is the human soul.

___ D. those concerned with the body are willing partners to those concerned with the soul.

3. Based on evidence within the passage, which of the following statements is
most acceptable in relation to the theme?

___ A. Undershaft and Bodger represent the primary evil in society.

___*B. Good and evil do not exist independently.

___ C. The church is being used as a shield by those who would escape from
a materialistic world.

___ D. The church welcomes evil men who are willing to contribute
money.[3] (31B)

~~~~~~

33.

A. Chance scores are relatively low with this item form, so go back
to *30A* and try again.

B. The stem of this question is not a complete statement. It would be
best to place "best known as a writer of" in the stem, reducing the amount
of reading and informing the student of the question before he reads the
choices.

Here are some additional guidelines. (4) All of the choices should be
correct grammatically. If this is not the case, the "test-wise" student can
eliminate some of the decoys, with a resulting reduction in efficiency of
the test. (5) Keep the length of the choices approximately the same. On
most teacher-made tests, a choice that is obviously longer than the rest is
usually the correct choice, with a resulting unwarranted benefit to the
"test-wise" student. (6) The answer to one item should not be given away
in another item. Carefully review the entire test after it is completed to be
sure that this flaw is not present. (7) The length of the items should be
short and the vocabulary relatively simple to keep the reading level as
low as possible. The user of multiple-choice items, as well as other forms,
should be conscious of the extent to which reading ability can affect a
student's score and should make every effort to keep the reading level as low
as possible. A test of achievement in home economics, for example, should
measure that achievement, not reading ability.

Evaluate these additional items.

a. Which of these composers were from the baroque period?
A. Stravinsky

[3] The extract and questions are reprinted from The Senior High School Examination Board, *Taxonomy of English 30 Objectives with Illustrative Test Items: A
Summary Description* (Edmonton, Alberta: Department of Education, 1968) pp.
98–102.

B. Schubert and Schulmann
C. Bach and Handel
D. Mozart   (30C)

b. The music of Schubert is characteristic of the period in which the music is

A. called baroque
B. called classical
C. called modern
D. mainly subjective with the emphasis upon emotion, freedom of expression and imagination.   (31C)

C. They *are* useful for testing the higher level objectives. Try another choice in *30A*.

~~~~~~

Variations

34.

A. We have now looked at the basic formats of test items but their applications are more diverse than would be indicated by the strictly verbal examples that have been used. For example, items based on pictures are often very useful, particularly in elementary schools. They are less dependent upon reading ability and can be used in conjunction with objective questions of many forms. For example, pictures of four different animals including a reptile might be followed by a true-false, multiple-choice, or completion item that requires the student to differentiate between reptiles and other animals.

One need not have artistic ability in order to use such items. Pictures of the needed items can usually be found quite easily and it is a simple matter to trace the essential elements onto the duplication master on which you are putting the test.

Picture items have the advantage of being less dependent on the students' reading ability.

__a. True (36A)
__b. False (37A)

B. Reread the section in *36A* and try the other choice.

~~~~~~

35.

A. Right! It is a systematic and uniform process established for evaluation purposes (in contrast to informal evaluation) but it is not limited to paper-and-pencil activities.

There are several versions of this technique. It can be used as a group approach or an individual approach; both have their limitations. If handled as a group activity, there usually must be enough materials for all students to use unless the entire group can view one set of materials without the need for manipulation. The individual approach, in which the teacher works with one student at a time, is limited by the great amount of teacher time consumed. For some evaluation purposes (e.g., evaluation of teaching practices or the instructional program), however, a sampling of student performance is completely adequate and is not a severe limitation.

Another way in which the various versions might be differentiated is in terms of the mode of response used by the students. With the group approach, the students must usually be restricted to a paper-and-pencil response, while oral responses are quite commonly used when the teacher is working with individual students. The paper-and-pencil responses can be in the form of multiple-choice, true-false, or matching items, but more commonly are a free-response type in which the student responds to a question in either the short-answer or a restricted essay mode.

The situation technique is restricted to use with individuals.

___a. True (36B)
___b. False (37B)

~~~~~~

36.

A. Yes! This is one of their advantages.

Another means of formal evaluation is based on the use of classroom materials such as those used for instructional purposes. These methods are sometimes referred to as situation techniques; the student is presented with an appropriate set of materials and asked to respond to the situation in a specified manner. For example, kindergarteners who have been working with various colors might be shown a set of small pieces of colored paper and asked to identify the colors; or senior high school industrial arts students might be shown examples of completed sheet metal products and asked to evaluate the quality of the workmanship. This type of systematic evaluation procedure is particularly appropriate in classes where the educational process includes work with concrete materials other than the books, papers and pencils usually used in the study of abstractions.

Situation techniques involve the use of educational materials in a systematic evaluation process.

___a. True (35A)
___b. False (34B)

B. No! You must not have read the section on *35A* very carefully. Read it again and try the other choice.

~~~~~~

37.

A. No! Reread this section in *34A* and try again.

B. Right! It can be used with individuals or groups. When considering the use of this technique, a key factor is whether or not this technique is the appropriate one for the objective you hope to evaluate. This, of course, is a key factor when considering the use of any technique.

Now that various types of measurement techniques have been examined we can turn our attention to tests as a whole and their role in making evaluations. This begins in section *38A*.

~~~~~~

Making Evaluations

38.

A. Now that we have examined a variety of test question forms, we can turn our attention to considering a test as a whole. In this regard, it has already been stated that the test should be constructed on the basis of the educational objectives, that it can be composed of more than one type of item (all of one type grouped together), and that good objective items can be retained and used in the future. Generally the same test should not be used repeatedly year after year, but a pool of items can be established from which most of a test can be composed when needed.

Because of the large amount of time required to construct good tests, some teachers would like to rely on published standardized tests or the tests which accompany some curricular materials. Although such tests are often useful, they usually fail to match satisfactorily the educational objectives of a given teacher's class and, as a result, most teachers do not find that they can rely upon them. Some curricular materials are accompanied by useful collections of test items which are intended as sources of items from which the teacher can select in constructing his own tests.

Published tests are generally adequate for a teacher's routine formal evaluation.

___a. True (40B)
___b. False (40A)

B. No, it should be halfway between a chance score on this type of test and a perfect score, not halfway between zero and a perfect score. Try again in *42A*.

~~~~~~

39.

A. No, if they did, why would he be making his next test easier? Try the other choice on *40A*.

B. Right. A chance score would be one out of every five or 20 percent. Halfway between a chance score and 100 percent would be 60 percent. The exact level of difficulty of a test is not of much concern, but it is important to note that tests can usually be much more difficult than they are. If so, they are *more discriminating,* as well as *more reliable,* and thus *more valid.*

Much of our study of test items and the tests which they constitute has been closely related to the assessment of the achievement of individual students. As noted earlier, however, evaluation is also helpful to the teacher in assessing the value of the educational practices he has been following. Within their formal evaluation procedures, teachers need to make provision for acquiring student judgments concerning their teaching practices. Thus, it is often appropriate to ask students their opinion of various facets of the class. Since it is opinion that is being sought, care must be taken to assure students that their opinion will not affect their grades or otherwise influence their standing with their teacher and their peers. These opinion questions should be clearly labelled as such, and if desired, can be put on a separate piece of paper which students hand in anonymously. Many formats are useful for this purpose but one that is particularly so is the Likert-type scale. An example follows:

Directions: The symbols below are SA (strongly agree), A (agree), ? (undecided), D (disagree), and SD (strongly disagree). For each item check the one that gives your opinion.

1. The municipal government study assignment was interesting.
   SA   A   ?   D   SD
   ( )   ( )   ( )   ( )   ( )
2. The municipal government study assignment was worth the amount of time spent on it.
   SA   A   ?   D   SD
   ( )   ( )   ( )   ( )   ( )
3. The teacher has not given us sufficient opportunity to discuss the issues involved in this unit.
   SA   A   ?   D   SD
   ( )   ( )   ( )   ( )   ( )

Opinion questions have no place in formal evaluation.

___a. True (42B)
___b. False (43B)

~~~~~~

40.

A. Right! Teaching and testing are intimately related. The teacher whose teaching is consistent with the uniqueness of his class will generally not find published tests to be sufficiently consistent with this uniqueness.

There is a widespread misconception that all passing students should be able to correctly answer 70 percent or at least 60 percent of the items on a test. Now, that expectation would be reasonable if a teacher had a well defined and complete set of objectives, a test which was a random sample of objectives, and a rational basis for deciding that mastery of 60 percent or 70 percent was the criterion for "passing." Rarely, however, is that the case, and unless it is, no one can treat a test as if it determines in absolute terms the degree of a student's *mastery* of a body of content. Actually, almost all tests used by teachers simply *discriminate* between students and provide a ranking of students which enables the teacher to *determine a student's achievement relative to the rest of the class rather than in absolute terms.*

A teacher has established 70 percent of the items on his test as the dividing line between passing and failing. After giving a test which a fairly large percentage of students failed, he said that he intended to make the next test considerably easier so an acceptable number of students would pass. Which of the following do his tests accomplish?

___a. determination of a students' mastery of the subject in absolute terms.
   (39A)

___b. discrimination between students in terms of their relative achievement. (42A)

B. No! In a few cases, yes, but this is not generally the case. Try the other choice in *38A*.

C. No; a chance score on this would not be the same as that on a true-false test; there are five options per item, not two. Try again in *42A*.

~~~~~~

41.

A. Fine! Most so-called absolute systems are really relative.

The most common grading practice is one in which grades are based on a student's performance relative to the rest of the class. A common procedure of this type is generally referred to as "grading on the curve." The strictest version of this procedure results in giving 7 percent of the class *A*'s, the next 23 percent *B*'s, the next 40 percent *C*'s, the next 23 percent *D*'s and the lowest 7 percent *F*'s (or some other fixed percentages of grades in each category). With this system, a fairer set of grades will result because the grading will not be influenced by variations in the level of difficulty of tests. There is a big problem, however, in that it is based on an erroneous assumption, which is that all classes have the same level of ability.

The best system is probably a modification of the above, in which grades are based on relative performance but dividing lines between grade categories are adjusted according to the average ability level of the class. Although there are fairly elaborate and good systems available for this kind of adjustment, most teachers find that they can do this satisfactorily with subjective adjustments based on their inspection of students' past grades and scores on aptitude tests.

The above approach is based on an individual student's ability and past performance.

___a. True (43C)
___b. False (44A)

B. Fine. The position taken in this chapter is that grades should not be based on effort. Although all persons need to experience success, there are many aspects of school life, other than academic endeavors, in which students can experience success. There is one place, however, where effort *must* be taken into consideration; this is in determining whether a student "passes" or "fails" a course. In making such a decision, the basic consideration is "Which option will be of greatest benefit to the student?" The effort expended by the student should be taken into account.

Whatever basis is used for determining grades, they should be based on a proper weighing of all measures of achievement which are available, not just on test scores. Evaluations of students' homework, reports, and classroom activity are all important. The time expended and educational objectives sought must be considered in determining what weight should be given to each measure of achievement.

The student who has mastered all that is contained in this chapter has answers to all questions concerning how to properly conduct evaluation in elementary and secondary schools.

___a. True (42C)
___b. False (44C)

～～～～～～～～～～～～～～～～～～～～～～～～～～～～

42.

A. Right! The fact that he intends to make his next test easier so more students will pass shows that his basis for determining who will pass is not the degree of mastery but relative performance. A discussion of the basis for determining where that dividing line should be is outside the scope of this section, but the fact that tests generally are used to determine relative ranking rather than mastery is relevant to another matter—the fact that teachers commonly fail to make tests as difficult as they should be.

Discarding the mastery myth (realizing, of course, that there are a few rare cases in which it is not myth) and recognizing that almost all tests are constructed and used for the purpose of discrimination, leads to desiring tests for which the *average* score rather than the *passing* score is in the neighborhood of 60 percent. The reason is that such tests give more discrimination. The test that provides the most discrimination is one in which the percentage of correct responses for each item is halfway between a chance score and a perfect score. For example, on a true-false test, the score which could be expected by chance alone for a student who knew nothing about the material on the test would be one out of every two or 50 percent; a perfect score would be 100 percent. The ideal level of difficulty would be halfway between the two or 75 percent.

What would be the desired level of difficulty for a multiple choice test with 5 options per item?

___a. 50%　(38B)
___b. 60%　(39B)
___c. 75%　(40C)

B. They do have a place. Try the other choice in *39B*.

C. You know better than that. Go back to *41B* and try the other choice.

~~~~~~

43.

A. This is a matter of opinion but the position taken in this chapter is that achievement grades should not be based on effort. Try the other choice in *44A*.

B. Correct! They have a place, although care must be taken to insure that they are not confused with and mixed with achievement assessment items. When used to evaluate the activities of a classroom, they can provide the teacher with valuable insights and give students more of a sense of involvement.

As mentioned earlier, a major use made of achievement measures is the assignment of grades. Grades have no precise meaning that can be depended upon. The grades assigned in one school cannot be compared to those from another school, and the grades given by two different teachers do not have the same meaning. What is worth a *C* to one teacher may be worth an *A* to another. In addition to variations in the level of achievement required for a given grade, there are variations in the bases used for determining grades. Some grades are said to be based on an absolute standard of achievement, some on achievement relative to the rest of the class, and others on achievement relative to the student's past performance. The teacher who claims to use an "absolute" system has specified a predetermined level of performance for a given grade and generally uses a percentage system of grading. This method of assessment is almost always unrealistic because of the variations in difficulty of tests, as pointed out earlier. Very few indeed, are the teachers who have specified in realistic operational terms what mastery is necessary for a given grade.

Grades based on absolute standards are often claimed but rarely found in reality.

___a. True (41A)
___b. False (44B)

C. There is a difference between using individual and group referents. Return to *41A* and try the other choice.

44.

A. Correct! In the above approach the percentage of people in the various categories is adjusted according to the ability level of the class as a whole.

A third basic approach is to base a student's grade on his ability or growth in achievement. If his performance is low but considerably improved he gets a high grade, whereas if his performance is high but not an improvement or is low with respect to his aptitude, he gets a low grade. This relative approach has difficulties. One argument against it is that evaluation "in real life" is not done in this manner. Possibly this is one reason why it is often misunderstood and disliked by parents. They expect a grade to tell them how their child is performing relative to the "world in general."

To avoid confusion, grades ordinarily should not be based on a student's effort, attitude, or deportment, but should be indicative of his achievement. Effort, attitude, and deportment are important and a good reporting system includes them. Much confusion is avoided, however, when these are not lumped together into one grade. A school's marking and reporting system should have separate categories for each. In addition, a school should have policies and procedures that encourage, as much as possible, a uniform meaning for grades throughout the school.

Grades should be based on effort since low ability children, like others, need to be able to achieve rather than fail constantly.

___a. True (43A)
___b. False (41B)

B. No, when examined carefully most absolute systems are not absolute. Try the other choice in *43B*.

C. Of course! This chapter has included much basic information but your actions will be influenced by further study, experience in the classroom, and good professional judgement. Your proficiency in evaluation will grow as you employ good judgement in conducting evaluations in accordance with what you have learned here and will learn in future study.

Selected References

EBEL, ROBERT, *Measuring Educational Achievement*. Englewood Cliffs, N.J.: Prentice-Hall, 1964.

This book is particularly good as a source of information on the construction of essay, true-false, and multiple choice items. The chapter on true-false items is probably the best available concerning the writing of this type of item, although more recent information casts doubt on the merits of the scoring system advocated for true-false items.

STANLEY, JULIAN C. AND KENNETH D. HOPKINS, *Educational and Psychological Measurement and Evaluation*. Englewood Cliffs, N.J.: Prentice-Hall, 1972.

An excellent general reference on measurement and evaluation, this book has thorough chapters on the construction of various types of test items. The description of a simplified procedure for item analysis is particularly valuable for the person who is interested in a means of evaluating and modifying test items which will be used again.

THE SENIOR HIGH SCHOOL EXAMINATION BOARD, *Taxonomy of English 30 Objectives with Illustrative Test Items: A Summary Description*. Edmonton, Alberta: Department of Education, 1968.

The booklet contains an extensive collection of multiple choice items that can serve as excellent models for the person wishing to construct items that test at the higher level of the *Taxonomy*. Although devoted entirely to English, it can provide insights to persons constructing items in other areas as well.

XEROX CORPORATION, *Science: A Process Approach, Parts A–G*. New York: Xerox Corporation, 1968–70.

This elementary school science program contains "competency measures" which can serve as models for the person constructing items of the situation-technique type. Although largely of the individual variety, many can be adapted to group use or provide insights into the construction of similar items in other subject areas.

Recognizing and assessing creativity

6

ALFRED DE VITO

Purdue University

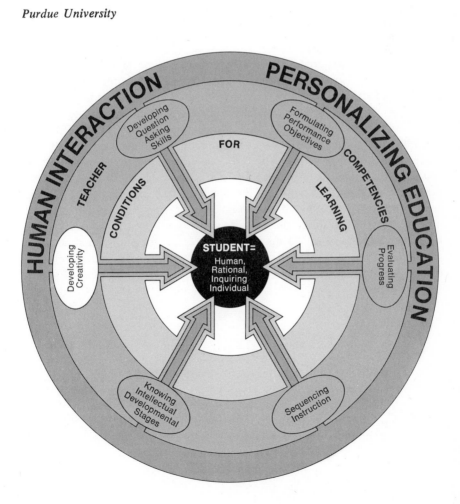

What is Creativity?

Much like other selected words in our vocabulary, creativity has become a hallmark of all that is good and desirable. To live creatively, to work creatively, and to think creatively is considered a desirable asset by many. People view creativity as the ingredient needed to solve problems of pollution, world population, food shortages, city planning, medicine, education, and so on. (We could go on and on.)

Creating is a thought process. It is the fusing together of knowledge gained from previous experience for the presentation of a *new* approach to the solution of a problem, or the design of a *new* technique or style for performing a familiar task.

Identify the Processes of Creativity

Does a definitive process of creativity exist? Some practitioners of the art of creativity say, "No." For purposes of clarification of the nebulous act of creativity, a model for the creative process of creativity is presented. (See Figure 6–1.) The first step in the process of creativity is the contact or the confrontation with a situation. One cannot be creative in a vacuum; one must have something to be creative about. The situation usually appears in the form of a problem. The problem is *analyzed* or defined, a process which involves a clarification and assessment of that which comprises the problem. As solutions are sought, ideas are *manipulated*. This sorting and manipulating of possible solutions may be accompanied by apprehension, frustration, or dismay. An *impasse* often occurs, leading to an apex. The problem seems unsolvable. Then, somehow, in some way, ideas jell, pieces seem to fall into place, and things seem suddenly to be clearly illuminated. You are over the apex. This is the magical *"Eureka,*

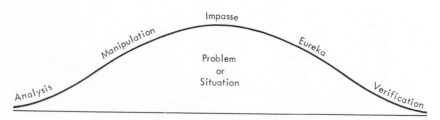

Fig. 6–1   A Model for Creativity

now I see it" stage. This may be followed by a *verification* or confirmation stage. Not all creativity follows this step-by-step process, but it approximates some of the events common to the process.

~~~~~~

Each statement below can be associated with a distinct process of the creative model. Read each statement and assign a corresponding number to the process which applies: 1. analysis, 2. manipulation, 3. impasse, 4. eureka, or 5. verification.

___A. Now I see it!
___B. I'm stuck.
___C. If it doesn't work this way, it must work this way. Hmm, not that way either.
___D. I see the solution!
___E. What type of problem are we dealing with here?
___F. I've got it!
___G. This seems to be the difficulty.
___H. It's impossible.
___I. How many variables are there?
___J. Let's check it out and make sure.

~~~~~~

Your numerical scoring of the above ten statements should have been 4, 3, 2, 4, 1, 4, 1, 3, 1, and 5. How well did you score?

~~~~~~

DISTINGUISH INTELLIGENCE FROM CREATIVITY

All individuals are creative. Although there is some correlation between IQ and creativity, creative contributions can come from all individuals. Intelligence has often been defined as the capacity to comprehend facts and situations, to perceive relations between them, and to reason about these relationships. Creativity is the creation of something, usually in reference to something new.

~~~~~~

Place a check before only those acts listed below which you think are creative acts.

___1. John just completed a complex algebra problem using the technique described in the text.
___2. Helen designed a new cover for the school newspaper.
___3. Scott made up a new vowel letter for the alphabet, increasing the number of letters from 26 to 27. He made up several rules for its application. He showed how this changed the present pronunciation of specific words.
___4. The entire class mastered all the week's spelling words.
___5. Jim wrote a poem relating the class members to Greek mythology.

~~~~~~

How did you rate these? *Two, three,* and *five* are creative acts. Do you agree?

~~~~~~

DISTINGUISH TALENT FROM CREATIVITY

Talent and creativity, like intelligence and creativity have much in common, so much, in fact, that the words are used interchangeably. And yet, the two traits are different. Someone may have a talent, a skill, or a proficiency for some action and still be considered uncreative. For example, a talented musician may be an excellent musician and still be uncreative. A talented artist may paint well, in the sense that he is a skilled craftsman, and yet he may be uncreative. A talent in this chapter is considered to be a proficiency of execution of some performance. Creativity, as stated earlier, is the creation of something new.

~~~~~~

Indicate by a check those items below which you think represent creative acts.

___1. Mother is a master in presenting innovative meals from simple leftovers.
___2. Sgt. Monahan is an excellent Marine drill sergeant.
___3. The local florist designs unique floral displays.
___4. The basketball star on the local team made 23 out of 25 foul shots from the foul line.

~~~~~~

One and *three* would be the correct responses for identifying creative acts as distinguished from talent.

~~~~~~

DISTINGUISH CRITICAL THINKING
FROM CREATIVE THINKING

The act of critical thinking is based on general reasoning, the ability to perceive problems, and the ability to organize facts and data for the solution of problems. Both inductive and deductive reasoning are components of critical thinking. The act of critical thinking is built on the premise that there is a reasonable explanation for every observed phenomenon, and if one can reason logically, an explanation will follow.

Teaching for critical or scientific thinking may establish some respect for the orderliness and simplicity of the universe. It does give the students a strategy for solving problems in a logical manner. This may cause the students to infer that, indeed, all nature is neat and orderly. This realization may tend to confine their thinking in a mental straight jacket and may even retard creative thinking. Critical thinking is an asset, but welding creativity to critical thinking creates a more potent asset. This creative addition would permit students to approach problems with a flexibility that welcomes the engagement of the mind with ambiguous, conflicting facts and data, hopefully making sense out of seeming disorder.

~~~~~~

Label the situations below as "C" if you believe them to represent creativity related to the solution of a problem.

____1. A student read in the local newspaper that dogs do not catch colds. He was puzzled by this discovery. Human beings catch colds, but dogs do not. This problem interested him. He attempted to reason through this phenomenon; he proposed several hypotheses, made some elementary considerations, and carried out a few simple experiments. His observations led him to infer that the only difference between dogs and human beings is the number of appendages and the presence of a tail in dogs. He concluded that animal forms with four legs and a tail do not catch cold.

____2. Another student read the same article. This problem interested him also. He wondered if animals other than dogs were so fortunate. He made studies to investigate the question. He tried to think of ways that dogs and other animals differ from human beings in their approach to keeping warm, dry, and so on. He attempted to learn if there was a tribe native to cold areas that existed without the use of clothes. He discovered that such a tribe existed in Tierra Del Fuego. He found that they rarely catch cold even though they sleep nearly nude outdoors in near-zero weather. He wondered about the fact that dogs had four legs, fur, and a tail. He attempted to relate the problem to other animals that more closely resembled human beings than dogs. This led him to search for information about monkeys. The study continued on with a major thrust directed at the initial problem, but all crossroads were considered, investigated, and their contributions held in abeyance until he felt closure was imminent.

If you selected situation number 2 you are correct.

~~~~~~

Techniques for Developing Creativity

SEEK NEW SOLUTIONS TO OLD PROBLEMS

If, indeed, creativity is to be the elixir for the ills of our present society, new solutions to old problems are needed. Someone once said, "If you are doing things the same way now as they were done ten years ago, there is a very good chance that there is presently a better way of doing them." Why must toothpaste come in a tube? Why must eyeglasses be worn in the same fashion? Why must all schools be built in nearly the same manner? Why? Why? Why not have a toothpaste toothbrush in which a toothpaste refill can be fitted in the handle? Why not have self adjusting glasses so that the wearer can make individual adjustments necessary for specific conditions such as reading, driving, or having degrees or portions of the lens capable of being tinted? Why can't we have schools built with bowling alleys, a theater area, a religious area, and a crafts area? This plan could enable the structure to be used for seven days and, if desirable, seven nights a week.

In winter, temperatures may drop to $-12°F$ with a chill factor of $-53°F$. It is cold! Heating a home is a problem. Furnaces and heating systems are working overtime. In the summer, the reverse temperatures overwork the air conditioners. Painting the exterior of the house is a nuisance. Installation of storm windows and screens is also a troublesome chore. Land is becoming more and more valuable. Overpopulation is rapidly making a megalopolis of previously rural areas. Trees are uprooted, grass is removed, and the surface of the earth is altered—not necessarily in the best interests of mankind. As a solution, skyscrapers, and high-rise apartments have been built. What can you offer as a solution to this problem? Would it help if you thought that "what goes up perhaps may also go down"?

Why not build houses underground? Surely there are many adjustments that must be made psychologically, mechanically, and in other ways, but creativity may solve these problems. A house built underground would have to be engineered differently, but that should not be a major problem for creative engineers. Homes built underground would be warmer in the winter and cooler in the summer. Exterior painting would never be needed.

This type of home would be safe from wind storms—perhaps even from atomic fallout. If the lack of light were a problem, we could build skylights. This type of home could be constructed so that it would be nearly burglar-proof. Heating units and other sources of possible fire hazards could be built underground a safe distance from the house. Does it sound practical?

~~~~~~

How many so-called unsolved problems can you think of that may need a creative application to arrive at a satisfactory solution? List several.

~~~~~~

DEVELOP A TECHNIQUE FOR PRIMING THE IDEA MECHANISM

Opening the flood gates of creativity may release only a trickle initially, but feeder lines can soon add to this trickle until you have released a creative stream. Where or how does it start? It was stated earlier that everyone has a creative potential; it needs only to be nurtured and primed in order to make it a viable part of your daily life. What are some of these creative priming techniques?

~~~~~~

Identify by checking the situation below which you think would contribute to priming the idea mechanism.

___1. You are just about ready to fall asleep. You get what appears to be a "flash of genius." You compliment yourself on thinking of the solution to what was previously a knotty problem. You roll over and say, "I will refine the idea in the morning." The morning arrives, but the idea has faded with the night.

___2. You are just about ready to fall asleep. You get what appears to be a "flash of genius." You compliment yourself, reach over for a pad and pencil and jot down the idea. In the morning you read your note and are ready to build on it.

If you identified situation *2* as a creative pump-priming technique, you are correct. Remember, "the dullest pencil can record what the sharpest mind can forget." A good technique for priming the creative pump is to carry a pad and pencil with you at all times. When you get a good thought, or idea, write it down. Keep an idea box. Each day jot down anything and everything that seems to be a worthwhile thought. At the end of the day, file the card. Occasionally review your idea file. Recapitulate ideas, cast out ideas, generate and integrate new ones. Try it; the creative pump will start working.

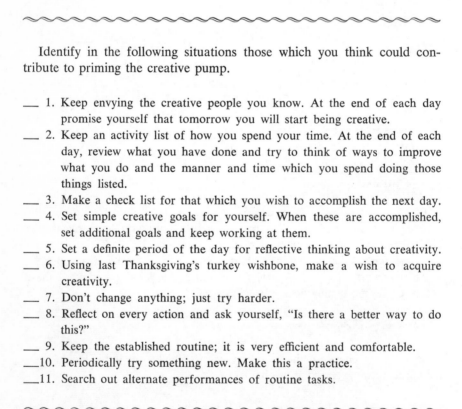

Identify in the following situations those which you think could contribute to priming the creative pump.

___ 1. Keep envying the creative people you know. At the end of each day promise yourself that tomorrow you will start being creative.
___ 2. Keep an activity list of how you spend your time. At the end of each day, review what you have done and try to think of ways to improve what you do and the manner and time which you spend doing those things listed.
___ 3. Make a check list for that which you wish to accomplish the next day.
___ 4. Set simple creative goals for yourself. When these are accomplished, set additional goals and keep working at them.
___ 5. Set a definite period of the day for reflective thinking about creativity.
___ 6. Using last Thanksgiving's turkey wishbone, make a wish to acquire creativity.
___ 7. Don't change anything; just try harder.
___ 8. Reflect on every action and ask yourself, "Is there a better way to do this?"
___ 9. Keep the established routine; it is very efficient and comfortable.
___10. Periodically try something new. Make this a practice.
___11. Search out alternate performances of routine tasks.

If you checked situations *2, 3, 4, 5, 8, 10,* and *11* as contributors to the creative pump-priming mechanism, you have selected the correct responses.

GIVEN A SERIES OF ITEMS OR SITUATIONS,
RECOMBINE THESE INTO MORE CREATIVE ACTS

Much emphasis has been placed on inquiry or discovery techniques in the learning process. Both of these techniques, and others by assorted names, are rooted in creativity. Manipulation of the materials when utilizing an inquiry or discovery approach to learning can give rise to a greater proliferation of ideas. This proliferation of ideas coupled with concrete manipulation of material objects facilitates the chaining or linking of ideas which is a valuable adjunct when directed towards the solution of a problem.

Imagine that a small toy car, a clock, an inclined plane, a meter stick, and various surface materials, such as a plywood board, a sheet of corrugated cardboard or a piece of corduroy material are provided. Many situations can be presented using these materials in different ways. Used in one manner the materials could complement a lesson on motion. Used in other ways, they might be part of a lesson about energy, force, and friction.

~~~~~~

If you were given a box of assorted colored rubberbands, list below as many ways as possible that you could use them to teach a lesson in any area of education.

~~~~~~

How well did you do? Did you relate this material to a math topic? Did you relate it to science? Could you have related this material to human nature? Some people have great elasticity; and all people get fatigued.

~~~~~~

DISCIPLINE THE MIND FOR CREATIVE PRODUCTION

Creativity is something everyone possesses in varying degrees. All individuals are born with some creative potential. Creativity can be developed if it is nurtured. How does one nurture creativity? One can nurture creativity by working and reflecting creatively; every action should be a challenge to your creative talents. Do you wash the dishes in the best manner, most economical of time, soap, wear and tear on the dishes, and so on? Do you take alternate routes to and from school to vary the view, looking for signs of change? Do you wear the same type of clothes every day? How can you dress more creatively? When was the last time you were puzzled by some observation? What did you do about it? What have you invented lately or at least thought about inventing? What in the design of some object such as a vacuum cleaner, lead pencil, or a new scouring pad has annoyed you? Did you attempt to alter it? Creativity, if not already exhibited, is a latent talent in everyone. It simply needs to be aroused and developed. When referring to creativity most people say, "But I can't paint, write, or play a musical instrument." These activities are and have long been associated with the identification of creativity. However, there are other avenues of creative expression. You can be creative in the kitchen—creating new recipes and new approaches to presenting the meals, varying the manner of serving, and so on. You can be creative in your shopping style. Make a list of the non-perishables you purchase week after week, for example, vinegar, catsup, mayonnaise, soaps. How could you creatively reduce your weekly shopping so that each week you only have to shop for the perishable items and the periodic palate tempters that are necessary for jaded appetites?

Creativity cannot be acquired on demand. It must be cultivated, almost coaxed, until creative thoughts cascade forth from the wellsprings of the mind.

You can start acquiring creativity by thinking creatively. Identify other creative people or creative groups and join them. Creativity is contagious; it can spill over and you can benefit from this "creative fallout." Involve yourself in something new or different. Join the "little theater" group, buy a beret and a smock and start painting, crochet fish-net hose, make something out of old tuna fish cans, but do *something*. When objects are manipulated and the mind is active, things seem to happen. Connections between seemingly extraneous ideas become obvious and new relationships "spring out" at you. Try it!

~~~~~~

Place a check mark before those activities which you feel discipline the mind for creative production.

___1. Continue thinking in much the same manner as you have been doing.
___2. Set aside a set period of the day to think about what you have done up

to that time and what you might have done differently and in a better manner.

___3. Get out more, rejoin the bridge club, get out your old bowling shoes and golf clubs and get back in the swing. From this move into new areas.

___4. Take a course in interior decorating or landscape design even though you feel you don't have the background.

___5. Take up one or more new hobbies or get involved in an area that is totally foreign to you but represents something that you always wanted to do.

___6. Study the arrangement of the furniture in your room, plan to rearrange and redecorate the room, spending as little money as possible.

___7. Wait to mature into a creative, innovative personality. Wish that things will move in this direction.

___8. Always admire creativity in others and envy their skill in resolving many situations to which you always respond by saying, "Why didn't I think of that?"

~~~~~~

Those techniques which might be designated as methods for disciplining your mind for active production are 2, 3, 4, 5, and 6. Did your responses agree with these?

~~~~~~

PROMOTE A SENSE OF FREE WHEELING THINKING
THROUGH PERIODIC BRAINSTORMING EXERCISES

Creativity, like many things in life, must be exercised to remain fluid in its application. The more it is exercised and used, the more productive it seems to become. A particular drill that seems to assist one in developing a free-wheeling style, producing a wealth of ideas, is called "brainstorming." Brainstorming is producing a multiplicity of ideas about some thought or problem. For example, a sign in a shoe shop reads, "We dye." Brainstorming, how many ways could this sign be altered to be a more creative sign? It might be altered to read, "We dye beautifully. We dye slowly. We dye daily. Dye, we do."

~~~~~~

For brainstorming, try this: You are given a man's old leather belt, a pair of suspenders, and a woman's silk stocking. Select one of these objects and list as many uses for this item as you can.

~~~~~~

How productive were you? Practice helps. If you were disappointed in the number of uses you discovered for the item you selected, choose another item from the list and repeat the process. The number of ideas should increase with practice. Did it?

~~~~~~

GENERATE NUMEROUS IDEAS FOR LATER SELECTIVE DISCRIMINATION OF THESE IDEAS IN SOLVING A PROBLEM

Not all exercises in creativity need to be directed toward immediate, practical problems. Exercises with situations that are hypothetical are excellent for developing a free-wheeling spirit of thinking. They free the mind for "loose" thinking. All contributions should be considered and no penalty should be attached to apparently extraneous or impractical contributions.

How many ways can you think of to re-ink or to re-use old typewriter ribbons? This may not be a practical problem, however, the question does provide an opportunity to generate new ideas. Some responses to this question might be: (1) Somewhere on the typewriter, place an atomizer ink sprayer that sprays the ribbon as it unwinds from a spool; (2) Have two ink pads that are re-inkable, allowing the ribbon to pass through and be re-inked; and (3) Have a set of ink brushes that brush against the ribbon as it unwinds. None, or all, of these ideas might be useful. Some may sound ridiculous. Any one of these ideas may be reworked, refined, and eventually resurrected so that it becomes a worthwhile solution to the problem.

~~~~~~

How good are you at generating ideas? Try this exercise. How many uses can you think of for the utilization of old Christmas cards? Generate in the space below as many ideas as possible in response to this question.

Analyze your responses. Which response is the best response? Which is the poorest?

~~~~~~

TRANSFER NON-CREATIVE FORMS OF IMAGINATION INTO PRODUCTIVE FORMS OF CREATIVITY

Imagination may take many forms such as dreaming, daydreaming, or sheer runaway imagination. For many people, these are pleasant excursions. Worrying, another form of imagination, occupies varying portions of everybody's thought time. In proper perspective all these soirées of the mind are healthy mental experiences, but for some people they occupy an inordinate amount of time. The point is not to eliminate any of these engagements, but to consider them as assets which can aid and abet creativity. Imagination, when channeled for use in the "real" world, can be a useful device. You can allow your mind to soar with the eagles, but then reel in your dreams and build foundations under them to make them come true. This, of course, is not always possible, but it is surprising how often it can be accomplished. Also, practice of this process increases the probability of success.

How would you answer these questions?

1. What was the wildest, most ambitious dream you have ever had?
2. Have you achieved it?
3. How much daily daydreaming do you involve yourself with? If the answer to this question is "None, I am too busy," re-evaluate the way you spend your time. A daily portion of your time spent daydreaming can add flavor to the day and to life, and it may lead to creative expression.

Worry can be a deterrent to constructive creative thinking if it occupies the major part of one's energies, or it can be a prime mover. Concern can be the drive that forces you to remove, rectify, or devise a solution; in such a case it can be considered a constructive creative force. Some people let worry wear them down; others learn to tolerate it, and perhaps, even to benefit from it.

~~~~~~

Check the following if they are true about you.

___1. I worry a little.
___2. I worry a lot.
___3. I worry, then I try to do something about it.

If you checked number 2, try to acquire the attitude described by statement number 3.

~~~~~~

Construct a Daily Creative Checklist

Read the following statements. Some of them, if followed daily, could assist you in developing your creativity. Place a check mark before those statements that appear to you to be components of a good daily creative checklist.

___ 1. Keep a record of activities done repeatedly, day after day. Ask myself if these need to be done in this manner and in this pattern. Is there a better way?
___ 2. Keep a record of what I did today that was new and different.
___ 3. What task did I perform in a fashion different from previous performances?
___ 4. Did I pause even briefly after each activity and ask myself, "Is this the best way? Is there another way? How could I have done it better?"
___ 5. Did I accept a challenge today?
___ 6. What puzzled me today? Did I look into things and wonder "How?" "Why?"
___ 7. What have I always dreamed of doing? Did I move a bit closer to it today?
___ 8. Did I constructively criticize some or all my performances today?
___ 9. Did I assume the role of the individual I have always longed to be? Was I brave today?
___10. Did I accept some criticism with the vigor of resolution?
___11. Did I attempt to arise from the quagmire of minutiae and see things in a more grandiose manner?
___12. How many times did I stick my neck out today?
___13. How many times did I question things today?

___14. What new project did I undertake today?

___15. Did I set aside a portion of my day to reflect about me, my actions, my destiny?

___16. How many "Eurekas" did I voice today?

___17. Did today count? What made it count? If not, what could I have done that would have made it count?

___18. Did I contribute anything to the improvement of something?

___19. What did I conquer today?

___20. Did I do something today that really pleased me?

All these activities are components of a good daily creative checklist. Go back over the list and check only those items that you practiced today. How do the two check lists compare?

~~~~~~

CONSTRUCT A SELF-EVALUATION PROGRAM RELATIVE TO CREATIVITY

A daily creative checklist is an excellent procedure for developing one's creativity. Your self-evaluation program could involve the same items listed in the daily creative checklist shown above. Which of the following action verbs would be the best indicator of a probability of creative acquisition?

1. I *could* be creative.
2. I *should* be creative.
3. I *will* be creative.

Yes, you *could,* you *should,* and you *will* be creative if you work at it. Try living creatively, thinking creatively, and teaching creatively.

~~~~~~

CREATIVE TRAITS

Amphyliboxia is a rare sickness. The symptoms are dizziness after prolonged deep breathing, heart palpitations, and a numbness in the ear lobes when exposed to long, dull conversations. By comparing the state of your health with these symptoms, you might infer that you may indeed have Amphyliboxia. Although creativity is not a disease, you can make similar comparative observations to determine if you possess personality traits that are related to creativity. E. P. Torrance [1] summarized the personality

---

[1] Reprinted from E. P. Torrance, *Guiding Creative Talent* (Englewood Cliffs, N.J.: Prentice-Hall, Inc., 1962), pp. 66–67, by permission of Prentice-Hall, Inc.

traits of highly creative persons in a list of forty-eight traits listed below. Make a tally mark before each creative trait which you feel you possess.

___strong affection
___altruistic
___always baffled by something
___attracted to mysteries
___attempts difficult jobs (sometimes too difficult)
___bashful outwardly
___constructive in criticism
___courageous
___deep and conscientious convictions
___defies conventions of courtesy
___defies conventions of health
___desires to excel
___determination
___differentiated value-hierarchy
___discontented
___dominant (not in a power sense)
___a fault-finder
___doesn't fear being thought "different"
___feels whole parade is out of step
___likes solitude
___industrious
___introversive
___keeps unusual hours
___lacks business ability
___makes mistakes
___not hostile or negativistic
___oddities of habit
___persistent
___receptive to ideas of others
___regresses occasionally
___reserved
___resolute
___self-starter
___sense of destiny
___shuns power
___sincere
___not interested in small details
___speculative
___spirited in disagreement
___tenacious
___thorough

___somewhat uncultured, primitive
___unsophisticated, naive
___unwilling to attempt anything on mere say so
___versatile
___willing to take risk

How well did you do? Did the blank spaces outnumber checked marks? Keep the items that were left blank by you in mind as you progress through this chapter.

~~~~~~

Creativity in the Classroom

GIVEN A CLASS OF CHILDREN, RECOGNIZE CREATIVE ACTS REVEALED BY OVERT ACTION OF SOME OF THE MEMBERS OF THE CLASS

Have you ever looked at a classroom filled with students? What do you see? A sea of faces—a galaxy of thoughts. Each a separate entity but bound inseparably to each other?

It was stated previously that all individuals have creative talents. How does a teacher recognize creative expressions? How does one discern a creative expression from an objectionable expression that seemingly is uncreative? How much creativity is strangled under the misinterpretation of an expression by children? Students come to the schools in their early years with high creative potential. An apparent lack of acumen quickly smothers this to the point where students recognize that creativity does not always pay off. You, as the teacher, set the market price for how much creativity costs within the four walls of your room. The students decide if they want to play the game and pay the price; usually it is too high.

A small styrofoam ball is thrown across the classroom. This may be called a creative act by the student but not necessarily identified as such by the teacher. We have to say it depends on circumstances, and so it does. At first this act may be interpreted as not being particularly creative, but we would have to correct some evidence before judging it. If the styrofoam ball were thrown to divert a bee from stinging a child who is seriously allergic to bee stings, we might say, providing that no one had been hurt, "Good thinking." We might even say "Very creative." If, after this event, the act was repeated for no apparent reason, the evaluation of the act might move from creative to uncreative. Thus, we might say that the rationale behind the act may aid greatly in discriminating creative acts from uncreative acts. Even though the creative acts do not always con-tribute to what you deem a "perfect" classroom situation, be tolerant of creative expression. For example, all your English compositions must conform to your organization. Mary has revised the writing of the name, date, and title each time she hands in an English exercise. Should you squelch her, compliment her, or forget the whole thing?

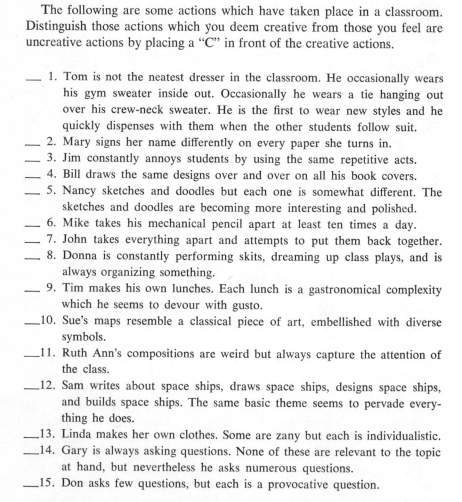

The following are some actions which have taken place in a classroom. Distinguish those actions which you deem creative from those you feel are uncreative actions by placing a "C" in front of the creative actions.

___ 1. Tom is not the neatest dresser in the classroom. He occasionally wears his gym sweater inside out. Occasionally he wears a tie hanging out over his crew-neck sweater. He is the first to wear new styles and he quickly dispenses with them when the other students follow suit.

___ 2. Mary signs her name differently on every paper she turns in.

___ 3. Jim constantly annoys students by using the same repetitive acts.

___ 4. Bill draws the same designs over and over on all his book covers.

___ 5. Nancy sketches and doodles but each one is somewhat different. The sketches and doodles are becoming more interesting and polished.

___ 6. Mike takes his mechanical pencil apart at least ten times a day.

___ 7. John takes everything apart and attempts to put them back together.

___ 8. Donna is constantly performing skits, dreaming up class plays, and is always organizing something.

___ 9. Tim makes his own lunches. Each lunch is a gastronomical complexity which he seems to devour with gusto.

___10. Sue's maps resemble a classical piece of art, embellished with diverse symbols.

___11. Ruth Ann's compositions are weird but always capture the attention of the class.

___12. Sam writes about space ships, draws space ships, designs space ships, and builds space ships. The same basic theme seems to pervade everything he does.

___13. Linda makes her own clothes. Some are zany but each is individualistic.

___14. Gary is always asking questions. None of these are relevant to the topic at hand, but nevertheless he asks numerous questions.

___15. Don asks few questions, but each is a provocative question.

Examples 1, 2, 5, 7, 8, 9, 10, 11, 13 and 15 are examples of creative expressions. How well did you do with scoring examples 1–15?

ABILITY TO CONTRAST A TRADITIONAL APPROACH WITH A CREATIVE APPROACH TO A TEACHING SITUATION

Much criticism has been directed at the so-called "traditional" approach to teaching. The author will not add to this criticism, defend the approach, or condone it. He will simply recognize it. Much good teaching has been accomplished under the mantle of "traditional" teaching, and much poor teaching as well. Creative teaching demands creative teachers who can alter existing styles to best meet the needs of an evolving curriculum involving children.

~~~~~~

Check one of the following suggested introductions to a lesson in elementary geometry which seems to be a more creative approach to initiating the lesson:

___A. "Okay, put away your spelling books," said the teacher. "We are going to start a new section in our math books. I think you will like it. Turn to page 139 in your math book."

___B. The teacher asked, "How many different routes can you think of to get to the pencil sharpener from your seat? Which route is the shortest? How can you tell? Measure. That's right. A section in our math book is concerned with measures on the earth. This study is called geometry. Who can tell me what section of the book is devoted to this study?"

If you selected *B* you have recognized that this approach involves an approach that is an alteration of a traditional approach and which should be novel and perhaps more interesting to the students.

~~~~~~

RECONSTRUCT A TRADITIONAL LESSON SO THAT IT WOULD BE CONSIDERED A VITAL, CREATIVE LESSON

The class had been studying a lesson in music. The assignment was to learn the various instruments that make up an orchestra. Part of this lesson dealt with the history of numerous instruments of the orchestra and how they evolved. The students were not very excited with the assignment. The teacher recognized this feeling and proposed instead that each student review the instruments that make up an orchestra. It was suggested that each student invent a variation for any one instrument that might give it a different sound, or design a new instrument combining the attributes of several orchestral instruments, or design a completely new instrument.

Each student was to assign a name to the newly-developed or designed instrument.

Does the above paragraph represent a creative departure from a rather traditional assignment? The author thinks that it does.

~~~~~~

Which of the following is representative of a more creative approach?

___"Write a short reaction to any situation in the story *Huckleberry Finn,*" instructed the teacher.

___"Write down as many nicknames as you can like "Huckleberry" that you could validly assign to yourself. Select one, and write a short paragraph describing how you acquired this nickname. Don't sign your name to the paper. They will be collected and read by other class members to see if the class can determine who in the class fits the nickname," said the teacher. The teacher will submit a paragraph describing a nickname assigned to him.

If you assigned a creative approach to assignment number 2, you are correct.

~~~~~~

GIVEN NUMEROUS SITUATIONS, DISTINGUISH THOSE TRAITS
WHICH BLOCK CREATIVITY FROM THOSE WHICH ENHANCE IT

Certain situations dampen creativity. The structure of the situation or the type of question may indeed thwart creativity. Overplanning, or accounting for every minute of the lesson with no room for deviations will inhibit creativity. Astute conformity to a predetermined norm can also retard creativity. Closed convergent questions which must lead to one correct answer accomplish the same purpose.

~~~~~~

Identify from the examples below only those situations you feel enhance creativity.

___A. The teacher holds an oriental bamboo backscratcher in the air. She asks, "Who knows what this is?" Either she continues probing the class until one student says, "A backscratcher," or she tells them.

___B. The teacher held up an oriental bamboo backscratcher in the air. She asked, "How many uses can you think of for this item?" The responses ranged from, "You can use it for a small garden rake" to "You can use it as a device for decorating icing on a cake." The responses totaled 53 uses before the teacher decided to bring the discussion to a halt.

___C. For the Christmas classroom party, one student suggested that portions of the room be decorated denoting Christmas around the world. The teacher responded, "We usually decorate the windows and put up a small tree."

___D. The teacher suggested that the students write a composition about what they did that was exciting over the summer vacation.

___E. Prior to the summer vacation, the teacher gave each child a map of the United States showing national parks, fashion centers, outstanding yearly events (for example, forthcoming fairs, world or local), outstanding landmarks of historical interest, and so on. She asked each student to study the map, select an area of the United States he might like to visit and explain why he would want to visit that particular place.

___F. As an assignment, the teacher asked each student to bring in a tool or small piece of equipment that seems to serve a puzzling purpose, for example, an apple corer or a unique bottle opener, to see if the other students in the class could identify the instrument or identify its purpose.

___G. The teacher prepared a detailed lesson that moved the students through the subject in a very logical order from simple to complex. Not much time was alloted for individual contributions because the schedule was extremely tight.

___H. The teacher was well aware of the objectives of the lesson. She knew where she was going, how she was going to get there, and she had an instructional device to let her know when she had arrived at this point. The lesson had structured into it opportunities for the students to digress and reflect on the material.

How well did you do? Those situations which might block creativity are A, C, D, and G. Situations B, E, F, and H would do more to enhance creativity. Were you able to identify these correctly?

~~~~~~

REVISE SUBJECT AREA LESSON FROM A CURRICULUM GUIDE
SO THAT THE STATED OBJECTIVES ARE REACHED IN A
CREATIVE MANNER OR DEVELOPED CREATIVELY OR BOTH

Lesson plans are blueprints for action. Unfortunately, some blueprints are followed so closely that few, if any, avenues for creativity are left open. Below are three lesson plans. Which of the following do you think represent a creative approach to the topic?

~~~~~~

DAILY LESSON PLAN: GEOGRAPHY

Concept: To show the relationship of populated regions of the earth to various land forms.

Lesson Plan 1.   Materials: sandbox, toothpicks, small flags, a 35 mm camera, film

The class is moved out into the elementary sand box area of the school-yard. The class creates in the sand box various land forms, such as hills, valleys, plateaus, river systems and oceans. The teacher designates farm-produce areas. Each student places a toothpick with a small name-flag on it in a spot in the sand box where he thinks he would like to live. Each student is asked to state why he or she selected that particular area as a good place to live.

Several students are assigned to construct in the sand box duplicate areas of specific portions of the world. Thirty-five millimeter slides are taken of the constructed areas. These slides are shown later in class and discussed by various groups pointing out the characteristics of the area, the populated areas, and the farm products which might be found.

Lesson Plan 2.   Materials: Textbook, a relief globe, a relief map of the United States

Procedure:
1. Point out high and low areas of the world.
2. Class locates on the globe the most heavily populated areas of the world.
3. The class relates the populated land areas of the world to the different land forms.
4. The class locates the major areas in which farm products are produced in quantities.

Summary: Students answer questions as to why people live where they do and why farm products are grown where they are.

Homework: Read pp. 75–86. Answer questions, 3, 5, 7, on p. 92 of the text.

Lesson Plan 3.   Materials: Textbook, balloons, papier-maché

Procedure: Each child blows up a balloon. Using papier-maché each child constructs a papier-maché sphere which depicts land-form reliefs. This is done in any manner chosen. The student orients the globe, placing a north and south pole at opposing ends of the sphere. Land and water masses are selected and colored in. Major river systems following the relief of the land are sketched in. Using the constructed globe, each individual plots the most advantageous places on his globe for a concentrated population and desired farm-produce areas to support this population.

Each student is asked to defend his placement of population plus the farm-produce areas.

Summary: Students discuss advantages and disadvantages of the various models.

Homework: The students individually compare their constructed world to the "real" world and point out advantages and disadvantages of both.

If you said 1 and 3 were creative in their approach to this subject, you are correct.

Which of the above lessons would you prefer to teach? Would it challenge you? Would it challenge the students?

~~~~~~

DISTINGUISH CREATIVE INTRODUCTORY STATEMENTS FROM UNCREATIVE INTRODUCTORY STATEMENTS

"Okay, time for music." Using a different inflection for each word of the previous statement, how many different implications do you think you could project? The vitality, spirit, anticipation, or the drudgery you superimpose on this statement is almost sure to be communicated to students and be mirrored back in a complementary performance.

~~~~~~

Place a "C" before the following introductory statements which you think would have appeal because they suggest a creative introduction.

___A. We are running over in the time allotted for math. We haven't done science for a week. Let's open our science books to page 97.
___B. Where did we stop yesterday in our English lesson?
___C. Class, can you think of any ways to study verbs today other than using our text books?
___D. Today's geography lesson will take place outdoors in the kindergarten sandbox (or the junior or senior high school broad-jumping pit).
___E. Would anyone like to play baseball instead of working math problems? Can we combine the two?

If you labeled introductory statements *C, D,* and *E* you are thinking creatively. These certainly are more creative introductions to lessons than either *A* or *B*.

~~~~~~

Develop Provocative Situations About Traditional Objects, Actions or Trends

Teachers in a sense are salesmen. They sell education. They are, among other things, performers. As performing salesmen, they occupy a fair share of the students' daily lives. It thus behooves teachers to be stimulating in their presentations. This occasionally means altering what might be termed a traditional approach so it becomes a new, provocative, creative approach.

Below are four examples. Check those which appear to be representative of a more creative approach.

___1. The teacher said, "Today we will start learning the 25 new words in our spelling book. Start reviewing them in preparation for Wednesday's test."

___2. "Examine the next group of spelling words," said the teacher. "Test yourself. Study those words that you miss or those that you are not sure of, and then write a short paragraph using as many of these words as possible."

___3. "An adjective is a modifier which describes or limits a substantive. Read through the descriptive paragraphs in your text and write down all the adjectives."

___4. The teacher assigned each student to cut out from magazines any three objects, for example, a bicycle, a can of tomato soup, and a football. All the pictures were collected and mixed, and each student was asked to pick out any three pictures. The class was divided into two teams, each of which was to write a short paragraph about the three objects picked at random, using as many adjectives as were presented in the previous day's assignment listing specific adjectives. The team with the most correctly used adjectives from the adjective list won.

Which situations seemed most provocative? If you identified items two and four as being creative approaches, you selected the correct ones.

Create an Environment Where Creative Activities Are Necessary, Not Merely Exercises

Unfortunately most learning seems to revolve around the clock. One period a day for mathematics, one period a day for reading, and so forth. Is this a creative approach? Creativity should not be turned off and on by the clock. It should be part of the total classroom environment. If subject areas of the curriculum are parceled into time blocks, let creativity be the "warp and woof" of your program. Its continuance can give continuity to the learning process. Creativity is a total process and should permeate the entire day and the entire curriculum. Creativity flourishes best in an environment where creativity is a *must* rather than an interjection into a program as a mere exercise pointed toward creative development. Some exercises may initially be desirable, but as quickly as possible, move these exercises out into the real world.

How many uses can you imagine for a light bulb, a brick, an old flashlight battery? This type of exercise is good. It does loosen up the mind and helps to develop a free-wheeling style of thought. Try to make it more applicable, however. For example, a teacher posed a problem relative to a science lesson dealing with plants. She was concerned with evaporation, transpiration, and liquid transportation within plants. She said, "School will be closed for ten days during spring vacation. No one will be available to water the plants. The school will be completely locked during this time. How can we take care of the needs of the plants during this period?"

A question like this is an exercise in creativity. It opens the door wider by making the problem relevant to the classroom situation. Thinking caps are adjusted and ideas pour forth from the students. Some responses are good and some are not so good. All solutions are entertained and finally the class moves closer to the solution of the problem by suggesting that the plants be placed in an aquarium lined with a gravel layer on top of sand saturated with water. The top of the aquarium would be covered by a plastic wrap with a few holes punched in it. Another group thought it best to suspend a bucket of water above the plants and to submerge coiled rope in the bucket leading down to the potted plants, wrapping around the stem at the base and resting on the soil. Both methods were implemented. The opening session of class after the semester break was a discussion about which plants survived and why.

~~~~~~

In the following exercises distinguish those creative acts which are simply exercises as opposed to those which are "exercises plus."

___1. Drop a blob of water color paint onto a piece of paper. Fold and press the paper quickly so that you make a mirror image smear. Make a list of the objects the resultant smear reminds you of.

___2. How many words can you substitute to describe a situation that is termed ridiculous.

___3. The teacher decided to label a section of the bulletin board as "What puzzled me today." Any child could tack up a notice posing a question that puzzles him. The class reviewed the questions and then attempted to resolve the puzzling question.

___4. Classroom space was a problem. Storage space, wall space, floor space, and so forth, seemed inadequate. The students redesigned the room, altering placement of chairs, clearing areas, and rearranging equipment.

Exercises 1 and 2 are straightforward creative exercises. Exercises 3 and 4 are exercises plus an application. If you selected 3 and 4 you are correct.

~~~~~~

GIVEN VARIOUS SITUATIONS IN THE DAILY CURRICULUM, DEVELOP DIVERGENT-THINKING PROCESSES AS WELL AS CONVERGENT-THINKING PROCESSES

The convergent approach moves things from the general to the specific. For example, the teacher holds up an object and says, "Who knows what this is?" Thirty children must "zero in" on one correct response. Divergent thinking, by contrast, is more dynamic than convergent thinking. For example, the teacher holds up an object, identifies it, and says, "How many other uses can you think of for this object?" This moves thinking from the specific to the general. Creativity springs from divergent thinking. Ideas escalate from this approach. The variety and multiplicity of ideas grow out of the interaction of the contributing members. Divergent thinking stimulates creativity. No responses can be considered wrong. The removal of the penalty for wrong answers frees the flow of ideas.

~~~~~~

Identify the following situations as convergent (C) or divergent (D) situations.

___1. I am thinking of the name of a city in Florida. It is a famous resort city.
___2. What could be done to Padre Island, Texas to make it an attractive resort area?
___3. This rock is one of what major classification of rocks.
___4. This part of the plant is called _____.
___5. What other names could you legitimately assign to each word in this sentence other than their correct part of speech names?
___6. Two and two are _____.
___7. How many ways can 3 and 2 be written?
___8. My watch stopped. How many ways can we use to determine what time it is?

Situations 2, 5, 7, and 8 are representative of divergent situations. Situations 1, 3, 4, and 6 would be classified as convergent situations.

~~~~~~

GIVEN A SERIES OF SITUATIONS THAT ARE CONVERGENT, ALTER THESE SO THAT THEY BECOME OPEN-ENDED EXPERIENCES

"I have a surprise" said the teacher. "Can any one guess what it is?" The children responded one by one, each attempting to identify the surprise. The teacher had one idea or in this case, one surprise. Thirty individuals were asked to focus in on one idea. If the first student guessed the surprise, the situation would have been drawn to a close with a rewarding comment to the lucky student. This situation has one answer and few rewards. The students were asked to converge on one idea. This is called a *convergent situation.*

Had the teacher said, "I have a surprise. What would you like it to be?", the flood gates would have been opened. Thirty children may have given 30, 60, 90, or more responses. No one's answer could be discredited and many rewards for excellent suggestions could be given.

"What is the capital of Indiana?" asked the teacher. How could this situation have been altered so that it would be an open-ended experience rather than a covergent question? This situation could have been altered by giving the students a map of Indiana in the year 1871 and a map of Indiana in the year 1971. On the current map, the teacher could show the populated areas, the industrial areas, railroads, rainfall, farm areas, and so forth. She may have stated that the capital of Indiana is Indianapolis. Looking at the current map of Indiana she asked the students, "Would you still place the capital at Indianapolis? If so, why? If not, why?" This opens up the discussion for many considerations.

~~~~~~

Try this: The teacher planted some seeds in two small flower pots. The seeds grew in one, but not in the other. Check those responses which are conducive to the extension of this event into an open-ended experience.

___1. Did I forget to water one of the plants?
___2. What could I have done wrong?
___3. Were the seeds in the one flower pot not fertile?
___4. I guess I don't have a green thumb.
___5. What could have happened to account for this?

Responses 2 and 5 would be considered open-ended questions. Did your answers correspond to these?

～～～～～～～～～～～～～～～～～～～～～～～～～

Assess the Adequacy of Numerous Proposed Ideas for the Task at Hand

Divergent thinking produces many ideas, and is advantageous because it proposes many suggestions for the solution of a problem. It does not necessarily *solve* a problem. One must select from these numerous suggestions the best or those best suggestions which seem most applicable for the solution of a specific problem. Thus, we move from a divergent approach to a convergent approach. This process is cyclic and can be repeated over and over until a satisfactory solution to a problem is reached. This cycle necessitates an evaluation of the proposed ideas and an assessment of priorities of consideration directed towards the solution of a problem.

A class was studying an area of historical geology concerned with ancient forms of life. A discussion had just transpired about the decline of dinosaurs. Someone noticed from viewing the geologic calendar that the cockroach had survived since mid-Paleozoic time. The teacher seized on a creative exercise. She suggested that the students think of all the animals they know. She then asked them to design an animal using any or all parts of these animals and create a new animal that would have the necessary characteristics to enable it to survive in the world of the future.

The class responded with many ideas. The following are a few:

1. The body of an elephant, the neck of a giraffe, webbed feet like a duck, and a tail like a monkey;
2. The body of a horse, wings like a condor, legs like a deer, a trunk like an elephant, and a hide like an alligator;
3. A body like a cougar, tusk like an elephant, feet like a horse, and a body covering like a duck;
4. A body like an armadillo, a head like an alligator, legs like an ostrich, feet like a mole, and a tail like a monkey;
5. A body like a gorilla with upper arms like a seal, a brain like a man, teeth like a bear, a body covering like a turtle, and a long tail.

All contributions, though given their just attention, cannot and do not warrant classroom discussion. This means that the teacher and the class must establish a priority. Some contributions are blind alleys. Others are fruitful, yielding worthwhile discussion in light of the question posed.

～～～～～～～～～～～～～～～～～～～～～～～～～

Which one of the above structures would you rank as the best construct for survival and most worthy of a classroom discussion?_____

Selection number 5 seems to be the best creation for survival. Why?

~~~~~~

FORMULATE RELEVANT QUESTIONS THAT PROMOTE CREATIVE THINKING SKILLS

Good questioning is considered the heart of good teaching. It is also considered the heart of good learning. How often have you heard the expression, "I guess I did not ask the right questions." Asking the right questions is as important to the teacher as he attempts to lead students to decision-making situations as it is for students to draw information out of the teacher or some other resource.

Let's try an example. Jim, during his Christmas vacation, decided to drive north for a skiing vacation. The car operated normally. It began to rain, then the rain turned to sleet, spewing mud and ice all over his windshield. He turned on his windshield wipers. They worked well, spreading the mud and ice in a nice even film. He turned on his windshield washers; nothing happened. The temperature outside was 0°F. The fluid was good for temperatures down to −5°F. He pulled into a gas station, and had to wait five minutes for the station attendant to service his car. In the meantime, the windshield wipers and the windshield washer were both operating, so he thought the problem was solved. Leaving the gas station, he noticed that the wipers and the windshield washer worked for the first mile; then the automatic washer stopped spraying fluid. Jim stopped at the next gas station, where the same thing happened: The automatic washer again began to operate. It later became inoperative about a mile down the road.

What relevant questions might you want to know the answers to in order to resolve this problem? Some sample questions might be: "Is the fluid really good for a temperature of −5°F?" "What is involved in the system?" The answer to the first question is "Yes." The answer to the second question is: A windshield liquid container, a hose from the container to a small motor, more hose leading to the windshield area, a small tube that is aimed at the windshield, and the dashboard switch.

How could you determine if any of these were operative? You could check the container to make sure it contained fluid. You could disconnect the hose to and the hose beyond the motor to make sure that they were not stopped up. You could replace the hose to the motor, turn the car motor on, turn the windshield washer switch on, and see if the motor does pump fluid through the hose. You could check to see if the small tubes leading to the windshield are free and open. You know the automatic fluid was dispensed when the car was stationary but stopped when the car traveled down the road about one mile. This would cause you to suspect that something about the motion of the car was responsible for the windshield washer becoming inoperative. Remember the fluid was safe for $-5\,°F$. The answer may not be clear yet, primarily because you may not have asked the right questions. The questions you have asked were good questions and the answers to each may have brought you closer to an explanation, but they did not furnish you with the correct explanation.

At this point in the problem, you have data which has not yet yielded a full explanation. Now you lead your students to the point where they can link these pieces of data together, perhaps asking another question or two which might enable them to come up with the magic "Eureka" as they see the explanation unfold.

Wet your finger. Blow on it slowly at first and then with greater force. What effect did the blowing stream of air have? Does this give you a clue as to the question that needs to be answered. What is it?

~~~~~~

If you said "What was the chill factor or reduction in temperature resulting from the motion of the car as it traveled the one mile distance?" you would be correct.

~~~~~~

TRAIN CHILDREN TO ASK SEARCHING QUESTIONS AS WELL AS CLOSURE QUESTIONS

We want children to be able to solve problems. In this process we want children to ask searching or open-ended questions. Open-ended questions stimulate the mind. Questions such as, "Can animals talk to one another? Are butterflies ever afraid of falling? Why must we all die? Do trees weep? Are trees ever happy?" may seem somewhat esoteric until considered. Individuals who may have responded to such questions by saying, "Gee, I never thought of that," might also wonder, "Why?"

Open-ended questions do not always lead to resolution, but they do expand the creative facilities of the mind. They stimulate individuals to pursue individualistic concerns about staid problems. Closure problems, presented in a formalized classroom setting, are usually pre-determined by the teacher or the text author. The child usually knows the answer has been found or can be found in the pages of the text. An example of an open-ended question in social studies is "Airplane travel is currently on the decline, why?" There are many considerations involved in the explanation of this phenomenon. Not all, and perhaps not any answers are in a given text. The students must "dig" for reasons to explain this phenomenon.

~~~~~~

Examine the following statements. Identify those which might be considered open-ended type statements by placing an *O* before them.

___1. A monocotyledon plant differs from a dicotyledon plant in what ways?
___2. How can one determine which part of a plant leaf grows the fastest?
___3. What might a rock composed of quartz, feldspar, and mica, having interlocking crystals, and a coarse texture be called?
___4. What would the world be like if all fear were eliminated?
___5. Do dogs laugh?
___6. What is the Beaufort symbol for a wind speed of 35 miles per hour coming from the northwest?
___7. Water can exist in what three states of matter?
___8. What kind of a world would it be if ice contracted instead of expanding upon freezing?
___9. Is smoking bad for you?

The open-ended statements are 2, 4, 5, 8, and 9. How well did you do?

~~~~~~

TEACH EACH SUBJECT NOT SIMPLY AS MASTERY BUT AS A TECHNIQUE TO SOLVE PROBLEMS

How often have you been a student in a classroom and wondered what you will be able to do at the end of the course that you could not do before it started? How often have you labored hard and long to master a topic only to wonder how it might help you either as a teacher or as an individual? How many of your assignments were concerned with memorization and recall without much application to thought-provoking questions that challenged your thinking ability? Thinking is just about the most important thing we do. Gaining knowledge which is not applicable to any situation is not necessarily a productive venture. Children learn a great deal in school. Opportunities for the application of this learning to the solution of problems are few. If you disagree with this statement make a profile chart of one or more students. Plot the amount of their time spent in applying information as opposed to time spent acquiring information on a day-to-day basis in the classroom. Much lip service is given to developing independent, decision-making students, but in reality little is done to promote this end. After you have learned something or taught something, ask yourself, "So what?" This may sound like a caustic approach to something we have long revered in the classroom but may have neglected: having children ask WHY and HOW: "Why do I need to know it and how can I use it?" Teach, assess the attainment of your objectives, and then place the students in real, "live" situations where they can see the value of the lesson. Place them in thought-provoking situations and allow them the opportunity to "think" their way out.

A lesson is taught about finding the area of a square. The formula, $A = l \times w$, is developed. This formula is carried further by asking students to find the total surface area of a cube. The formula for finding the total surface of a cube is developed and practiced.

In a creative extension that affords students an opportunity to apply this information, the teacher gives each student eight sugar cubes and some glue. He instructs the students to construct any geometric solid they so desire, using all eight sugar cubes. When they have completed the construct, they must calculate the total exposed surface area. Having done this, each student swaps his construct with a classmate. Each student computes the total surface area of the new construct and then the students compare their calculations.

~~~~~~

As you read through the following information about a fictitious country, be thinking of questions which would aid your students in developing problem-solving skills. San Royale is a fictitious country, consisting of 29 states, two territories, and a Federal District. Munez is one of these 29 states. It is located in the northeast section of San Royale and borders the United States of America. Its area is 30,000 square miles and its population is 1,000,000. The capital of the State of Munez is Montamunez.

Center of a rich farming and dairying region, Montamunez—often called San Royale's Pittsburgh—is a modern, Americanized, commercial metropolis built at the meeting place of Cisco coal and Humboldt iron ore. Here are numerous big industries and golf courses, country clubs, pure water, and also crime and juvenile delinquency. Wealthy, ambitious, and progressive Montamunez symbolizes the San Royale of tomorrow. Montamunez ranks second as a railroad center.

The geographic area of Munez is termed a low-latitude steppe. It is a land of thorny bushes, acacia, and short grasses where sheep, goats, and cattle graze. Wheat is raised in more humid sections, and in the irrigated lower Grande Aqua section, citrus and truck crops flourish.

Munez is a land of stark desert landscape cut by deep serrated canyons. Dry and healthy, with an average elevation of 3,000 to 4,000 feet, this vast, sparsely populated tableland shares with the United States an unguarded border. The mean temperature is 68 to 72 degrees, and the area is often referred to as "the land of eternal springtime."

~~~~~~

Which of the following questions would aid a student in solving problems? Indicate your response by placing a check in the appropriate space.

___1. San Royale consists of how many states?

___2. This is a picture of Arizona's terrain. Contrast this with Munez.

___3. A section of southern Texas borders on Munez. This area has a relatively dry, healthy climate. The average temperature is about 70 degrees and the mean elevation is 1,500 feet. This area has some thorny bushes, cacti, and short grasses. What similar products might come from both this portion of Texas and Munez?

___4. What is the population of Munez?

___5. Utilizing the facts contained above in the description of San Royale, describe the potential for Munez becoming a cotton and tobacco-producing state.

___6. The border between the two countries (United States and San Royale) is unguarded. San Royale and the United States have had a long history of hostility. Under what considerations should we have an unguarded border there?

___7. What is the capital of Munez?

___8. Describe the differences and similarities of the people that live on each side of the border as affected by the geographical conditions.

While all the above questions may be justified in the learning process, certain ones assist students in obtaining experiences with problem solving. You would have been correct if you had listed 3, 5, 6, and 8 as problem-solving promotional questions.

~~~~~~

DISSECT PROBLEMS INTO SIMPLER COMPONENTS FOR SUB-ANALYSIS OF THESE SEGMENTS FOR CONTRIBUTORY EFFECTS TO THE TOTAL PROBLEM

When confronted with a problem, most students are at a loss as to how to begin. They may observe a phenomenon or formulate their observations into a stated problem, but the attack for the resolution of the problem leaves many students feeling at loose ends. They do not know where to begin. Not all problems are solved using the same strategy. Creativity is essential to the productivity of a diversified attack for the resolution of numerous problems. Students who have not yet reached this level of expertise need a strategy or at least a starting point. This starting point may well be the application of their powers of observation. Using all their senses, ask them what they observe. Is there a pattern to their observations? Is there a change over a period of time? Is there a change due to some application? Simply, what is asked is, "What do you see?" This may be followed by "What is involved?" and finally by, "What do I know about what I observed?" This is like isolating the parts of a puzzle to determine how they might fit together or relate to the total picture. The very play of ideas may be likened to a kaleidoscope wherein the process of manipulation brings into view new mosaics; so it is with ideas.

The weather outside the classroom was very cold. Early in the morning the windows in the classroom were clear. The temperature outside did not rise during the day. By mid-day the classroom windows were all covered with steam. The teacher asked the class, "Why?"

What did the students see?

1. They saw clear windows early in the day.
2. They saw steam or condensation on the windows from mid-day on.

What is involved:

1. No temperature change outdoors.
2. They might infer the temperature increased within the classroom as the day wore on.
3. The classroom did not have anyone in the room overnight.
4. Thirty students had been in the classroom from early morning on.

What do they know about what they observed?

1. They read somewhere that a person loses two to three pounds overnight simply by breathing and exhaling. The exhalation carried off moisture from the body.
2. When there is a number of passengers in a car on a very cold day, the windows fog.

Do you agree that this process, though just one process, may lead students to the solution of "Why?" It is only one strategy, but it may provide some students with a "handle" with which to grip problems.

Matches, when burned, curl upward; try burning one. How would you explain this? What observations did you make? What is involved? What do you know about what you see? Did you come up with an explanation?

~~~~~~

DEVISE UNIQUE METHODS FOR DEVELOPING CREATIVITY WITH CHILDREN

Creativity is what creative people do. What you do with the children in your classroom paves the way for their creative development. This fact means that you will need to put into action the creativity you have developed within yourself and transmit it to others. It means not only being creative yourself, but allowing children to get involved in the creative process.

A teacher was teaching a lesson about letter writing. She was struggling to get the children to remember the major components of a letter such as the heading, the salutation, the body, the closing, and the signature. Using a creative approach, she had the class construct a bulletin board about letter writing components. She received a clue for an idea from the word *salutation* which she associated with the base word, *salute*. She asked the class if they could use this in some way to communicate the components of letter writing. She asked, "Who salutes?" The responses were many and from this the class evolved a model of a soldier saluting. The figure of a saluting soldier was sketched on the bulletin board. The teacher asked the students to relate the nomenclature of letter writing to the figure. The class labeled parts such as the saluting arm as "salutation," an arrow pointing inside the head of the soldier read, "The Inside Heading—Who am I saluting?" The soldier's body was labeled simply. "The Body," The closing was a sign that said, "Corresponds to the formality of the salutation." Another sign was labeled, "The Signature—Who is saluting whom?" The class enjoyed the exercise. It was creative and learning and retention were improved.

~~~~~~

You are in charge of the gym period as well as the other duties of the self-contained classroom. The class has played much the same games in gym as they have played for a number of years. They still enjoy the gym period, but they are showing signs of boredom with playing the same games over and over. Which of the following situations would be fruitful for developing creativity if you investigated it?

___1. I have thought up a new game. Would you like to play it?

___2. I have a surprise for you today: We are going to play Bozoball. This is a new game. It is played with a whiffle ball, three chairs, and a wooden paddle.

___3. I have a tennis racket, six ping-pong balls, four small croquet type baskets. How many ways can we think of to use this equipment in playing a game? When we are done we will play the game. What shall we call it?

___4. Make a list of your favorite games. Arrange these in order of the preference you have for playing these games. From the three games you like best, invent a totally new game using the equipment involved in your three favorite games. Give it a name.

___5. The librarian has given me a book of games. Let's divide into groups. Each group, in turn, will review the book and suggest new games for us to play during our gym period.

Three and four look like the best contributors for the development and creativity in children. Did you agree?

~~~~~~~~~~~~~~~~~~~~~~~~~~~~~~~~~~~~~~~

ORGANIZE RECALL CONTENT INTO A CREATIVE GAME

The teacher had taught a unit about percentage. She realized that the students understood the basic idea, but had little experience with actual application. During a spelling contest, she got the idea to divide the class into two groups. Each correctly spelled word was worth ten points. Each misspelled word discounted the team's total score at the moment of the error by 10 percent. Each student had to compute the opposing team's score. They could not communicate with each other. A running total was kept for the 25 minutes duration of the spelling contest. At the end of the spelling contest those students with the wrong score for the opposing team had to forfeit 5 points to the opposing team. The class had a spelling exercise, applied some mathematical concepts, and loved it. It was new, it was different, and it made learning fun.

In a lesson in earth science the class was learning that eight elements made up 98 percent of the earth crust. These elements are: Oxygen, 46.60%; Silicon, 27.72%; Aluminum, 8.13%; Iron 5.00%; Calcium, 3.63%; Sodium, 2.83%; Potassium, 2.59%; and Magnesium 2.09%.

The teacher thought memorization of these elements was essential, but the class had trouble memorizing these elements, the order, and the percentages of composition.

~~~~~~~~~~~~~~~~~~~~~~~~~~~~~~~~~~~~~~~

Which of the following exercises represents a creative game directed towards the learning of these elements:

___1. The teacher listed the initial letters of each element in descending order of abundance in the earth's crust. She wrote the letters O,S,A,I,C,S, P,M on the blackboard. She asked each student to make up a sentence using these letters in the order given, for example, "Oh say, am I clever, smart, polite, and masterful?" She thought this would be a good way to assist the students in memorizing the order of the eight basic elements.

___2. She constructed a cross word puzzle utilizing these eight basic elements.

___3. She made flash cards with the names of each element on one side and the percentage of composition of the earth's crust on the reverse side. She drilled the class on the descending order and percentages of the earth's crust composition of the eight elements. Then she put the names of the eight elements in a shoe box and the percentages of composition of the earth's crust in another shoe box. Two teams were selected. Each individual had to pick two cards and place the selected element in its proper descending order and assign the name to the percent card that corresponded to one of the eight elements. The student received one point if he correctly identified one of the cards. If he correctly identified both cards, he received three points. Final team scores were compared.

If you agree with the author, you selected exercise number 3 as the best creative game directed towards a learning situation.

~~~~~~

GIVEN A LIST OF ASSIGNMENTS, IDENTIFY THOSE ASSIGNMENTS THAT ARE MOST LIKELY TO DEVELOP CREATIVITY

Students attend school on the average of 180 school days a year. They usually attend twelve years of public school. How many assignments are meted out to students in this interim? How many are repetitive exercises of busy work? How many could have been fun, a challenge, an exercise that might have sent the mind racing with reckless abandonment as one pursues a desired goal?

~~~~~~

Read the following list of assignments and rank them from 1 through 4; number 1 being assigned to the least creative assignment and number 4 being assigned to the most creative assignment.

___A. Now that we have learned how to translate numbers in a base ten system to base two, five, and eleven, translate numbers in a base ten system to numbers in a base nine and base twelve system.

___B. For your assignment finish the page.
___C. Select any five words of your 25 spelling words and see how many new words you can construct from the letters that make up each word.
___D. Think of the United States of America with its present topography inverted; in other words, the high areas become the low areas and vice versa. The depths now correspond to the previous heights. With this type of topography, how might the westward expansion of the United States have been affected?

How did you rank the above? Selection *B* is clearly the most uncreative assignment and should have been labeled 1. *D* is clearly the most creative assignment and should have been labeled 4. *A* and *C* are evenly matched. Thus your ordered sequence for the above assignments could have been either 2, 1, 3, 4 or 3, 1, 2, 4.

~~~~~~

To impart information in a more effective, interesting manner is only part of the creative development necessary for you to teach more creatively. The creative classroom revolves around *you*. It is your listening to creative cues as they spring from your students, and it is your creative reactions to these cues that will develop creativity in you and in your students. Your job is to encourage those in your charge and those around you to develop self expression and to realize their internal dream of self fulfillment.

The foregoing chapter material is a brief compendium of ideas and suggestions in that area called creativity. Hopefully, it has whetted your desire to be more creative and to continue to expand your creativity in and out of the classroom.

Selected References

MIEL, A. (ed.), *Creativity in Teaching*. Belmont, Calif.: Wadsworth Publishing Company, 1961.

OSBORN, A. F., *Applied Imagination* (rev. ed.). New York: Charles Scribner's Sons, 1963.

PARNES, S. J., *Creative Behavior Guidebook*. New York: Charles Scribner's Sons, 1967.

SMITH, JAMES A., *Setting Conditions for Creative Teaching in the Elementary School*. Boston: Allyn and Bacon, Inc., 1966.

SMITH, PAUL (ed.), *An Examination of the Creative Process*. New York: The Hasting House, Publishers, Inc., 1959.

TAYLOR, CALVIN W., *Creativity: Progress and Potential*. New York: McGraw-Hill Book Company, 1964.

TORRANCE, PAUL E., *Guiding Creative Talent*. Englewood Cliffs, N.J.: Prentice-Hall, Inc., 1962.

————, AND R. E. MEYERS, *Creative Learning and Teaching*. New York: Dodd, Mead & Co., 1970.

Developing
7 teacher competencies in
interpersonal transactions

DEWAYNE KURPIUS

Indiana University

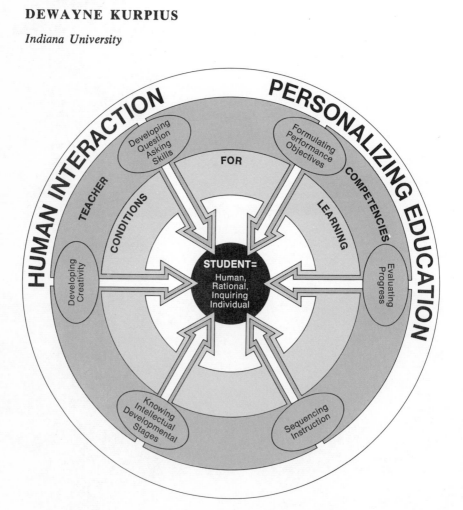

Current educational literature suggests that the humanistic teaching-learning dimension is a necessary condition for total learning to take place. Although suggested in the literature, at least in a philosophical manner, little evidence exists that this necessary condition for learning is represented in the teaching-learning enterprise. It appears that the philosophers have outlined the necessary conditions, but the behavioral scientists have not come forth with functional models for implementation. Perhaps the best statement to define humanistic teaching and learning is represented in the *Articles of Association of the American Association for Humanistic Psychology.* They define humanistic approaches as not a new psychology, but a new approach to the psychology of learning, which is described as follows:

> Humanistic psychology is primarily an orientation toward the whole of psychology rather than a distinct area or school. It stands for respect for the worth of persons, respect for differences of approach, open-mindedness as to acceptable methods, and interests in exploration of new aspects of human behavior. As a "third force" in contemporary psychology, it is concerned with topics having little place in existing theories and systems: e.g., love, creativity, self, growth, organism, basic need-gratification, self-actualization, higher values, being, becoming, spontaneity, play, humor, affection, naturalness, warmth, ego-transcendence, objectivity, autonomy, responsibility, mean, fair-play, transcendental experience, peak experience, courage, and related concepts.[1]

As you look at the descriptive words in the above statement, how many do you recognize as a part of your own educational process? Have you experienced love, creativity, warmth, or humor? Perhaps we can think of unique cases where these conditions are present; however, seldom can we remember when these conditions were contiguous. Therefore, it is the intent of this chapter to focus on human interaction as it affects the growth and development of human beings.

Human interaction is the most common of all personal experiences but one about which we probably know the least. How we interact, relate, and transact with others, and the reciprocal impact of this phenomenon, form the single most important aspect of our existence. Man's nature is such, in fact, that only through interaction with others can he become aware of his own identity. Although this identity is singular, we can very quickly conceptualize a person as representing two component parts. One of the components represents the internal self or man's attitudes, values, feelings, and beliefs; and the second component is that of the external self or man's behavior. Another way to describe internal and external self is to think of the internal self as being observable only through man's behavior. Hence, man's internal self is only made known to others by his

---

[1] *Articles of Association of the American Association for Humanistic Psychology.*

external self or behavior, since how you feel, for example, is made known to others only through the behavior attached to that feeling at that specific moment. Therefore, in the growth and development stages of man, his combination of and interaction between internal and external selves provide the raw material for the development of the total person. So as the person progresses through his development, he is *acquiring* new material for both his internal and external selves, he is *maintaining* selected portions of his internal and external selves, and he is experiencing the stage of *change* or *modification* in which human beings decide both consciously and unconsciously how to change or modify themselves as persons. The uniqueness of the acquisition, maintenance, and modification of self is related to the fact that only through interaction with other human beings can these three human stages be activated. Man remains dependent upon other human beings to determine his own makeup. Consequently, this process begins at infancy and continues until death for all human beings.

The internal feeling of security which develops from having been loved and respected from infancy is one of the most basic determinants of one's behavior toward others. Insofar as a person possesses this feeling, he is able to approach new experiences and other people who are a part of those experiences in a confident manner. If during the child's pre-school years, he has been brought up in the atmosphere of respect and affection, in which he is valued rather than rejected, he will be ready to meet new experiences outside of himself. It is out of these internal and external experiences that man begins to develop and build his concept of self. As the child continues to experience the acceptance and the attributed worth of others, he includes these feelings in his framework of how he views himself. As a result, a sense of personal value and confidence is built into his internal makeup, and the internal feelings are openly manifest to the external self through his behavioral experiences. As the child meets various happenings in his environment, he is able to distinguish ways of reacting which are personally meaningful and acceptable. Hence, a reciprocal sequence is developed between self and others, and the self concept continues to grow.

Development and learning are enhanced as long as the child has an internal security base and an external environment he can trust, such as the family or school, in which to test himself. As he continues to measure himself meaningfully through his behavior, the characteristics of the child will indicate his acceptance of others, his curiosity and desire to test new ideas, and his demonstration of confidence in his value and reality testing. This behavior is a sign of his trust for self and others. A child who has not experienced a meaningful existence and who has not developed a security base will manifest observable behavior which will be less than socially acceptable. He will often exhibit bragging, attention getting, or revengeful behavior toward authority figures. He may also become possessive and selfish and try to use his power and influence to win over others.

A child who has had external affect deprivation also may show signs of withdrawal. He has learned through his contact with people in his environment that because of his lack of interaction skill with people, the easiest way to reduce pain is to withdraw from people.

Schutz [2] states that affection is based on the testing and retesting of emotional and affective experiences and the eventual understanding of the consequences of the feelings and behaviors related to affect. In addition, he suggests that there are three phases of development of human relationships. Phase I is *inclusion*. Phase II is *control*, and Phase III is *affection*. During the first encounter or the inclusion phase, the persons involved must decide if the experience is worthy of continuation of the relationship. If the people involved decide that their relationship is worthy of continuation and expansion, they immediately move into the second phase, that of confronting one another in relation to the control factors in the relationship. In the control phase each is testing the other in order to understand what kind of control is being used on him, what is expected of him in the relationship, and whether or not he is able to control the other person or whether he is the more controlled. Each also learns the kinds of behaviors that will be most functional for controlling the other as well as the behaviors that are most effective in restricting or dissipating control. If during the control phase each party decides that the relationship has meaning and should be continued, control factors will be tested and worked out in a satisfactory fashion at least for the immediate time. This interaction will move the relationship into Phase III, the stage of affection. This stage is typically the one in which more risk is involved, more genuineness is exchanged, more freedom and spontaneity to test and experiment with the relationship enter in, and the relationship begins taking on the potential to become a lasting one.

Schutz and others have described two dimensions of interpersonal relationships, one being related to the underpersonal individual and the other being identified, in the continuum, as pertaining to the overpersonal type of person. Persons who lack the understanding and experiences of affection, the underpersonals, are likely to avoid close relationships with others. They generally will feel most comfortable in smaller groups and many times on a one-to-one basis. Such a person's interaction even on the one-to-one basis tends to be cognitive and intellectual and oftentimes superficial. The underpersonal type of individual tends to seek out another person like himself since each feels most comfortable with the other; however, neither person places any demands on the other to develop growth and affectional rela-

[2] William C. Schutz, *Joy: Expanding Human Awareness* (New York: Grove Press, Inc., 1967), pp. 117–120.

tionships. It is hypothesized that on a near-conscious or even unconscious level this person wants more meaningful and closer relationships; at the same time that he experiences the need for close personal associations, however, he feels that he is not worthy of another individual's sharing of himself on a personal level. He feels he is not wanted and behaves accordingly. If people do show interest in caring for him, he immediately becomes suspect and tends to pull away or make statements which cause the other person to leave. If the underpersonal individual reaches a level of discomfort sufficiently potent, he may become impolite, highly verbal, boring, or if necessary, completely out of touch with the people to whom he is talking, closing the conversation or the relationship. In less demanding situations, he may appear to be outwardly friendly to almost anyone. This outward friendliness allows him the power to control the relationship in the way in which he wants it to go, thereby protecting himself from becoming involved in a personal relationship with anyone; for

> The deepest anxiety for the underpersonal, that regarding the self, is that he is unlovable. If people got to know him well, he believes, they would discover the traits that make him so unlovable. As opposed to the inclusion anxiety that the self is of no value, worthless, and empty, and the control anxiety that the self is stupid and irresponsible, the affection anxiety is that the self is nasty and unlovable.[3]

At the other end of the continuum, the overpersonal individual as described by Schutz is one who attempts to develop close personal relationships with all the people he meets. Schutz interprets this approach as resulting from thinking such as the following: " 'My first experiences with affection were painful, but perhaps if I try again they will turn out to be better.' " [4] The style of approaching people and attempting to develop close personal relationships in almost all cases is anxiety reducing to the person in that it continually proves to him that he is worthy and that people do care for him and do show him respect and love. Although he is assuring himself periodically at the intellectual level, he is well aware at a deeper level that this is not the true situation. He believes that he is not worthy of relationships, that he is not worthy of someone else's caring for him, and that he does not possess the kind of characteristics that other people will respect.

Consequently, the outward behaviors of the overpersonal and the underpersonal are communicating the same message from their internal selves. Both are in need of close personal relationships with others, and both have considerable doubt about their worthiness of being accepted by others or their capabilities for dealing with and relating to others.

[3] *Ibid.,* pp. 174–175.
[4] *Ibid.,* p. 175.

As Schutz states, "The primary interaction of the affection area is that of *embrace,* either literal or symbolic." [5] This interaction requires the expression of the deeper feelings that a person is experiencing. Oftentimes deeper feelings represent very strong positive kinds of feelings, but they may also represent strongly negative or hostile kinds of feelings. There is little reason to fear the expression of anger or allowing the feelings of anger to be expressed because typically persons in our society have an equal amount of difficulty allowing others to express strong positive feelings. As you have noticed, each of the personal characteristics mentioned indicates individual behaviors which are observable.

Since it is the person's behavior which he uses to negotiate himself through life, it is necessary for an individual to know what behaviors work most effectively for him. Once again, as the child experiences success as he uses his behavior to interact with others, he is continually building his security base for continuous existence. As the child goes on interacting in his environment, he becomes aware of the limitations and responsibilities he must live by. Although it is a difficult task for adults to interpret the environment to the child, such interpretation contributes to perhaps the most significant of all child-adult relationships, for it is during this process that the child experiences the level of respect and positive regard which others, both peers and adults, model for him.

Perkins has described a portion of the child's significant adult relationships as being in the family. He suggests the family as representing four basic types of emotional climates: affection, rejection, inconsistency, and over-protection.[6] I feel that the classroom teacher also should be aware of the significant effects his behavior has on the class climate in general, as well as on selected individuals within the class. Thus, the four descriptions which follow here are useful in looking at both family-parent-child relationships and classroom-teacher-child relationships.

As Perkins suggests, a person who exists in a climate of affection feels wanted and valued. Consequently,

he learns that he can depend upon others for support and help. Such a child gains a certainty of his own worth and thus is freed from his own anxiety. He is able to express affection for others and to work to progress toward growth and maturity. In short, his interactions with others confirm and reinforce his conception of his own value, thereby providing himself with a firm feeling of security.[7]

[5] *Ibid.,* p. 176.
[6] Hugh V. Perkins, *Human Development and Learning* (Belmont, California: Wadsworth Publishing Company, Inc., 1969), pp. 104–132.
[7] *Ibid.,* p. 112.

On the other hand, some individuals experience lack of acceptance in the family or in the classroom in which relations are cold, indifferent, hostile, or rejecting. In such an atmosphere the child feels uncertain of his own worth and

> consequently, feels threatened, anxious, and in constant conflict. Burdened by these emotions, he cannot make optimum progress in learning and development and often behaves aggressively. Thus, the child who tries intentionally to hurt others or himself or behave in other ways which are sure to result in punishment is really grasping for crumbs of attention as a substitute for the affection or acceptance he has been unable to secure. Such a child is emotionally crippled; he has simply not learned that he can gain love and acceptance by socially acceptable behavior.[8]

In a climate of inconsistency, however, the parental or teacher relationship with the child varies:

> On some days the parent [or teacher] may be overindulgent, generous, and affectionate toward the child; at other times, for no apparent reason the parent [or teacher] may be critical, punishing, hostile, or rejecting. This inconsistency deprives the child of adequate perceptual cues to the behavior desired of him. Not knowing for sure how this parent [or teacher] will respond to his behavior in any given situation, he becomes anxious and immobile. Although he is loved and valued at times, the overall inconsistency of the treatment he receives from his parents creates within the child an uncertainty and a fear of taking changes—qualities that are inimical to learning and the development of a well-integrated personality.[9]

Just as harmful as a school or home atmosphere of rejection or inconsistency is that of over-protection. Brought up in such a climate, a youngster cannot develop the independence he needs to meet new experiences in the larger world. Unequipped to develop meaningful relationships with others, such a child may indeed be smothered with love. This type of love represents a distortion, however, because it is not productive in nature. Parents and/or teachers who create this climate do not provide for positive learning in children, for they

> overindulge them, establishing no firm or realistic limits for their behavior or accede to their every whim. As a result, they become overdependent and self-centered and gain a distorted perception of their own importance. The indulgent and over-protective adult [or teacher] often has emotonal problems of his own. Over-protection may be evidence of irrational fears concerning the safety and health of an only child or handicapped child, or it may serve as compensation for emotional needs left unfilled by the marriage.[10]

[8] *Ibid.*
[9] *Ibid.*, pp. 112–113.
[10] *Ibid.*, p. 113.

If the child is brought up in an atmosphere of affection, however, his sense of security will allow him to become involved with more people as he expands his experiences. If he is brought up in a climate which departs sufficiently from that of affection, his perception of the social world or interpersonal environment may be a distorted one. Approaching new experiences with this distorted view, he is able to learn and develop his potential to only a limited degree.

According to the authors of the *Taxonomy of Educational Objectives,* Volume II, there is a point in the continuum of the affective domain where "Provision must be made . . . for emotional quality. . . . Further, . . . the range of emotion from neutrality through mild to strong emotion" (*positive or negative*) must be dealt with. A continuum was designed by ordering the components as follows: (1) individual *"aware* of a phenomenon" and *"able to perceive it,"* (2) individual *"responds* to the phenomenon with a *positive feeling,"* (3) individual goes *"out of his way* to respond," (4) individual *"organizes"* the "conceptualizations" of his behavior, and (5) that "structure . . . *becomes his life outlook."* [11]

"Internalization" is the term used to describe "the process by which the phenomenon" successfully becomes "a part of the individual." The use of internalization in the continuum "gave an ordering" to some of the learning theories that take "place with affective objectives." It placed "the focus of learning within the individual, and it constructed a continuum of his behavior." [12]

"At the lowest levels of the internalization continuum," emotion plays a small part. "At the middle levels, emotional response is recognized" and is a "critical part of the behavior. . . . As the behavior becomes completely internalized and routine, this emotion decreases. . . ." The lower level is termed *responding,* whereas "The next level is titled *valuing* to indicate that the control is becoming internal." [13]

As pointed to in the *Taxonomy,* other definitions have been associated with the process of internalization. Pitts uses the term to replace identification when it "refers to one's taking on the values and attitudes of another." The "child internalizes the father figure to form the superego. . . ." Using other means in addition to modeling to develop attitudes and values, "the school furthers the differentiation of the supergo, providing models to replace the parent. . . ." [14] On the other hand Kelman's use of internalization pertains to a theory of attitude change. He points to three different processes by which an individual conforms to or accepts influence —compliance, identification, and internalization:

[11] David P. Krathwohl, Benjamin S. Bloom and Bertram B. Masia, *Taxonomy of Educational Objectives: The Classification of Educational Goals, Handbook II: Affective Domain* (New York: David McKay Company, Inc., 1964), pp. 26–27.

[12] *Ibid.,* p. 28.

[13] *Ibid.,* p. 30.

[14] *Ibid.,* p. 31.

1. "Compliance can be said to occur when an individual accepts influence because he hopes to achieve a favorable reaction from another person or group."
2. "Identification can be said to occur when an individual accepts influence because he wants to establish or maintain a satisfying relationship to another person or group. . . ."
3. "Internalization can be said to occur when an individual accepts influence because the content of the induced behavior—the ideas and actions of which it is composed—is intrinsically rewarding." [15]

"The *Taxonomy* uses the term 'internalization' to encompass all three of Kelman's terms, recognizing them as different stages in the internalization process." The inclusion of Krathwohl's model here is to provide the reader with a guide for viewing stages of learning. That is, compliance "corresponds to a very early level," identification "is treated in the middle stages of the continuum," and internalization "refers to the end product. . . ." [16]

Learning theories, on the other hand, focus mainly on cognitive behavior. Even attitudes and feelings are defined in cognitive terms. Rokeach believes that the two systems, cognitive and affective, hold "congruent" characteristics.[17] He thinks that "If we know something about the way a person relates himself to the world of ideas we may also be able to say in what way he relates himself to the world of people and to authority." [18] If a teacher, for example, knows how she relates to the world of ideas, she may be more able to see how she relates to people.

The teacher's knowledge of teaching techniques, however, must be transferred into a situation so that each instructor understands the impact his attitudes, values, feelings, and behavior have on each child. For example, does the teacher treat a child who is bright, productive, and respectful differently than he treats a slow learning youngster who may not respect adults or schools? It is obvious that the latter child needs differential treatment, but the kind and schedule must be clearly defined and systematically applied. It is this second aspect that is so difficult in education, since the teacher's attitude, values, feelings, and behavior can become very complex and confusing to the perceptions of a child.

We know that the teacher takes his full self, attitudes, values, feelings, and behavior into the classroom each day, but that he uses only his behavior to represent himself. If we observe and respond to a person suggesting that he has a positive attitude, we are making this decision on his observable behavior, either verbal or non-verbal. If we observe a person destroying something of value, we may quickly interpret this behavior as

15 *Ibid.*, p. 32.
16 *Ibid.*, p. 32.
17 *Ibid.*, p. 46.
18 *Ibid.*, p. 55.

representing an angry person possessing an unbalanced value system, that is, with a bad attitude toward learning. Usually this type of student behavior elicits a selected teacher behavior. Although there are many responses to such student behavior, certain responses will be more helpful to child and teacher than others. If the instructor responds from a source of authority and control, the youngster may continue to resist. If the teacher can understand the kind of feelings that the child is presently experiencing, perhaps the teacher would respond differently. It is the instructor's ability to understand his own internal and external styles, as well as his capacity to attend to understanding the child's internal and external selves, that is so important for true education of the whole child.

Although there is ample justification for attending to a more specific and systematic approach to human interaction, why are we so archaic in our teaching-learning procedures? Harbeck states that most educational goals related to the affective domain are often "stated in some obscure document such as a school philosophy," but that they are mostly disregarded when planning for instruction takes place. Teachers tend not to "teach or test for objectivity in the affective domain." We seem to have developed an assumption based on faith that each person will develop his affective self naturally as he grows.[19]

Krathwohl states that "If affective objectives and goals are to be realized," (1) the goals "must be clearly defined;" (2) proper "learning experiences . . . must be provided;" and (3) "systematic means of appraisal must be developed." [20] Krathwohl also "lists five categories in the affective domain: receiving, responding, valuing, organization of values, and characterization by a value system." He states that no learning comes about without an individual's receiving and responding.[21] The training program related to this chapter will focus directly on a person's capacities for receiving and responding; and it includes goals which are clearly defined, learning experiences which are specified, and a system for appraisal which accompanies the goals and experiences.

~~~~~~

Definition of Terms

Selected terms have been defined to help you to more quickly develop a language system with similar meaning.

[19] Mary B. Harbeck, "Instructional Objectives in the Affective Domain," *Educational Technology*, X, No. 1 (January 1970), 49.

[20] Krathwohl, Bloom, and Masia, *Taxonomy*, p. 23.

[21] Harbeck, "Instructional Objectives," p. 50.

Feelings The term is difficult to define, but it tends to refer to the internal experiencing of the self which is distinctly different from the intellectual knowing part of the self. Oftentimes the words *feeling, affection, empathy,* and *emotion* are used interchangeably, especially when contrasted with cognition.

Empathy Listening to another person in a manner in which we put ourselves into the frame of reference of another so that the other person's thinking, feeling, and behaving are completely understood, even to the point of being predictable. When I attend and listen as directly and closely as described here, I have developed the ability to follow another person on whatever level he experiences himself with his feelings regardless of how superficial or how deep these feelings go.

Respect Respect is present when the helper does not judge the helpee but accepts his present functioning as a part of that person at that time. As the interaction continues, the helper will indicate understanding, acceptance, and warmth which is observable and reinforcing to the helpee.

Helper Any person who is functioning in a way helpful to another person. (Usually a conscious effort.)

Helpee Any person being helped by another person. (Usually a conscious effort.)

Intrapersonal Communication A method of communicating to the self. It is how you talk to yourself about the way you are behaving and feeling and/or the way you would like to behave and feel. (Also called introspection.)

Interpersonal Communication The ability to transmit attitudes, values, feelings, ideas, beliefs, and knowledge from one person to another. Verbal and nonverbal behaviors are the most common among human beings.

Perception Identifying and using information from the environment. It is the prime process which influences and is influenced by the internal and external self. As perceptions are broadened through experience so is the internal and external self; therefore, greater experiences are extracted from the environment.

Listening An art of interpersonal exchange when the person listening tries to perceive the various levels of communication including both content and intent.

Attending Conscious focusing of internal and external self on the other person and at the same time blocking out other internal feelings and external behaviors. It is the ability of a person to act internally or externally in a given direction to a given situation.

Values That which is personally prized by an individual and considered as worthwhile and desirable.

Acceptance Both an attitude and a behavior through which the teacher communicates that he is interested in the student and that he wants to understand and accept what the student is saying both verbally and nonverbally.

Approval A behavior by which the teacher communicates his acceptance or rejection of a particular attitude or behavior of the student. Approval is a very strong reinforcer and will greatly influence the behavior of the other person. Approval should be genuine and both verbal and nonverbal behavior should be congruent. Indiscriminate approval may prove aversive over time in that the student begins to recognize that there are times when the teacher is role-playing.

Assurance A powerful reinforcer in that it tends to reduce anxiety and cause the person to feel more secure. Assurance aids the student in developing greater ego strength and developing a more stable self-concept. The teacher needs to be aware of the methodology through which to transfer assurance reinforcement, which tends to cause dependency, to self-assurance reinforcement, which encourages a more independent style.

Advising A straightforward process in which the teacher instructs the student in a manner suggesting exactly what the student should do. Theoretically, the advisement is justified in that the teacher has a greater repertoire of experiences and behaviors and that advisement is beneficial for that particular student. Perhaps a lesser manner of advising is to suggest to the student, since suggestion provides more space for the student to reject the advisement.

Threat A technique used by persons in authority both consciously and unconsciously. It is usually used as the last resort measure to cause a high degree of fear of the consequences and thereby convince the person to conform to the user's suggestion.

Clarification Device for the teacher to restate the meaning that she has heard so that both parties are relating and communicating from the same frame of reference. A secondary payoff of clarification is that the student is given a chance to see how well someone else understands him and is given an opportunity to clarify his own communication.

Interpretation   It consists of seeing beyond the verbal and non-verbal behavior and feelings of the individual and describing to the other person that which you see. There are many different levels of interpretation, all of which can be helpful or harmful. In classroom settings it is generally best to use interpretation in a way so that the student may reject, with comfort, the interpretation you have made. Sample—Teacher: "John, you sure look happy today. I'll bet it's because you did so well on the math exam yesterday." John's response: "No, it's not that at all. It's because we are not going to have school this afternoon." In this short statement the teacher indicated that she was not sure what the cause was but did make a minor interpretation. In a sense the teacher was saying, "Could it be that you are happy today because of the math exam?" The student response immediately indicates that this is a setting in a student-teacher relationship where the student can disagree with little emotion involved.

Content Reflection   A simple style of merely repeating almost verbatim the words the student has just used. It may be useful for the student to hear the words that he has used so that he has a better understanding of how they sound. Sample—Student statement: "I failed the exam because I didn't read the chapter." Teacher response: "You failed the exam because you didn't prepare properly."

Reflection of Feeling   Oftentimes the student will make a response to the teacher in which the words describe a very cognitive kind of statement while the feeling of the student is at a much deeper level. This technique is used to tell the student that you really do understand how he feels about what he is saying even though he is not verbalizing it. Sample—Student statement: "I failed the exam because I didn't read the chapter." Teacher response: "You feel bad because you failed the exam and you're kicking yourself for not preparing properly."

Selective Reflection   A technique in which the teacher isolates one thought or feeling from a group of thoughts or feelings and either restates in a content reflection fashion back to the student or reflects in a feeling fashion back to the student. This technique is very useful in that it helps the student very quickly isolate the message which he hopes to communicate. If the teacher responds in a non-authoritarian manner by introducing his statement with, "It seems that" or, "Could it be that," the student is allowed the opportunity to say, "No, I don't feel that way," and then the student will volunteer, "but I do feel this way." If the student does not volunteer his true feelings, perhaps the teacher could ask the student, "Could you tell me how you are feeling?" In this way, neither the teacher nor the student feels that he is getting into an uncomfortable interaction and yet they are moving very rapidly to the cause of the problem and perhaps to the solution.

Probing   A technique in which a series of direct questions are posed to the student for the purpose of getting information about the student and/or his concerns. While probing may be useful in some cases, it may be more harmful, especially if the student is not aware of why he is being questioned or what the teacher will do with the information she receives from him. Generally, students resist personal probing. Some even resist intellectual probing. A full chapter in this text is dedicated to the systematic approach to question asking.

Silence   A non-verbal technique which the teacher may use in many different ways. Oftentimes silence can mean anger; usually this can be observed by the expression on the person's face. Silence also may be a very positive reward situation, in that the teacher is willing to wait and allow the student time to respond to the question or to the situation. It is interesting to note in the research literature that the length of silence between the teacher's asking a question and the student's response is directly related to the achievement level of that particular student. The findings are that the teacher will wait 2–3 seconds for a response from a low-achieving student and will wait up to 10 seconds for a high-achieving student.

Length of Utterance   It is related to the length of the teacher's statement in responding to a student. Research evidence also indicates that the longer the teacher utterance time, the fewer responses and the less accurate responses will be received from the student.

Operant Conditioning   It refers to a process in which the frequency of occurrence of an identified bit of behavior is modified by the consequences of that behavior. Operant conditioning is a method of focusing upon the relationship between the behavior of the organisms and their environment. The operant conditioning approach to understanding behavior is based on gaining knowledge of the factors which modify behavior.

Behavior   Anything which the organism does which is observable and recordable, *i.e.,* motion and sound.

Classroom Environment   It includes everything that has an effect on the person whether it be internal or external.

Internal Personal Make-up   It includes a person's attitudes, values, feelings, beliefs, and thinking.

External Self   The person's behavior.

Consequences   An event which follows the behavior. Examples are:

1. Behavior: Student arrives late to class.
   Event: Teacher punishes.
2. Behavior: Teacher rewards child positively.
   Event: Child smiles.
3. Behavior: Bell rings
   Event: Students rush to the door.

Probability   What is the frequency or rate of occurrence at which this behavior will follow a similar stimulus? Sample—Does the teacher respond the same when any child comes late to the classroom?

Environmental Events   Events which regularly precede a response.

~~~~~~

Introduction to Training Program

The following programs have been designed to aid teachers, students, and parents to become more effective in how they listen and respond to others. Although it sometimes appears that human interaction is quite simple, there are many times when we feel that others do not understand the real message we are communicating or intending to communicate. Within this realm, there are three elements of communication which seem most significant in most all human interaction. These three are the ability to listen and respond with *empathy, respect,* and *concreteness.* Each element seems so obviously important when we think of how human beings interact and the impact this interaction has on our personal growth and development. However, there is universal evidence that listening (both intrapersonal and interpersonal) and responding to oneself and others are areas where most humans need assistance in developing. Often the person asking for help and understanding is not even aware of what he is asking for. Hence, it is the responsibility of the listener to aid in the process of exploring and defining the problem. Even in task meetings such as committee meetings, and certainly in regular class meetings, there are many hurts experienced by both teacher and students which are either missed completely or misunderstood. Some are very minor and some are quite significant. Often many minor problems collect, problems which if recognized earlier would not have grown into major ones.

A simple example of a minor problem with potential for becoming a major one might develop for a student who is late for class. Lateness has very different meanings for different people. Usually the magnitude of being late for class is a function of the teacher's or professor's reaction to the situation. Occasionally, a student will simply oversleep and feel quite embarrassed and even guilty about coming late. If, when the student enters the classroom, the instructor responds from his own internal self, he may recognize only his own feelings rather than those of the student. For example, the teacher could internally experience himself as follows: (1) "No one comes late to my classes," or (2) "The policy of the school does not allow lateness; therefore, I would look bad if I did not shape this student's behavior," or (3) "I can't stand students interrupting me after class begins." Regardless of the internal impact, a personalized response will follow if the student's frame of reference is not considered or listened to. From this point in the relationship a barrier may begin between student and teacher. If the student is "put down" for being late, one "set" is beginning between student and teacher; but if the teacher recognizes the embarrassment of the student and responds from the student's internal self rather than his own, a different kind of "set" occurs and a different and usually more positive relationship develops.

The purpose for the brief example is to suggest how what may be perceived as a very minor incident can grow into a major misunderstanding between two people. These minor occurrences are most important because they tend to set the pattern of interaction between these two people, and even carry over into other relationships.

The three elements of *empathy, respect,* and *concreteness* are perhaps the most generalizable of all communication elements. If we know how the other person feels and how he is experiencing the situation (empathy) and if we know our true feeling for this person (respect) and if we can listen and respond to the whole message (concreteness), there is high probability that the outcome of that interaction will be more meaningful and productive than if the three elements were missing or were being performed at a very low level.

Therefore, it is the purpose of the following programs to aid you in developing skills to listen and to respond to others with *empathy, respect,* and *concreteness*. Each training program is presented separately. For example, Program I will focus totally on empathy. In addition, Program I is divided into 5 lessons with each lesson sequenced into several steps. Each program, lesson, and step has specific directions for you to follow.

Although three programs are presented independently, they are sequenced in a fashion which allows them to be collective. You are now ready to begin Program I: Empathy Training. The approximate total time to complete Program I is 2 hours; however, each lesson has an approximate time required ranging from 15 to 30 minutes.

~~~~~~

Program I: Empathy Training

LESSON ONE: EMPATHY TRAINING
(Approximate time required: 30 minutes)

Four standardized student statements have been selected for your first training experience to help you explore your present ability to understand and respond to a communicated message. There are no right or wrong answers in Lesson I, so proceed as naturally as possible.

PROCEDURE: Complete each step before proceeding to the next step.

Step A:

1. Student statements *1* through *4* to be presented in the following material cover a wide range of values, feelings, and attitudes (internal self) and behavior (external self).
2. All statements represent the same student.
3. Read each statement as if it were being said by a student in your class seeking help and understanding.
4. Read student statement number *1* as many times as necessary to complete the following:
   a. Identify the *content* communicated (verbal message) and write it on the score sheet provided at the end of the chapter.
   b. Identify the *intent* communicated (feeling and emotions) and enter it on your score sheet.
   c. Formulate a response you would make to this person who has come to you for understanding and help and add it to your score sheet.

~~~~~~

STUDENT STATEMENTS [22]

1. I feel so bad—I have no friends. Nobody likes me. All the other kids lunch together and play together. They always leave me out—as if they don't even care about me. Sometimes when I'm alone and all the other kids are

---

[22] Student statements selected from Robert R. Carkhuff, *Helping and Human Relations: A Primer for Lay and Professional Helpers,* Vol. II (New York: Holt, Rinehart and Winston, Inc., 1969), 251.

together I feel like crying. Why doesn't anyone like me? I try to be nice, but nothing seems to work. I guess there is nothing I can do.

2. It makes me so mad! Everybody is always telling me what to do and what not to do. When I'm at home, my parents tell me what is best for me. At school it's the teacher. Even my friends bother me. Everybody pushes me around. Sometimes I feel like punching them all in the nose! They had just better leave me alone and let me do things the way I want to.

3. I'm so excited and everything is going so great! I ran for president of my class and I won; I guess the other kids really like me. And today my teacher said I was one of the best students she had ever had; she makes me feel all warm inside. And next week, during spring vacation, I'm going to have a great time with my family. I'm so happy. It's unbelievable. Some people make me feel so good.

4. I just don't know what to do. I try very hard in school, but nothing seems to sink in. I guess I'm not very smart. Nobody seems to care that I try. What really hurts is when I see my parents bragging to others about how smart my brother is; they never even mention me—they even change the subject when I'm mentioned. Oh, I wish I could do better, but I can't. The smart kids are really lucky—everybody likes them because they are smart. Sometimes I even get mad at myself because I can't do any better.

Step B:

5. Repeat (a) through (c) from number 4 above for student statements *2, 3,* and *4.*

Step C:

6. You have now been exposed to the *content* of a communicated message, the *intent* of a communicated message, and your response to each. In order to better understand your responses read (a) through (c) before beginning and then follow the directions given:
   a. Identify the *content* communicated in your written responses and enter at number 4 on your score sheet.
   b. Identify the *intent* communicated in your written response and write it at number 5 on the score sheet.
   c. Complete (a) and (b) above for your response to *each* student statement before going on to the remaining statements.

Step D:

You have just completed a brief introduction to how you understand and respond to communicated messages. Chances are that identifying the content of the messages was easier than identifying the intent. Perhaps most difficult was deciding how you wanted to respond to the person in the excerpt. Identifying the content and intent of your responses should have been helpful, however, in cueing you to how you respond to others, especially people asking for understanding. In order to aid you in improving your interpersonal communication skills, a systematic approach has been developed to help you to improve your ability to understand and help others.

The key to accurate communication is supported by Carkhuff in this statement:

> Empathy is the key ingredient of helping. Its explicit communication, particularly during early phases of helping, is critical. Without an empathic understanding of the helpee's world and his difficulties as he sees them there is no basis for helping.[23]

Therefore, the following scales have been developed for the purpose of teaching listening and responding skills in communication. The scales are designed to sequence from Level I, the lowest level of functioning to Level V which is the highest level of functioning. Each scale level has three parts: (1) the description of the level, (2) an example of the level, and (3) a summary of that level. Read the empathy scale until you understand the sequencing related to the levels of communication.

~~~~~~

SCALE 1:
EMPATHIC UNDERSTANDING IN INTERPERSONAL PROCESSES
A SCALE FOR MEASUREMENT [24]

Level 1 The verbal and behavioral expressions of the helper either *do not attend to* or *detract significantly from* the verbal and behavioral expressions of the helpee(s) in that they communicate significantly less of the helpee's feelings and experiences than the helpee has communicated himself.

> *Example:* The helper communicated no awareness of even the most obvious, expressed surface feelings of the helpee. The helper may be bored or disinterested or simply operating from a preconceived form of reference which totally excludes that of the helpee(s).

In summary, the helper does everything but express that he is listening, understanding, or being sensitive to even the most obvious feelings of the

---

[23] Carkhuff, *Helping and Human Relations,* Vol. I, 173.
[24] The following five levels are quoted from Robert R. Carkhuff, *Helping and Human Relations: A Primer for Lay and Professional Helpers,* Vol. I (New York: Holt, Rinehart & Winston, Inc., 1969), 174–175.

helpee, and does so in such a way as to detract significantly from the communications of the helpee.

Level 2 While the helper responds to the expressed feelings of the helpee(s), he does so in such a way that he *subtracts noticeable affect* from the communications of the helpee.

>   *Example:* The helper may communicate some awareness of obvious, surface feelings of the helpee, but his communications drain off a level of the affect and distort the level of meaning. The helper may communicate his own ideas of what may be going on, but these are not congruent with the expressions of the helpee.

In summary, the helper tends to respond to something other than that which the helpee is expressing or indicating.

Level 3 The expressions of the helper in response to the expressions of the helpee(s) are essentially *interchangeable* with those of the helpee in that they express the same affect and meaning.

>   *Example:* The helper responds with accurate understanding of the surface feelings of the helpee but may not respond to or may misinterpret the deeper feelings.

In summary, the helper is responding so as to neither subtract from nor add to the expressions of the helpee. He does not respond accurately to how that person really feels beneath the surface feelings, but he indicates a willingness and openness to do so. Level III constitutes the minimal level of facilitative interpersonal functioning.

Level 4 The responses of the helper *add noticeably* to the expressions of the helpee(s) in such a way as to express feelings at a level deeper than that with which the helpee was able to express himself.

>   *Example:* The helper communicates his understanding of the expressions of the helpee at a level deeper than they were expressed and thus enables the helpee to experience and/or express feelings he was unable to express previously.

In summary, the helper's responses add deeper feeling and meaning to the expressions of the helpee.

Level 5 The helper's responses *add significantly* to the feeling and meaning of the expressions of the helpee(s) in such a way as to accurately express feelings some levels below that which the helpee himself was able to express or, in the event of ongoing, deep self-exploration on the helpee's part, to be fully with him in his deepest moments.

> *Example:* The helper responds with accuracy to all of the helpee's deeper as well as surface feelings. He is "tuned in" on the helpee's wave length. The helper and the helpee might proceed together to explore previously unexplored areas of human existence.

In summary, the helper is responding with a full awareness of who the other person is and with a comprehensive and accurate empathic understanding of that individual's deepest feelings.

~~~~~~

When you feel you have an understanding of the levels of recognizing and responding to communicated empathy, proceed to Lesson II, where you will have an opportunity to expand and extend your knowledge and application of empathic communication.

~~~~~~

LESSON TWO: EMPATHY TRAINING
(Approximate time required: 20 minutes)

PROCEDURE: Complete each step before continuing to the next step.

Step A:
1. Class members select partners and form into dyads.
2. Next each person rates his own written responses to the four student statements, using the Empathy Scale to aid in identifying the empathic level of his responses. Write your evaluations on a scratch sheet, *but do not share them* until number 4 in Step B.

Step B:
3. Now exchange your four written responses to the statements with your partner and evaluate his written responses on a scratch sheet, using the Empathy Scale as a guide.
4. As soon as you have completed the ratings, transfer your self-evaluation and your partner's rating of your responses to numbers 6 and 7 on your score sheet. Then share your self-scoring and your partner's scoring by discussing agreement and/or disagreement. Also review each other's content and feeling statements by pinpointing the content and intent first of each excerpt and second of each written response.

Step C: (Note to instructor)

5. At this point, the entire class may briefly discuss and clarify questions related to the content and feeling responses, empathy scales, or ratings.

Step D:

You have now completed your first lesson in focusing on the content and intent of communications. This experience will help you in the remainder of the programs and lessons. If your ratings were in the 1 and 2 range, you are functioning at beginning levels and should use the scales as a guide for the exercises to follow. If you received ratings of 2 and 3, you are doing very well. If you consistently received scores of 3, 4, and 5, you may be over-rating yourself. Ratings of 4 and 5 are exceptional, and perhaps you should refer to the scales to verify validity and reliability.

Step E: (Brief summary and integration of ideas)

During the early stages of developing skills in empathic listening and responding there are several factors which may be helpful to you. These are:

1. Refresher on the definition of empathy. Empathy is listening to a person in a manner in which we put ourselves into the frame of reference of another so that the other person's thinking, feeling, and behaving are completely understood.

2. Use of reflection of content. A simple style of merely repeating almost verbatim the words the student has just used. It may be useful for the student to hear the words that he has used so that he has a better understanding of how they sound. Sample—Student statement: "I failed the exam because I didn't read the chapter." Teacher response: "You failed the exam because you didn't prepare properly."

3. Use of reflection of feeling. Oftentimes the student will make a response to the teacher in which the words describe a very cognitive kind of statement while the feeling of the student is at a much deeper level. This technique is used to tell the student that you really do understand how he feels about what he is saying even though he is not verbalizing it. Sample—Student statement: "I did it again, I failed the exam because I didn't read the chapter." Teacher response: "You feel bad because you failed the exam and you're kicking yourself for not preparing properly."

4. Be aware that not only does the level of empathic response from the helper affect the level of response from the helpee, but the helpee's response level also affects the helper's subsequent responses. This may be called a reciprocal response effect.

The developmental stages of empathic communication are supported by Carkhuff in "Stage 1 of Empathy" in which he describes this process:

Generally, it enables the helper to gauge the level at which the helpee is functioning and thus his readiness for entering further phases of empathic understanding and helping. Specifically, it enables the helper to estimate the helpee's depth of understanding in relevant areas. Similarly, it allows the helpee to determine how well the helper can comprehend his world as he has expressed his experience of it. Thus, while Stage 1 of Empathy establishes the helper's readiness to proceed to higher or deeper levels of functioning, it also helps to establish a secure base for the helpee's readiness to proceed to the next level of attempted self-understanding. It is as if the helpee were saying, "If the helper can stay with me and be with me as I present myself, then there is basis for my attempting to explore and understand myself at levels that I have not yet successfully reached.[25]

You are now ready to proceed to Lesson III in which you will develop your own content for rating.

~~~~~~

LESSON THREE: EMPATHY TRAINING
(Approximate time required: 15 minutes)

PROCEDURE: Complete each step before proceeding to the next one.

Step A:
1. Class members form triads.
2. Each triad identifies a helper, helpee, and observer.
3. The helpee requests help on a simple problem.

　　The observer allows *one minute* of interaction to follow, such as this sample exchange between a person asking for understanding and help, in a normal, everyday type of interaction, and a person whom he respects:

　　The helpee tells something about himself to the helper, such as, "This is an interesting experience talking to you about me, but I'm not sure what I should tell you."

　　The helper responds, "You are not sure how much you want me to know about you."

4. At the end of the one-minute dialogue, turn to the appropriate score sheet at the end of the chapter, and record your levels of empathic interaction, using the following as a guide to the Empathy section of your rating diagram:
　a. The helper and helpee each rate themselves.
　b. The helper and helpee each rate the other.
　c. The observer rates both the helper and the helpee.
5. After all rating has been recorded, the observer reads all the evaluations to the group in the sequence stated above. Attempt to resolve quickly your disagreements and rotate roles so that each member plays the parts of helper, helpee, and observer. Rate and share your evaluations following each rotation.

[25] Robert R. Carkhuff, *Helping and Human Relations,* Vol. II, 84.

Step B:

This is your first exercise involving you in genuine interaction for the purpose of improving your listening and responding skills. As before, if your ratings are 1 and 2, you should refer to the Empathy Scale. If you have ratings of 2 and 3, you are doing well. Ratings above 3 are great and you are to be commended for your rapid progress. Do remember, however, to refer to the Empathy Scale for validation of scores of 4 and 5, since these ratings are unusually high.

Step C:

Reading the following summary of empathy will clarify Lesson III and prepare you for Lesson IV.

A second stage of development related to empathy training is a continuation of the first stage; however, the helper extends his limits of understanding and helping by:
1. Listening for more intent and feeling in the helpee's statements. (See definition of terms)
2. Moderately interpreting (see definition of terms) or asking the helpee a question to help each other better understand the true message. A sample response which the helper might make is: "Could it be that you fear teaching in front of a class of 30 students while being observed by your supervisor." With an introduction of "could it be", the helpee can agree that you are following accurately or suggest that you had not heard the total message. In the latter case, the helper merely responds with, "Would you help me better understand what you are saying?"

Carkhuff supports this approach in the following statement:

Whereas the helper must usually initiate entrance into this stage—since the helpee is reluctant to go where he has not been before, at least in a constructive way—in its more successful instances this stage becomes a highly interactional process during which both helper and helpee enable the other to move to deeper and deeper levels of understanding. Again whether or not the helpee achieves the deepest possible levels of self-understanding is contingent upon the depth to which the helper understands himself; indeed, over the course of helping the helper often comes to expand his self-understanding.[26]

~~~~~~

LESSON FOUR: EMPATHY TRAINING
(Approximate time required: 20 minutes)

In Lesson III you created your communication content from your own

[26] *Ibid.,* p. 84.

triad. Lesson IV is similar except that the helpee is to talk to the helper for *two minutes*. Try to increase your scores by one-half level in this lesson.

PROCEDURE: Complete each step before proceeding to the next one.

Step A:
1. Remain in your present triad of helper, helpee, and observer.
2. The observer allows the helper and helpee to communicate with each other for *two minutes,* as in the example below:

   Helpee statement: "Every time I find myself in a situation where someone is getting to know me better, I feel uncertain."

   Helper statement: "You feel uncertain when talking to someone about yourself, and you're wondering why this occurs."
3. During the two-minute interaction the observer focuses on the empathic levels of functioning for the helper and helpee. At the end of the two-minute period, rate the level of communication and enter your evaluations on your rating diagram in the following sequence, but do not share your ratings until all notations are completed:
   a. The helper and helpee each rates himself.
   b. The helper and helpee rate each other.
   c. The observer rates both helper and helpee.
4. After all rating has been recorded, the observer reads all the evaluations to the group in the sequence stated above. Attempt to resolve quickly your disagreements and rotate roles so that each member plays the parts of helper, helpee, and observer. Rate and share your evaluations following each rotation.

Step B:

How did you do? Were you able to increase by one-half level? If you are averaging ratings of 2.5, you are doing very well. If not, you may need to select a person to practice with a few more times on your own.

Now read the summary statement on empathic communication in preparation for Lesson V.

Carkhuff suggests that the final stage of understanding and helping concentrates upon problem solving.[27] Sometimes the problem identification, selection of alternatives, and decision making are quite clear and relatively easy to make. Other times, however, the helpee is not ready to act upon the problem. In this case, the helper should not proceed in advance of his helpee, but meet him at his level of self understanding and functioning. Oftentimes a break in time of a few days between talk sessions will allow the helpee to become more objective in his decision making.

You are now ready for Lesson V.

~~~~~~

[27] *Ibid.,* p. 85.

LESSON V: EMPATHY TRAINING
(Approximate time required: 25 minutes)

PROCEDURE: Complete Step A before going on to Step B.

Step A:

1. Change triads by forming into threes with class members you have not worked with on the previous communication exercises.
2. Maintain roles of helper, helpee, and observer.
3. Helpee begins by asking for help and understanding from the helper in an area of personal concern, though the problem need not be of a particularly serious nature.

   The helper attempts to respond to the feeling and meaning of the request. Try to maintain brief, but meaningful, responses for both helper and helpee.

   This interaction should be as genuine as possible. Since you are beginning to focus on feelings, it may be beneficial for the helper to start with "You feel" and then continue with the feeling he is picking up in the interaction, as illustrated in the following example:

   > Helpee statement: "Sometimes I feel like coming to class has no meaning. I just can't seem to find how I fit into all of this. Maybe I'm not cut out to be a teacher."

   > Helper response: "You can't find a direction in life which you want to pursue, and some days you feel confused about why you are considering teaching as your future."

4. Continue the interaction for *two minutes*. During this time the helper should focus on the person as well as on the concern, listening as fully as possible to all that the person is saying. His concentration should be upon both content and intent.
5. Following the two-minute interaction, the observer will take a more active role by focusing on specific areas of the interaction. He will ask the helper and helpee to record the empathy levels on their score sheets for each of the following questions:
   a. Helpee rates self: At what level of empathy did you observe yourself requesting help from your helper?
   b. Helpee rates self: At what level of empathy did you want to request help from your helper?
   c. Helpee rates self: At what level of empathy did you want your helper to receive your statement?
   d. Helper rates self: At what level of empathy did you observe yourself receiving your helpee's concern?
   e. Helper rates self: At what level of empathy did you want to receive your helpee?
   f. Helper rates helpee: At what level of empathy did you want your helpee to receive you?
6. Rotate so that each person functions in each role of helper, helpee, and observer.

Step B: Summary

This is the completion of Program I: Empathy Training. You should be receiving scores which average between 2.5 and 3 in your ability to listen and respond to another person with feeling. Since developing empathic communication skills is of greatest importance, you will have additional chances to develop this skill in Programs II and III.

Keep up the good work and continue practicing outside of class until you can function consistently at or near level 3 when people are asking you for help and understanding.

You are now ready to proceed to Program II, which concerns learning how to understand and communicate the condition of respect.

~~~~~~

Program II: Respect Training

INTRODUCTION:

As you learned in Program I, the single greatest skill in communication is the ability to listen, understand and respond to both the content and intent or feeling of an interpersonal message. This skill has been termed *empathy*.

Perhaps the second greatest requirement for effective interaction relates to the level of *respect* communicated between the helper and helpee. In order to focus on this topic, it is necessary to learn the meaning and levels of respect transmitted in human interaction.

Program II, *Respect Training,* provides specific guidelines for you to understand and learn the levels and functions of communicating respect to another person. Please read Scale 2 of Respect Training until you understand the description and meaning of the different levels.

SCALE 2:
THE COMMUNICATION OF RESPECT IN INTERPERSONAL PROCESSES
A SCALE FOR MEASUREMENT [28]

Level 1   The verbal and behavioral expressions of the helper communicate a clear lack of respect (or negative regard) for the helpee(s).

Example: The helper communicates to the helpee that the helpee's feelings and experiences are not worthy of consideration or that the helpee is

[28] These five levels are quoted from Carkhuff, *Helping and Human Relations,* Vol. I, 178–179.

not capable of acting constructively. The helper may become the sole focus of evaluation.

In summary, in many ways the helper communicates a total lack of respect for the feelings, experiences, and potentials of helpee.

Level 2   The helper responds to the helpee in such a way as to communicate little respect for the feelings, experiences, and potentials of the helpee(s).

Example: The helper may respond mechanically or passively or ignore many of the feelings of the helpee.

In summary, in many ways the helper displays a lack of respect or concern for the helpee's feelings, experiences, and potentials.

Level 3   The helper communicates an openness to the prospect of the helpee's position and concern for the helpee's feelings, experiences, and potentials.

Example: The helper communicates an openness to the prospect of the helpee's ability to express himself and to deal constructively with his life situation.

In summary, in many ways the helper communicates the possibility that who the helpee is and what he does may matter to the helper, at least minimally. Level III constitutes the minimal level of facilitative interpersonal functioning.

Level 4   The helper clearly communicates a very deep respect and concern for the helpee.

Example: The helper's responses enable the helpee to feel free to be himself and to experience being valued as an individual.

In summary, the helper communicates a very deep caring for the feelings, experiences, and potentials of the helpee.

Level 5   The helper communicates the very deepest respect for the helpee's worth as a person and his potentials as a free individual.

Example: The helper cares very deeply for the human potentials of the helpee and communicates a commitment to enabling the helpee to actualize this potential.

In summary, the helper does everything he can to enable the helpee to act more constructively and emerge most fully.

~~~~~~

Following training in empathy, training in the discrimination of respect has both theoretical and experiential meaning. To be sure, the dimension of respect is often incorporated within a high-level empathy communication, although such is not always the case as is particularly prominent in communications of the detached comments of a more diagnostic kind of empathy. Similarly, respect may be communicated to the helpee even in the absence of high levels of empathy. In this regard, although warmth often receives separate and distinct considerations, we view warmth as one of several possible vehicles for communicating respect; it is a critical vehicle that is essential under many and specifiable conditions, but nevertheless it is only one vehicle for respect. In any event, without respect by the helper for some critical helpee characteristic, helping is not possible.

When you feel you have an understanding of the levels of recognizing and responding to communicative respect, proceed to Lesson I in which you will have an opportunity to expand and extend your knowledge and application of communicating respect.

~~~~~~

LESSON ONE: RESPECT TRAINING
(Approximate time required: 20 minutes)

Four additional standardized student statements have been selected for your second training experience to help you explore you present ability to understand and respond to a communicated message. As in Program I, there are no right or wrong answers, so proceed as naturally as possible.

PROCEDURE: Complete each step before proceeding to the next one.

Step A:

1. Student statements 5 through 7 cover a wide range of values, feelings, and attitudes (internal self) and behavior (external self).
2. All statements represent the same student.
3. Read the statement as if it were being said by a student in your class seeking understanding and help.
4. Now read student statement number 5 below as many times as necessary to complete the following:
   a. Identify the *content* communicated (verbal message) and enter on your score sheet.
   b. Identify the *intent* communicated (feelings and emotions) and write it on the score sheet.

c. Formulate a response you would make to this person who has come for understanding and help and enter it on your score sheet.

STUDENT STATEMENT: [29]

5. Each day I get up at the crack of dawn and people wonder why; I do because I have a longing to learn about myself and the things around me. It's so exciting! Each moment I see or learn something new—caterpillars become butterflies, the sun is actually bigger than the earth, or my body is made of many tiny cells. I feel like I'm bubbling over with excitement. I want to learn and discover things all day long!

Step B:
5. Repeat (a), (b), and (c) above for student statements 6 and 7 below.

STUDENT STATEMENTS: [30]

6. Whenever we divide up to choose sides to play I'm always the last one picked. I'm so awkward and I don't seem to play the way others want me to. No one ever wants me on their side. It really makes me feel bad to be the last one left. When everybody is playing I just lean against the nearest wall —sometimes I could cry; when I do I simply feel worse than ever and all the other kids laugh at me then. I hate my body; why couldn't I have gotten a different one?

7. People get me so mad! Sometimes I feel like really letting them have it. That would at least make them stop making fun of the way I look. Just because I'm bigger than most kids my age, they call me names. The other kids call me "lardy" or "fatso." Sometimes my teacher says I'm a big bully. Even my dad and mom don't like the way I look; they kid me by saying, "You'll grow out of it, we hope." Well, they just better watch out because I'll show them I can really be a bully if I want to. I'm not going to let them make fun of me and get away with it.

Step C:
6. Rate your responses for student statements 5–7 for *empathy* and *respect* and enter the results on your score sheet.

Step D:
7. You have just completed your first exercise on recognizing and responding with respect. Please proceed to the comments on the first stage of respect and read them carefully for greater clarification.

~~~~~~

[29] Carkhuff, *Helping and Human Relations,* Vol. II, 252.
[30] *Ibid.*

STAGE 1 OF RESPECT

Similar to the operation of empathy, in early stages the emphasis upon unconditionality or unconditional positive regard enables both the helper and the helpee to experience the helpee as fully as possible. The essential communication, which often is implicit, is, "With me you are free to be who you are." This is not to say, however, that there are no limits set. There are limits, but they primarily involve those behaviors that are harmful or potentially harmful to the helpee or others. In this sense the terms *unconditionality* or *unconditional positive regard* are misnomers, for no one is totally unconditional in relation to another. While the communication of warmth may be a modality for communicating respect, translated functionally, *unconditionality merely involves the suspension of all potentially psychonoxious feelings, attitudes, and judgments on the part of the helper—that is, those that might have a restrictive or destructive effect upon the expressions and behaviors of the helpee.* Such a communication establishes the basis for a secure relationship within which the helpee can experience and experiment with himself. Furthermore, it provides the basis for the helper as well as for the helpee to come to know the helpee well enough to discern those aspects of the helpee that are deserving of positive regard, the second stage of respect.[31]

Lesson II provides an opportunity for you to practice developing better skills in recognizing and responding with respect. Please proceed to Lesson II.

~~~~~~

LESSON TWO: RESPECT TRAINING
(Approximate time required: 20 minutes)

PROCEDURE: Complete each step before proceeding to the next step.

Step A:
1. Class forms into groups of four.
2. Groups assign one helper, one helpee, and two observers.
3. Helpee engages helper in a *two-minute* relationship of asking the helper to aid him in understanding an area of concern in his life, as in the example below:

> Helpee's statement: "I have been wondering if teaching is really what I want to do. Sometimes I feel like dropping out of class and changing majors."

> Helper's response: "Some days you are not sure what you want to do; you feel like teaching is not for you, and yet you are not sure what other areas may interest you more."

[31] *Ibid.,* p. 86.

4. The two observers each rate the interaction in the following manner: Observer 1 records empathy for both helper and helpee on the score sheet at the end of the chapter. Observer 2 records respect for both helper and helpee.

Observer 1:

a. Identify and record level of empathy sending for helper.
b. Identify and record level of empathy receiving for helper.
c. Identify and record level of empathy receiving for helpee.
d. Identify and record level of empathy sending for helpee.

Observer 2:

a. Identify and record level of respect sending for helper.
b. Identify and record level of respect receiving for helper.
c. Identify and record level of respect receiving for helpee.
d. Identify and record level of respect sending for helpee.

5. Helper rates level of empathy and respect sending for self.
6. Helper rates level of empathy and respect receiving for self.
7. Helpee rates level of empathy and respect receiving for self.
8. Helpee rates level of empathy and respect sending for self.

Step B:
1. Rotate all roles so each member experiences each role.

Step C:
2. Compare all scores. As stated earlier, a score of 1 or 2 can be classified as low, 2 or 3 as average but good, and above 3 as excellent. If your scores are consistently at 3 and above, either you are an excellent communicator or you need to validate scores. The additional lessons will help you confirm your scores. Use the empathy and respect scales to aid in the discussion. Now read Stage 2 of Respect to prepare you for Lesson III.

~~~~~~

STAGE 2 OF RESPECT

As the helper comes to know the helpee, then, he comes to experience aspects of the helpee to which he can respond positively. If he cannot do so, there is no basis for continuing further, since there is no hope that the helpee will come to have respect for his own capacities for making appropriate discriminations and acting with responsibility in relevant areas. The principal modalities for communicating positive regard involve the communication of accurate or attempted empathic understanding and, to a lesser degree, the genuinely positive responses of the helper to the helpee. In particular, the degree to which the helper is committed to and can with intensity understand the helpee will reflect the degree to which he communicates respect in its second stage. At a minimum the communication, "You are worthy of my effort to understand" establishes a basis for the helpee's experience of his own self-worth. At a maximum a depth of understanding on the part of the helper communicates his readiness and desire to be able to know the helpee more fully. In a sense we might view the respect dimension in more traditional behavioristic terms. We need first to know who this person is before we can respond positively to some or all of his assets. However, since not all of his characteristics are functional and thus deserving of positive reinforcement, we must also deal with those that are nonfunctional and even self-destructive. This consideration leads readily to the third stage of respect.[32]

Proceed to Lesson III.

~~~~~~

LESSON THREE: RESPECT TRAINING
(Approximate time required: 20 minutes)

HOMEWORK ASSIGNMENT: Two audio recorders needed.

The class should select two groups of six persons each to prepare two audio tapes. The purpose of the taping session is to record taped samples to be played and rated by the remainder of the class or other classes. With the previous training and understanding of levels of empathy and respect communication, the taping groups should have little difficulty preparing the taped program.

PROCEDURE: Read all of Lesson III (1 through 15) before beginning.

1. Provide one audio tape and recorder for each group.
2. Class selects six tapers for each group.
3. Specify nature of the task.

For Tapers Only:

4. Group I should prepare an empathy training tape and Group II should prepare a respect training tape.
5. Each group should select a quiet place to work, but the two should work near each other.
6. Each group should form three helper-helpee pairs and take turns practicing their roles while being recorded. When this is completed, play back the tape and decide who will function best at a low verbal interaction level (levels 1 to 2 on the rating scales), at an average verbal interaction level (level 3 on the rating scales, and at a high verbal interaction level (any rating above 3 on the scales).

[32] *Ibid.,* pp. 86–87.

7. Decide who should work together to prepare two taped samples at the 1 to 2 level of verbal interaction, at the 3 level of verbal interaction, and at the 4 to 5 level of verbal interaction.
8. Begin working on your task with pair one interacting and recording at levels 1 and 2 while the other two pairs are rating. Rate and give feedback at short (one to two-minute) intervals to help the tapers work at their assigned levels. You should complete two one-minute samples at your assigned level for your task.
9. Each pair should complete two one-minute samples at their assigned level for their task.
10. After taping, rating, editing, and agreeing on each level and task in your group (e.g., level 1 to 2 verbal interaction with task of preparing an empathy training tape), the groups should randomly sequence their 12 one-minute statements with a 10-second silence between statements. You are now ready to present your tape for class rating.

Playing Tapes to Class for Rating:

11. You have 12 one-minute tape samples for two topics (empathy and respect) at three levels (1 to 2, 3, 4 to 5).
12. Divide the class into two groups of equal size. Request Group I to rate for topic one, empathy, and Group II to rate for topic two, respect.
13. Request each group to turn to their score sheets. While the tapes were prepared to teach levels of empathy and respect training separately, it will be beneficial for both groups to rate each of the 12 statements. Play the 12 statements without stopping. If necessary, the tape could be replayed for all statements. Do not play statements an unequal number of times.
14. When the tape has been played and score sheets are complete, record the scores on the chalkboard for Group I, empathy, and Group II, respect, for each of the 12 statements. Compute the means and compare scores to the ratings assigned by the tape makers. If 75 percent agreement cannot be reached on a statement within each group, consider that statement invalid. Remember to use the empathy and respect scales for rating or to clear up disagreements.
15. Your mean score for empathy should be between 2.75 and 3, and your mean score for respect should be between 2.25 and 2.75. If your scores are as stated, you are progressing at an above average pace. If your scores are at the top of those stated above, or higher, you are doing very well and should congratulate yourselves. This is also a good time to thank your tapers for their extra contribution to the training program.

You are doing well; therefore, you are ready to proceed to concreteness and specificity of expression. As you know, the two most important skills in interpersonal communication are empathy and respect; perhaps the next most important skill is that of *communicating with concreteness.* In order to expand on the communication of respect, please read Stage 3 of Respect.

~~~~~~

STAGE 3 OF RESPECT

As we come to know the helpee fully we determine that there are many aspects of his behavior that we want to reinforce positively and many that at a minimum we want to extinguish and at a maximum to reinforce negatively or punish. In a very real sense, Stage 2 has already initiated an extinction process by the selective reinforcement of some behaviors and the absence of reinforcement for others. In this context, Stage 3 is more critical in rehabilitation treatment processes than it is in socioeducational processes. The last stage of respect, then, emphasizes a conditionality of respect. That is, "Given your developmental stage, I will respect you *only if* you function at your highest level." *The central message of this stage involves not accepting an individual at less than he can be.* The main modality for its communication is the genuineness of the helper, a level of spontaneity that allows the helper to disclose fully in his attitudes and behaviors both his positive and his negative feelings about the helpee's behaviors. To be sure, many helping processes may never reach this stage. In the ideal, however, successful completion of the helping process will dictate a helpee who has incorporated a standard of not accepting himself as being less than he can be. At the highest levels, this has implications for full and creative productivity, and, indeed, self-actualization. The helper's conditionality is not predicated upon "doing things as I do them" but rather upon "finding your own way, employing me as a model for someone who strives to be fully himself not only in the moment but in life."[33]

Please proceed to Program III which is the last training program before learning how to apply your recently acquired skills in a classroom setting.

~~~~~~

Program III: Concreteness and Specificity of Expression

Two prime skills of verbal interaction have been achieved—empathic styles of communicating and communicating respect to another person. Perhaps the next most significant element in communicating with others is to do so in a concrete and specific manner.

The following scale has been developed to aid the communicator in

[33] *Ibid.,* p. 87.

focusing on the specificity of his message. Please read the scale until you feel you understand the levels and sequencing of it.

~~~~~~

SCALE 3:
PERSONALLY RELEVANT CONCRETENESS OR SPECIFICITY
OF EXPRESSION IN INTERPERSONAL PROCESSES
—A SCALE FOR MEASUREMENT [34]

Level 1   The helper appears to lead or allow all discussions with the helpee(s) to deal only with vague and anonymous generalities.

> *Example:*   The helper and the helpee discuss everything on strictly an abstract and highly intellectual level.

In summary, the helper makes no attempt to lead the discussion into the realm of personally relevant specific situations and feelings.

Level 2   The helper frequently appears to lead or allow even discussions of material personally relevant to the helpee(s) to be dealt with on a vague and abstract level.

> *Example:*   The helper and the helpee may discuss "real" feelings but they do so at an abstract, intellectual level.

In summary, the helper does not elicit discussion of most personally relevant feelings and experiences in specific and concrete terms.

Level 3   The helper is open and at times facilitative of the helpee's discussion of personally relevant material in specific and concrete terminology.

> *Example:*   The helper will help to make it possible for the discussion with the helpee(s) to center directly around most things that are personally important to the helpee(s), although there will continue to be areas not dealt with concretely and areas that the helpee does not develop fully and specifically.

In summary, the helper is open to consideration of personally relevant specific and concrete instances, but these are not always fully developed. Level III constitutes the minimal level of facilitative functioning.

[34] These five levels are quoted from Carkhuff, *Helping and Human Relations,* Vol. I, pp. 182–183.

Level 4   The helper appears frequently helpful in enabling the helpee(s) to fully develop in concrete and specific terms almost all instances of concern.

   Example: The helper is able on many occasions to guide the discussion to specific feelings and experiences of personally meaningful material.

In summary, the helper is very helpful in enabling the discussion to center around specific and concrete instances of most important and personally relevant feelings and experiences.

Level 5   The helper appears always helpful in guiding the discussion so that the helpee(s) may discuss fluently, directly, and completely specific feelings and experiences.

   Example: The helper involves the helpee in discussion of specific feelings, situations, and events regardless of their emotional content.

In summary, the helper facilitates a direct expression of all personally relevant feelings and experiences in concrete and specific terms.

At minimally facilitative levels the helper demonstrates an openness to and may periodically enable the helpee to become involved in discussion of personally relevant material in specific and concrete terminology. In accordance with the operation of many other dimensions, whether or not an area is discussed fully and specifically appears more a function of the helper's interests or disposition rather than of what is most urgent or necessary for the helpee. At lower levels the helper leads or allows almost all discussion to deal with vague and anonymous generalities. While this approach may be helpful at times, particularly as an entry into troublesome material, it does not enable the helpee to come to grips with the specifics of his experience or the realities of his situation. At higher levels, in turn, the helper facilitates full, fluent, direct, and complete discussion by the helpee of specific feelings and experiences.

Thus, at relatively low levels of concreteness the helper might discuss all parental concerns on strictly an abstract or highly intellectual level: "One can't help but surmise that your current difficulties with your parents are a function of the long development of complex and heterogeneous inter-actions with them." At relatively high levels, in turn, the helper attempts to involve the helpee in the discussion of specific feelings, situations, and events regardless of their emotional content: "Although it's not easy for you to talk about because of strong feelings of guilt, it does seem that every time you make a move to find your own direction, your own autonomy, your mother gets sick and you get pulled back from your goal."

At more intermediate or minimally facilitative levels the helper responds in a manner that is at least in part concrete and helpful: "In some way maybe you have related your mother's recurrent illness to your struggles."

~~~~~~

You now have a general idea of how being more specific and concrete as a listener also aids you in responding more specifically and concretely to another person. It is very common to hear or read about the need in education to become more objective in what to teach, how to teach, and the outcomes of "what" and "how." Setting objectives is useful and necessary, though very difficult, in human interaction. At this point, there is little question that there is a direct relationship between a person's attitudes, values, feelings, and knowledge (internal self) and his behavior (external self).

We are in question as to the influence each has on the other. Should we focus on the behavior of the person, in this case helping someone become more concrete and specific in his interpersonal (self to others) communication; or should we focus on the internal make-up of the person and attempt to uncover the emotional dynamics which will hopefully explain the reason for nonspecific interpersonal communication? It is the intent of Program III to focus on both the *content* and *intent* of interpersonal communication, so helpers and helpees become more alert and sensitive to what is being verbalized and to responding in more helpful and meaningful ways.

We have taken the position that communicating with empathy and respect is an element in interpersonal interaction which precedes being more specific in how we listen and respond to others. However, there are times when we cannot be objective with ourselves, even on the simplest of concerns. For this reason, we have introduced Program III and have attempted to objectify and sequence both the training and application of communicating more specifically both the *content* and *intent* of verbal interaction between people. Please proceed to Lesson One on *Concreteness Training*.

~~~~~~

LESSON ONE: CONCRETENESS TRAINING
(Approximate time required: 20 minutes)

PROCEDURE: Complete each step before proceeding to the next one.

Step A:
1. Class forms into groups of three.

2. Each group assigns one helper, one helpee, and one observer.
3. Helpee engages helper in a *one-minute* relationship by asking the helper to aid him in understanding an area of concern in his life, as in this example:

> Helpee's statement: "It seems that I have difficulty making myself clearly understood when I speak to others, especially when I want the other person to know exactly how I feel."

> Helper's response: "When you want others to most understand you, they seem to respond inappropriately and you are not sure if it is the way you are telling them or the way they are listening."

4. The observer will:
   a. Identify and record level of concreteness sending for helpee, based on the scale for concreteness.
   b. Identify and record level of concreteness receiving for helper.
   c. Identify and record level of concreteness receiving for helpee.
   d. Identify and record level of concreteness sending for helper.
5. The helper records level of concreteness sending for self.
6. The helper records level of concreteness receiving for self.
7. The helpee records level of concreteness receiving for self.
8. The helpee records level of concreteness sending for self.
9. After all ratings have been recorded on the score sheets, the observer will read all ratings. Attempt to resolve quickly your disagreements and rotate roles so each member functions in each role of helper, helpee, and observer. Rate and share your appraisals following each rotation.

Step B:

This is your first exercise in learning how to become more specific in listening and responding to both the *content* and the *intent* of verbal interaction in a helper-helpee relationship. Chances are that it was difficult for you to know if you were on the right wave length regardless of whether you were a helper or a helpee. Try not to *interpret* (refer to definition of terms) each other, but do concentrate on the words (content) as well as the feelings (intent) of the interaction. Try to rely on the observer and the scales to settle disagreements. Don't feel bad if you have scores of 1 and 2 since this is perhaps the most difficult of the three programs. Now proceed to Stage 1 of Concreteness which will give you a greater understanding of the meaning of concreteness.

~~~~~~

STAGE 1 OF CONCRETENESS

During the initial stage, then, the helper employs his resources to influence the helpee to discuss fluently, directly, and completely specific feelings and experiences regardless of their emotional content. Again the helper influences the helpee through the critical sources of learning. He may employ specificity in his own communications, whether basically reflective or interrogative, so that he enables the helpee not only to have the facilitative experience of having the specifics of his problems understood but also the experience of being encouraged to make his own relevant discriminations and communications. In addition, the helper provides the helpee a role model for a person who can deal concretely with problem areas, his own as well as those of others. Finally, the helper may didactically teach the helpee to communicate concretely in both his questions and his directions. In summary, then, during stage 1, the helper's concreteness serves several critical functions: . . . it insures that the helper's response does not become too far removed emotionally. . . .[35]

You are now ready to proceed to Lesson II of *Concreteness Training.*

~~~~~~

LESSON TWO: CONCRETENESS TRAINING
(Approximate time required: 20 minutes)

In Lesson II the previously developed tapes for respect and empathy training are to be played. Even though the tapes were not developed for the purpose of training concreteness, they will provide stimuli for training better listening skills in concreteness.

PROCEDURE: Complete each step before proceeding to the next one.

Playing Tapes for Concreteness Training:

Step A:
1. Class members turn to their score sheets.
2. The 12 one-minute tape samples are played to the class and each person is asked to rate the verbal interaction using the concreteness scale. The tape should be played only once.
3. After all 12 statements have been played, tally the raw score and the mean score of concreteness for each of the one-minute tape samples. If the class is large, it may be necessary to divide into several smaller groups, with each group developing their own mean score for each tape sample. Following this task, someone can quickly write the group mean scores on the chalkboard for the computation of the class mean scores for each taped sample. If there are extreme differences on one or two of the samples, do not use them for your assessment. If there is wide disagreement on several of the one-minute samples, it may be beneficial to replay the tape a second time. This time, however, start the tape at the fifth, sixth, or seventh sample and play the first samples last. This reversal will reduce the imprinting to use scores from the first rating. After completion of the tape training exercise, please read about the second stage of concreteness.

~~~~~~

[35] Carkhuff, *Helping and Human Relations,* Vol. II, p. 88.

STAGE 2 OF CONCRETENESS

Stage 2 of Concreteness is something quite different, for, having enabled the helpee to deal with the specifics of his problem areas, it now becomes imperative for the helper to decrease his emphasis on this dimension in an attempt to achieve a fuller, freer exploration on the part of the helpee. Thus, in the intermediary phase the helper may not only allow but also actively encourage the helpee to explore himself in more abstract, less specific ways. In particular, in dealing with material that is not readily available to the helpee's awareness it would seem most effective to facilitate a more vague and general course of exploration. Suffice it to say that this is the form that less conscious or unconscious processes take and it is simply not effective to attempt to impose concreteness on what is not concrete. The modalities of the second stage involve nonspecific probing and free associations on the part of both the helper and the helpee. Although not always apparently immediate in relevance, the second stage enables the helpee to break the binds of rigid cosmologies, restricted thinking, and blunted emotionality. Such a course enables both the helpee and the helper to return once again to the relevant areas with a new and fresh perspective necessary to discern and design a constructive course of action during the last stage.[36]

You are now ready to proceed to the third and final training session. Please proceed to Lesson III of *Concreteness Training*.

~~~~~~

LESSON THREE: CONCRETENESS TRAINING
(Approximate time required: 25 minutes)

PROCEDURE: Complete each step before proceeding to the next step.

Step A:
1. Class forms into groups of five.
2. Each group identifies one helper, one helpee, and three observers.
3. The helper engages the helpee by asking him for a spontaneous response to personally relevant information from the helpee's own life. The helpee should not talk longer than *15 seconds*. Continue this exercise until the helpee and helper have responded to each other three times.
4. The observers have the following responsibilities:
   a. Identify yourselves as Observer 1, 2, and 3.
      Observer 1 will always rate Empathy;
      Observer 2 will always rate Respect;
      Observer 3 will always rate Concreteness.

[36] *Ibid.,* pp. 88–89.

b. After each utterance by the helper–helpee, a recording should be entered on score sheet number 10 as follows:

    1) Observer 1—Empathy

        a) Enter your name in the column marked Observer 1.

        b) Enter the helper and helpee names in the columns marked.

    2) Observer 2—Respect

        a) Enter your name in the column marked Observer 2.

        b) Enter the helper and helpee names in the columns marked.

    3) Observer 3—Concreteness

        a) Enter your name in the column marked Observer 3.

        b) Enter the helper and helpee names in the columns marked.

5. Compare all scores after each rating. Once again, your concreteness scores will probably be lowest. If you received ratings or 2.5 to 3 for empathy and respect and 2 to 2.5 for concreteness, you are doing very well. Also, as you have probably learned by now, learning also takes place when you are the observer.

6. Rotate all roles so that each member experiences the role of helper, helpee, and observer.

Step B:

Please read about the third stage of concreteness in order to help you understand better the full meaning of this quality in successful communication.

~~~~~~

STAGE 3 OF CONCRETENESS

During the final stage the dimension of concreteness once again takes on a critical function of the helping process. Whereas it initially served responsively as a necessary supplement to understanding all specific and relevant aspects of the helpee's problem area, now it functions actively to consider all specific and relevant aspects of educative or remedial action. Concreteness is, at this point, the key to a consideration of potential preferred modes of treatment. It involves a consideration of alternative courses of action, including in particular the details of the advantages and disadvantages of each. At this point, its modalities include both questions and answers on the part of both the helper and the helpee. It may also include, among many other possibilities, representational balance sheets, topological portrayals, and specific homework assignments. The second stage, having provided new and fresh perspectives, lays the base for breakthroughs in the development of modes of problem resolution. On the one hand, it becomes apparent to the helpee that he has many more degrees of freedom available to him than he once thought he had. On the other hand, in conjunction with a depth of self-understanding, the helpee's improved discriminations allow him to discern the subtle cues that determine the course of action most suitable for him. It should be underscored that many would-be helpers attempt to move to this stage prematurely.[37]

~~~~~~

Summary for Training Program in Communication Skills

Since the scale levels have been standardized, the score numbers have the same meaning for all scales. If you are scoring between 2.5 and 3 consistently, you have done well, but perhaps you need a few more practice sessions to increase your scores. Scores consistently below 2.5 suggest that you should perhaps begin with Program I and practice with each program until you are scoring consistently between 2.5 and 3. Regardless of your score, always check the validity and reliability of your scores to make sure your scoring matches your performance.

If you feel, however, that an additional performance test is needed, a standardized post-test has been included. The post-test provides eight student statements followed by four response choices for each statement. You are to read the statement and, as in Program I, Lesson One, first write an appropriate response and second, after writing your response, turn to the four responses included and select the one you think is most helpful. Correct answers are provided in Table 7–1.

If you think this exercise will be helpful to your present growth rate, please proceed to the post test. If not, turn to page 292 and read the last paragraph of this chapter.

POST-TEST
(Approximate time required: 20 minutes)

You have now completed the three programs on empathy, respect, and concreteness. Although you have had several opportunities to assess your levels of verbal interaction, it is also important to take a standardized test to help you determine the helpfulness of your responses.

PROCEDURE: Complete each step before proceeding to the next step.

Step A:
1. Read each student statement and formulate a brief written response on your score sheet to include your highest possible level of empathy, respect, and concreteness. Complete your written response to each student statement before proceeding.

~~~~~~

[37] *Ibid.,* p. 89.

Student Excerpts [38]

1. I don't know if I am right or wrong feeling the way I do. But, I find myself withdrawing from people. I don't seem to socialize and play their stupid little games any more. I get upset and come home depressed and have headaches. It all seems to be superficial. There was a time when I used to get along with everybody. Everybody said, "Isn't she wonderful. She gets along with everybody. Everybody likes her." I used to think that was something to be really proud of, but that was who I was at that time. I had no depth. I was what the crowd wanted me to be—the particular group I was with.

2. Gee, those people! Who do they think they are? I just can't stand interacting with them anymore. Just a bunch of phonies. They leave me so frustrated. They make me so anxious. I get angry at myself. I don't even want to be bothered with them anymore. I just wish I could be honest with them and tell them all to go to hell! But I guess I just can't do it.

3. They wave that degree up like it's a pot of gold at the end of the rainbow. I used to think that, too, until I tried it. I'm happy being a housewife; I don't care to get a degree. But the people I associate with, the first thing they ask is, "Where did you get your degree?" I answer, "I don't have a degree." Christ, they look at you like you are some sort of freak, some backwoodsman your husband picked up along the way. They actually believe that people with degrees are better. In fact, I think they are worse. I've found a lot of people without degrees that are a hell of a lot smarter than these people. They think that just because they have degrees they are something special. These poor kids that think they have to go to college or they are ruined. It seems that we are trying to perpetuate a fraud on these kids. If no degree, they think they will end up digging ditches the rest of their lives. They are looked down upon. That makes me sick.

4. I get so frustrated and furious with my daughter. I just don't know what to do with her. She is bright and sensitive, but damn, she has some characteristics that make me so on edge. I can't handle it sometimes. She just—I feel myself getting more and more angry! She won't do what you tell her to. She tests limits like mad. I scream and yell and lose control and think there is something wrong with me—I'm not an understanding mother or something. Damn! What potential! What she could do with what she has. There are times she doesn't use what she's got. She gets by too cheaply. I just don't know what to do with her. Then she can be so nice and then, boy, she can be as ornery as she can be. And then I scream and yell and I'm about ready to slam her across the room. I don't like to feel this way. I don't know what to do with it.

5. I finally found somebody I can really get along with. There is no pretentiousness about them at all. They are real and they understand me. I can be myself with them. I don't have to worry about what I say and that

[38] These student excerpts are quoted from Carkhuff, *Helping and Human Relations,* Vol. I, pp. 115–122.

they might take me wrong, because I do sometimes say things that don't come out the way I want them to. I don't have to worry that they are going to criticize me. They are just marvelous people! I just can't wait to be with them! For once I actually enjoy going out and interacting. I didn't think I could ever find people like this again. I can really be myself. It's such a wonderful feeling not to have people criticizing you for everything you say that doesn't agree with them. They are warm and understanding, and I just love them! It's just marvelous!

6. I'm so thrilled to have found a counselor like you. I didn't know any existed. You seem to understand me so well. It's just great! I feel like I'm coming alive again. I have not felt like this in so long.

7. No response. (Moving about in chair.)

8. Gee, I'm so disappointed. I thought we could get along together and you could help me. We don't seem to be getting anywhere. You don't understand me. You don't know I'm here. I don't even think you care for me. You don't hear me when I talk. You seem to be somewhere else. Your responses are independent of anything I have to say. I don't know where to turn. I'm just so—doggone it—I don't know what I'm going to do, but I know you can't help me. There just is no hope.

Step B:

2. Reread each student statement and select the best response of the four listed for each comment. List the number of your responses from 1 through 4 on your score sheet. Complete your selection for the eight student statements before you proceed.

Step C:

3. Refer to the score sheet at the end of the chapter for the correct responses as rated by trained judges. In each case only two responses are listed. As stated at the top of the table, the remaining two responses were not rated as helpful and, therefore, they are not listed. If your selection matches 7 to 8 of those selected by trained judges, you have done very well. If you have selected 5 to 6 of the correct responses, you are doing average work. With a score range from 5 to 8, you should find that you are now able to both listen and respond with more meaning to people in general and especially to people asking for help and understanding.

Step D:

4. Form groups of two to six to exchange and compare your written responses to those of the best standardized responsees by looking for key words in the standardized comments as well as in your written responses. Hypothesize the rating your response would receive if it were rated by trained judges. If time is available, you may wish to rate the empathy, respect, and concreteness for each of your comments by referring to the training scales. You may also want to design your own training program for this or other classes.

HELPER RESPONSES [39]

Helper Responses [to Statement 1]:

1. You know you have changed a lot. There are a lot of things you want to do but no longer can.
2. You are damned sure who you can't be any longer but you are not sure who you are. Still hesitant as to who you are yet.
3. Who are these people that make you so angry? Why don't you tell them where to get off! They can't control your existence. You have to be your own person.
4. So you have a social problem involving interpersonal difficulties with others.

Helper Responses [to Statement 2]:

1. They really make you very angry. You wish you could handle them more effectively than you do.
2. Damn, they make you furious! But it's just not them. It's with yourself, too, because you don't act on how you feel.
3. Why do you feel these people are phony? What do they say to you?
4. Maybe society itself is at fault here—making you feel inadequate, giving you this negative view of yourself, leading you to be unable to successfully interact with others.

Helper Responses [to Statement 3]:

1. You really resent having to meet the goals other people set for you.
2. What do you mean by "it makes me sick"?
3. Do you honestly feel a degree makes a person worse or better? And not having a degree makes you better? Do you realize society perpetuates many frauds and sets many prerequisites such as a degree? You must realize how doors are closed unless you have a degree, while the ditches are certainly open.
4. A lot of these expectations make you furious. Yet, they do tap in on something in yourself you are not sure of—something about yourself in relation to these other people.

Helper Responses [to Statement 4]:

1. So you find yourself screaming and yelling at your daughter more frequently during the past three months.
2. Why don't you try giving your daughter some very precise limitations? Tell her what you expect from her and what you don't expect from her. No excuses.
3. While she frustrates the hell out of you, what you are really asking is, "How can I help her? How can I help myself, particularly in relation to this kid?"
4. While she makes you very angry, you really care what happens to her.

[39] These helper responses are quoted from *Ibid.,* pp. 116–122.

Helper Responses [to Statement 5]:

1. Sounds like you found someone who really matters to you.
2. Why do these kinds of people accept you?
3. That's a real good feeling to have someone to trust and share with. "Finally, I can be myself."
4. Now that you have found these people who enjoy you and whom you enjoy, spend your time with these people. Forget about the other types who make you anxious. Spend your time with the people who can understand and be warm with you.

Helper Responses [to Statement 6]:

1. Gratitude is a natural emotion.
2. This is quite nice but remember, unless extreme caution is exercised, you may find yourself moving in the other direction.
3. That's a good feeling.
4. Hey, I'm as thrilled to hear you talk this way as you are! I'm pleased that I have been helpful. I do think we still have some work to do yet, though.

Helper Responses [to Statement 7]:

1. You can't really say all that you feel at this moment.
2. A penny for your thoughts.
3. Are you nervous? Maybe you haven't made the progress here we hoped for.
4. You just don't know what to say at this moment.

Helper Responses [to Statement 8]:

1. I have no reason to try and not to help you. I have every reason to want to help you.
2. Only when we establish mutual understanding and trust and only then can we proceed to work on your problem effectively.
3. It's disappointing and disillusioning to think you have made so little progress.
4. I feel badly that you feel that way. I do want to help. I'm wondering, "Is it me? Is it you, both of us?" Can we work something out?

~~~~~~

This, of course, has been a brief training period, and it may be necessary to check occasionally your skill levels in each of the three programs. Perhaps the best way would be to refer to one of the lessons described in this chapter or to develop your own training program to fit the exact needs of your situation. As a classroom teacher, you may want your class to receive the exact training program described here, or you may want to modify the lessons to better fit your age group. Experience suggests that the program presented here is acceptable from junior high students to adults depending upon the nature of the group.

Be aware, however, that the purpose of the newly acquired skills is not to play "one upsmanship" on others, but to incorporate your newly developed skills into your attitudinal and behavioral frame in order to become more sensitive to your own communication competencies and the ability to understand and help others understand themselves better.

〜〜〜〜〜〜〜〜〜〜〜〜〜〜〜〜〜〜〜〜〜〜〜〜〜〜〜〜

Table 7–1   Key to Helper Responses

Student statement	I	II	III	IV	V	VI	VII	VIII
Best response in order of helping	2, 1	2, 1	4, 1	3, 4	3, 1	4, 3	1, 4	4, 3

Note: *The following responses for each student statement are those rated by trained judges as most helpful to those asking for help. The first number indicates the best response, and the second number was rated as next best. The remaining two responses were rated as not helpful and therefore not listd.*

Selected References

CARKHUFF, ROBERT R., *Helping and Human Relations: A Primer for Lay and Professional Helpers,* Volume I: *Selection and Training.* New York: Holt, Rinehart & Winston, Inc., 1969.

————, *Helping and Human Relations: A Primer for Lay and Professional Helpers,* Volume II: *Practice and Research.* New York: Holt, Rinehart & Winston, Inc., 1969.

DREIKURS, RUDOLF, M.D., *Psychology in the Classroom, A Manual for Teachers* (2nd ed.). New York: Harper & Row, Publishers, 1968.

EKMAN, PAUL, "Communication Through Nonverbal Behavior: A Source of Information about an Interpersonal Relationship." Unpublished research supported by a postdoctoral research fellowship.

GALE, RAYMOND F., *Developmental Behavior: A Humanistic Approach.* New York: The Macmillan Company, 1969.

GLASSER, WILLIAM, M.D., *Schools without Failure.* New York: Harper & Row, Publishers, 1969.

GREENBERG, SELMA, *Selected Studies of Classroom Teaching: A Comparative Analysis.* Scranton, Pa.: International Textbook Company, 1970.

GUERNEY, BERNARD G., JR., *Psycho-Therapeutic Agents: New Roles for Nonprofessionals, Parents, and Teachers.* New York: Holt, Rinehart & Winston, Inc., 1969.

HARBECK, MARY B., "Instructional Objectives in the Affective Domain," in *Educational Technology,* Volume X, No. 1, January, 1970, 49–52.

JONES, RICHARD M., *Fantasy and Feeling in Education.* New York: New York University Press, 1968.

KAGAN, NORMAN, AND DAVID R. KRATHWOHL, "Empathy: The Measurement and Characteristics of Affective Sensitivity," *Studies in Human Interaction: Interpersonal Process Recall Stimulated by Video-Tape.* Educational Publication Services, Michigan State University, December, 1967.

KELLER, FRED S., "Good-bye, Teacher . . . ," *Journal of Applied Behavior Analysis,* Volume I, No. 1, Spring, 1968, 79–89.

KRATHWHOL, DAVID R., BENJAMIN S. BLOOM, AND BERTRAM B. MASIA, *Taxonomy of Educational Objectives: The Classification of Educational Goals, Handbook II: Affective Domain.* New York: David McKay Company, Inc., 1956.

KURPIUS, DEWAYNE J., "The Affective Class Meeting." A paper prepared for the Indiana State Department of Public Instruction, 1970.   •

————, "The Use of Small Group Procedures for Classroom Settings." A chapter in preparation for publication in a book edited by Anthony Riccio, Ohio State University, and Richard Tierman, Penn-Harris-Madison School Corporation, Mishawaka, Indiana.

LAING, R. D., H. PHILLIPSON, AND A. R. LEE, *Interpersonal Perception: A Theory and a Method of Research.* New York: Springer Publishing Company, 1966.

LAZARUS, RICHARD S., *Patterns of Adjustment and Human Effectiveness.* New York: McGraw-Hill Book Company, 1969.

MEACHAM, MERLE L., AND ALLEN E. WIESEN, *Changing Classroom Behavior: A Manual for Precision Teaching.* Scranton, Pa.: International Textbook Company, 1970.

MEHRABIAN, ALBERT, *Tactics of Social Influence.* Englewood Cliffs, N. J.: Prentice-Hall, Inc., 1970.

MOUSTAKAS, CLARK, *Personal Growth: The Struggle for Identity and Human Values.* Cambridge, Mass.: Howard A. Doyle Publishing Company, 1969.

PERKINS, HUGH V., *Human Development and Learning.* Belmont, California: Wadsworth Publishing Company, Inc., 1969.

ROGERS, CARL R., AND BARRY STEVENS, *Person to Person: The Problem of Being Human.* Lafayette, Calif.: Real People Press, 1967.

ROGERS, CARL R., AND WILLIAM R. COULSON, *Freedom to Learn.* Columbus, Ohio: Charles E. Merrill Publishing Company, 1969.

ROSENBLITH, JUDY F., AND WESLEY ALLINSMITH, *The Causes of Behavior: Readings in Child Development and Educational Psychology,* (2nd ed.). Boston: Allyn and Bacon, Inc., 1969.

ROSENTHAL, ROBERT, AND LENORE JACOBSON, *Pygmalion in the Classroom: Teacher Expectation and Pupils' Intellectual Development.* New York: Holt, Rinehart & Winston, Inc., 1968.

SCHULTZ, WILLIAM C., *Joy: Expanding Human Awareness.* New York: Grove Press, Inc., 1967.

TOMKINS, SILVAN S., AND CARROLL E. IZARD, eds., *Affect, Cognition, and Per-*

sonality: Empirical Studies. New York: Springer Publishing Company, Inc., 1965.

WANN, T. W., ed., *Behaviorism and Phenomenology: Contrasting Bases for Modern Psychology*. Chicago: The University of Chicago Press, 1964.

WINTER, WILLIAM D., AND ANTONIO J. FERREIRA, eds., *Research in Family Interaction: Readings and Commentary*. Palo Alto, Calif.: Science and Behavior Books, Inc., 1969.

SCORE SHEET NUMBER __1__ FOR EMPATHY TRAINING – Lesson One (Steps A, B, and C) and
Empathy Training Lesson Two
(Steps A, B, and C)

Steps A: 4a and B:5
1. Content of   (1)_____
   Statements
   1-4   (2)_____

                  (3)_____

                  (4)_____

Steps A: 4b and B
2. Intent of   (1)_____
   Statements
   1-4   (2)_____

                  (3)_____

                  (4)_____

Steps A: 4c and B
3. Your Written   (1)_____
   Responses to
   1-4   (2)_____

                  (3)_____

                  (4)_____

Step C: 6a
4. Content of   (1)_____
   Your Written
   Responses   (2)_____
   to
   1-4   (3)_____

                  (4)_____

Step C: 6b
5. Intent of   (1)_____
   Your Written
   Responses   (2)_____
   to
   1-4   (3)_____

                  (4)_____

Lesson Two; Step B:4
6. Self Rating | Levels: | Circle the response level for each statement. | | | |
   of Your |---------|------|------|------|------|------|
   Responses | (1) | 1 | 2 | 3 | 4 | 5 |
                  | (2) | 1 | 2 | 3 | 4 | 5 |
                  | (3) | 1 | 2 | 3 | 4 | 5 |
                  | (4) | 1 | 2 | 3 | 4 | 5 |

7. Lesson Two; Step B:4
   Partner Rating | Levels: | Circle the response level for each statement. | | | |
   of Your Responses |------|------|------|------|------|------|
                  | (1) | 1 | 2 | 3 | 4 | 5 |
                  | (2) | 1 | 2 | 3 | 4 | 5 |
                  | (3) | 1 | 2 | 3 | 4 | 5 |
                  | (4) | 1 | 2 | 3 | 4 | 5 |

SCORE SHEET NUMBER __2__ FOR EMPATHY TRAINING – Lesson Three (Step A, Numbers 4 and 5)

Sample: The helper will circle "Helper" in Column one, enter his last name in Column Two, circle his self rating in Column Three and circle his rating of the helpee in Column Four

Circle your role	Enter your last name	Helper Score (Circle chosen score)	Helpee Score (Circle chosen score)
Helper	_____	1 2 3 4 5	1 2 3 4 5
Helpee	_____	1 2 3 4 5	1 2 3 4 5
Observer	_____	1 2 3 4 5	1 2 3 4 5
Average Score			

Circle your role	Enter your last name	Helper Score (Circle chosen score)	Helpee Score (Circle chosen score)
Helper	_____	1 2 3 4 5	1 2 3 4 5
Helpee	_____	1 2 3 4 5	1 2 3 4 5
Observer	_____	1 2 3 4 5	1 2 3 4 5
Average Score			

Circle your role	Enter your last name	Helper Score (Circle chosen score)	Helper Score (Circle chosen score)
Helper	_____	1 2 3 4 5	1 2 3 4 5
Helpee	_____	1 2 3 4 5	1 2 3 4 5
Observer	_____	1 2 3 4 5	1 2 3 4 5
Average Score			

SCORE SHEET NUMBER __3__ FOR EMPATHY TRAINING – Lesson Four (Step A, Numbers 3 and 4)

Circle your role	Enter your last name	Helper Score (Circle chosen score)	Helpee Score (Circle chosen score)
Helper	_____	1 2 3 4 5	1 2 3 4 5
Helpee	_____	1 2 3 4 5	1 2 3 4 5
Observer	_____	1 2 3 4 5	1 2 3 4 5
Average Score			

Circle your role	Enter your last name	Helper Score (Circle chosen score)	Helper Score (Circle chosen score)
Helper	_____	1 2 3 4 5	1 2 3 4 5
Helpee	_____	1 2 3 4 5	1 2 3 4 5
Observer	_____	1 2 3 4 5	1 2 3 4 5
Average Score			

Circle your role	Enter your last name	Helper Score Circle chosen score)	Helper Score (Circle chosen score)
Helper	_____	1 2 3 4 5	1 2 3 4 5
Helpee	_____	1 2 3 4 5	1 2 3 4 5
Observer	_____	1 2 3 4 5	1 2 3 4 5
Average Score			

SCORE SHEET NUMBER 4 FOR EMPATHY TRAINING –
Lesson Five (Step A, Numbers 5 and 6)

Step A #5

Role	Questions Asked by Observer Observer Name _____	Circle chosen score
Helpee Name _____	a. Level observed self requesting help:	1 2 3 4 5
	b. Level you wanted to request help:	1 2 3 4 5
	c. Level you wanted request received:	1 2 3 4 5
Helper Name _____	d. Level observed self receiving:	1 2 3 4 5
	e. Level you wanted to receive helpee:	1 2 3 4 5
	f. Level you wanted helpee to receive you:	1 2 3 4 5

Step A #6

Role	Questions Asked by Observer Observer Name _____	Circle chosen score
Helpee Name _____	a. Level observed self requesting help:	1 2 3 4 5
	b. Level you wanted to request help:	1 2 3 4 5
	c. Level you wanted request received:	1 2 3 4 5
Helper Name _____	d. Level observed self receiving:	1 2 3 4 5
	e. Level you wanted to receive helpee:	1 2 3 4 5
	f. Level you wanted helpee to receive you:	1 2 3 4 5

Step A #6

Role	Questions Asked by Observer Observer Name _____	Circle chosen score
Helpee Name _____	a. Level observed self requesting help:	1 2 3 4 5
	b. Level you wanted to request help:	1 2 3 4 5
	c. Level you wanted request received:	1 2 3 4 5
Helper Name _____	d. Level observed self receiving:	1 2 3 4 5
	e. Level you wanted to receive helpee:	1 2 3 4 5
	f. Level you wanted helpee to receive you:	1 2 3 4 5

SCORE SHEET NUMBER __5__ FOR RESPECT TRAINING – Lesson One (Steps A, B, and C)

1. Content of Statements 5 - 7	(5)_____ _____ (6)_____ _____ (7)_____
2. Intent of Statements 5 - 7	(5)_____ _____ (6)_____ _____ (7)_____
3. Your Written Responses to 5 - 7	(5)_____ _____ _____ (6)_____ _____ _____ (7)_____ _____

4. Self Rating of Your Written Responses in Empathy

Levels: Circle the empathy level of your responses

(5)	1	2	3	4	5
(6)	1	2	3	4	5
(7)	1	2	3	4	5

5. Self Rating of Your Written Responses in Respect

Levels: Circle the respect level of your responses

(5)	1	2	3	4	5
(6)	1	2	3	4	5
(7)	1	2	3	4	5

SCORE SHEET NUMBER _6_ FOR RESPECT TRAINING
Lesson Two (Step A, Numbers 4,5,6,7 and 8)

Step A #4	Helper Ratings		Helpee Ratings	
	Sending	Receiving	Receiving	Sending
Observer 1 Empathy Rating	1 2 3 4 5	1 2 3 4 5	1 2 3 4 5	1 2 3 4 5
Observer 2 Respect Rating	1 2 3 4 5	1 2 3 4 5	1 2 3 4 5	1 2 3 4 5

Step A #5, 6

Empathy

Helper Self Rating

Sending	Receiving
1 2 3 4 5	1 2 3 4 5

Respect

Sending	Receiving
1 2 3 4 5	1 2 3 4 5

Step A #7, 8

Helpee Self Rating

Empathy

Receiving	Sending
1 2 3 4 5	1 2 3 4 5

Respect

Receiving	Sending
1 2 3 4 5	1 2 3 4 5

300

SCORE SHEET NUMBER __7__ FOR RESPECT TRAINING – Lesson Three

Listen to each tape sample statement and circle the number which represents your task rating score for each.

Your Name _____ Your Task _____

Empathy Rating	Respect Rating
1. 1 2 3 4 5	1. 1 2 3 4 5
2. 1 2 3 4 5	2. 1 2 3 4 5
3. 1 2 3 4 5	3. 1 2 3 4 5
4. 1 2 3 4 5	4. 1 2 3 4 5
5. 1 2 3 4 5	5. 1 2 3 4 5
6. 1 2 3 4 5	6. 1 2 3 4 5
7. 1 2 3 4 5	7. 1 2 3 4 5
8. 1 2 3 4 5	8. 1 2 3 4 5
9. 1 2 3 4 5	9. 1 2 3 4 5
10. 1 2 3 4 5	10. 1 2 3 4 5
11. 1 2 3 4 5	11. 1 2 3 4 5
12. 1 2 3 4 5	12. 1 2 3 4 5

Note 1. The rating scores from each tape sample rating will need to be added together and divided by the number of group members in order to acquire an average or mean score.

Note 2. Compare the group rating of each of the twelve tape samples to the rating and task assigned by the tape makers. If there is one full score point difference on any item, either rescore the item by playing the tape again or remove that item from the training program.

SCORE SHEET NUMBER __8__ FOR CONCRETENESS TRAINING - Lesson One (Step A, Numbers 4-8)

Note: Circle the number which corresponds to your rating.

Step A #4-8

	Helper Ratings		Helpee Ratings	
	Sending	Receiving	Receiving	Sending
Observer Rating Name_____	1 2 3 4 5	1 2 3 4 5	1 2 3 4 5	1 2 3 4 5
Helper Self Rating Name_____	1 2 3 4 5	1 2 3 4 5		
Helpee Self Rating Name_____			1 2 3 4 5	1 2 3 4 5
Summary				

Step A #9

	Helper Ratings		Helpee Ratings	
	Sending	Receiving	Receiving	Sending
Observer Rating Name_____	1 2 3 4 5	1 2 3 4 5	1 2 3 4 5	1 2 3 4 5
Helper Self Rating Name_____	1 2 3 4 5	1 2 3 4 5		
Helpee Self Rating Name_____			1 2 3 4 5	1 2 3 4 5
Summary				

Step A #9

	Helper Ratings		Helpee Ratings	
	Sending	Receiving	Receiving	Sending
Observer Rating Name_____	1 2 3 4 5	1 2 3 4 5	1 2 3 4 5	1 2 3 4 5
Helper Self Rating Name_____	1 2 3 4 5	1 2 3 4 5		
Helpee Self Rating Name_____			1 2 3 4 5	1 2 3 4 5
Summary				

SCORE SHEET NUMBER _9_ FOR CONCRETENESS TRAINING – Lesson Two (Step A, Number 3)

Tape Samples	Your Ratings Name:	Small Group Score	Total Group Score
1	1 2 3 4 5		
2	1 2 3 4 5		
3	1 2 3 4 5		
4	1 2 3 4 5		
5	1 2 3 4 5		
6	1 2 3 4 5		
7	1 2 3 4 5		
8	1 2 3 4 5		
9	1 2 3 4 5		
10	1 2 3 4 5		
11	1 2 3 4 5		
12	1 2 3 4 5		

SCORE SHEET NUMBER __10__ FOR CONCRETENESS TRAINING – Lesson Three (Step A, Numbers 4,5 and 6)

Helper Name:	Helpee Name:	Observer 1 Name:	Observer 2 Name:	Observer 3 Name:

Utterances	Utterances	Empathy Ratings		Respect Ratings		Concreteness	
		Helper	Helpee	Helper	Helpee	Helper	Helpee
1	1	1 2 3 4 5	1 2 3 4 5	1 2 3 4 5	1 2 3 4 5	1 2 3 4 5	1 2 3 4 5
2	2	1 2 3 4 5	1 2 3 4 5	1 2 3 4 5	1 2 3 4 5	1 2 3 4 5	1 2 3 4 5
3	3	1 2 3 4 5	1 2 3 4 5	1 2 3 4 5	1 2 3 4 5	1 2 3 4 5	1 2 3 4 5
Average Ratings for Each		1 2 3 4 5	1 2 3 4 5	1 2 3 4 5	1 2 3 4 5	1 2 3 4 5	1 2 3 4 5

Step A #5

Helper Name:	Helpee Name:	Observer 1 Name:	Observer 2 Name:	Observer 3 Name:

Utterances	Utterances	Empathy Ratings		Respect Ratings		Concreteness	
		Helper	Helpee	Helper	Helpee	Helper	Helpee
1	1	1 2 3 4 5	1 2 3 4 5	1 2 3 4 5	1 2 3 4 5	1 2 3 4 5	1 2 3 4 5
2	2	1 2 3 4 5	1 2 3 4 5	1 2 3 4 5	1 2 3 4 5	1 2 3 4 5	1 2 3 4 5
3	3	1 2 3 4 5	1 2 3 4 5	1 2 3 4 5	1 2 3 4 5	1 2 3 4 5	1 2 3 4 5
Average Ratings for Each		1 2 3 4 5	1 2 3 4 5	1 2 3 4 5	1 2 3 4 5	1 2 3 4 5	1 2 3 4 5

Step A #5

Helper Name:	Helpee Name:	Observer 1 Name:	Observer 2 Name:	Observer 3 Name:

Utterances	Utterances	Empathy Ratings		Respect Ratings		Concreteness	
		Helper	Helpee	Helper	Helpee	Helper	Helpee
1	1	1 2 3 4 5	1 2 3 4 5	1 2 3 4 5	1 2 3 4 5	1 2 3 4 5	1 2 3 4 5
2	2	1 2 3 4 5	1 2 3 4 5	1 2 3 4 5	1 2 3 4 5	1 2 3 4 5	1 2 3 4 5
3	3	1 2 3 4 5	1 2 3 4 5	1 2 3 4 5	1 2 3 4 5	1 2 3 4 5	1 2 3 4 5
Average Ratings for Each		1 2 3 4 5	1 2 3 4 5	1 2 3 4 5	1 2 3 4 5	1 2 3 4 5	1 2 3 4 5

Step A #5

Helper Name:	Helpee Name:	Observer 1 Name:	Observer 2 Name:	Observer 3 Name:

Utterances	Utterances	Empathy Ratings		Respect Ratings		Concreteness	
		Helper	Helpee	Helper	Helpee	Helper	Helpee
1	1	1 2 3 4 5	1 2 3 4 5	1 2 3 4 5	1 2 3 4 5	1 2 3 4 5	1 2 3 4 5
2	2	1 2 3 4 5	1 2 3 4 5	1 2 3 4 5	1 2 3 4 5	1 2 3 4 5	1 2 3 4 5
3	3	1 2 3 4 5	1 2 3 4 5	1 2 3 4 5	1 2 3 4 5	1 2 3 4 5	1 2 3 4 5
Average Ratings for Each		1 2 3 4 5	1 2 3 4 5	1 2 3 4 5	1 2 3 4 5	1 2 3 4 5	1 2 3 4 5

Step A #5

Helper Name:	Helpee Name:	Observer 1 Name:	Observer 2 Name:	Observer 3 Name:

Utterances	Utterances	Empathy Ratings		Respect Ratings		Concreteness	
		Helper	Helpee	Helper	Helpee	Helper	Helpee
1	1	1 2 3 4 5	1 2 3 4 5	1 2 3 4 5	1 2 3 4 5	1 2 3 4 5	1 2 3 4 5
2	2	1 2 3 4 5	1 2 3 4 5	1 2 3 4 5	1 2 3 4 5	1 2 3 4 5	1 2 3 4 5
3	3	1 2 3 4 5	1 2 3 4 5	1 2 3 4 5	1 2 3 4 5	1 2 3 4 5	1 2 3 4 5
Average Ratings for Each		1 2 3 4 5	1 2 3 4 5	1 2 3 4 5	1 2 3 4 5	1 2 3 4 5	1 2 3 4 5

Enter a brief written response to each student statement.

1._____
_____
_____

2._____
_____
_____

3._____
_____
_____

S 4._____
T _____
U _____
D
E
N 5._____
T _____
   _____
S
T 6._____
A _____
T _____
E
M
E 7._____
N _____
T _____
S

8._____
_____
_____

Score Sheet for POST TEST SUMMARY (Step B, Number 2)

Circle Best Helper Responses

1.   1   2   3   4   ___   4.   1   2   3   4   ___   7.   1   2   3   4   ___

2.   1   2   3   4   ___   5.   1   2   3   4   ___   8.   1   2   3   4   ___

3.   1   2   3   4   ___   6.   1   2   3   4   ___

Note: After completing your ratings, please turn to Table 7-1 (p. 293) and copy
       the responses rated by trained judges as "Best", on the line after each
       choice.

8 Assessment of teacher competencies

JAMES D. RUSSELL

Purdue University

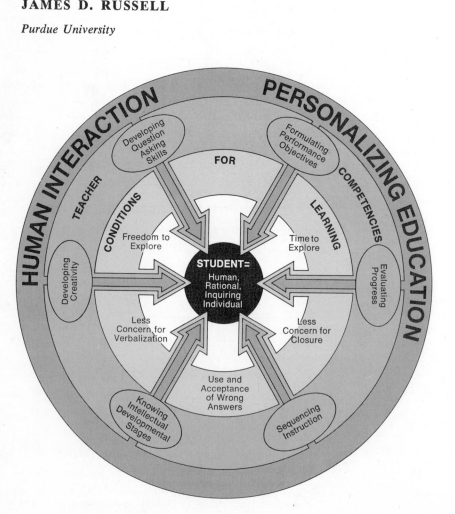

Introduction

Now that the development of teacher competencies has been discussed, how do you, as a teacher, evaluate your own competence? We want to look at several ways to assess teacher competencies; to do this we must observe the teaching process itself and collect as much objective data as possible.

A technique which has been utilized since the beginnings of formal education is evaluation by someone other than the teacher himself. The evaluator could be an administrator, another teacher, or even a student. Usually classroom conditions change when an outsider is present. The degree of change will depend upon the evaluator and the particular classroom. However, it is possible to assess and improve instruction when there is mutual trust, open communication and cooperation between the teacher and the evaluator. Pairs of teachers have found it effective to observe each other, then sit down together and discuss openly each other's performance in the classroom.

In studying teaching and teacher competence, our observations must be as objective and accurate as possible. If we as teachers try to remember what went on during our own lessons, our recall will often be colored or biased by our prejudices, as well as by what has occurred since the lesson. We would conclude we did a "good job" when in reality it was a complete failure. Other times we tend to be more critical of our classroom performance than we should be.

AUDIO TAPE RECORDINGS

The miracles of modern electronics have made it possible for the teacher to sit back and actually "observe" his own performance. The earliest and most commonly used device is the simple audio tape recorder. The tape recorder can objectively and accurately record classroom sounds (teacher talk, student questions and commotion) for instant replay. It offers the advantage of being easy to operate, portable and readily accessible. Many teachers have their own recorders or can borrow one from their school's audio-visual center. Once a tape has been made, the teacher can play it back at his own convenience, after school or at home. Techniques for analyzing the classroom performance recorded on the tape will be discussed later. The audio tape recorder has the limitation of recording only audio— more goes on in the classroom than just sounds.

VIDEO TAPE RECORDINGS

A more recent development is the video tape recorder which records both sights and sounds for instant replay. Before the days when video tape was available for use by an individual teacher, some educators experimented with sound movie film, but they found it too expensive. There was also the disadvantage of a long delay between shooting and viewing due to development time. Today, video tape recording systems are relatively inexpensive. These units are also becoming more portable; some weigh as little as thirty pounds. Some schools have larger, more elaborate equipment which allows television cameras to be positioned in the classroom and operated by remote control to record teacher behavior and classroom interaction without an outside individual being present. Video tape units are still not as accessible and reliable in their operation as the audio tape recorder.

Once a tape has been made, the teacher can view it or listen to it as often as he wishes; each time evaluating it for different competencies. Analyzing classroom behavior should be done quantitatively as well as qualitatively. One technique for making quantitative observations is to use a checklist or rating scale.

ANALYSIS OF TAPE RECORDINGS

By listening to an audio tape recording of your classroom performance, you as a teacher can make many objective observations. You might discover that you are dominating the classroom, and not giving your students a chance to participate in the discussion. It is usually advisable to listen to the tape once just to get a general impression of the class session. Then you might want to get a stopwatch. Start the tape and flip the watch on when you are talking, then off when a student is talking. The time on the watch divided by the total time will give you the percentage of time you spent talking. How much of that time did you spend lecturing? Asking questions? Criticizing student behavior? You also might want to check on the number of different students participating in class discussions. How often do your students interact with each other?

Educational psychologists tell us that praise is very important in the classroom. A tape of your classroom performance will allow you to determine how many times you praise or encourage students. You might also note how many times you really meant it. What happened after you praised the student? Listen to your directions very carefully. Are they concise and accurate? Or do you just ramble on and on and on . . .

Roberson has developed a checklist or code which he calls the "Roberson Teacher Self-Appraisal System." [1]

Part One of the code deals with verbal interaction in the classroom. Watching another teacher's performance or listening to your own by means

[1] Paul M. Allen, William D. Barnes, Jerald L. Reece and E. Wayne Roberson, *Teacher Self-Appraisal: A Way of Looking Over Your Own Shoulder* (Worthington, Ohio: Charles A. Jones Publishing Company, 1970), p. 44.

TEACHER CODE			
	Categories	Tally	Total
Verbal	1. Teacher Talks	ɪ̄N̄ʲ ɪ̄N̄ʲ ɪ̄N̄ʲ	15
Verbal	2. Student Talks	IIII	4
Verbal	3. Silence	I	1
Facial	4. Teacher Smiles	ɪ̄N̄ʲ I	6
Facial	5. Teacher Frowns	II	2
Facial	6. Neutral Expressions	ɪ̄N̄ʲ ɪ̄N̄ʲ II	12
Method	7. Lectures	ɪ̄N̄ʲ ɪ̄N̄ʲ IIII	14
Method	8. Questions	IIII	4
Method	9. Directs	II	2

Fig. 8—1

of a recording, you record a tally at a fixed interval, such as one every ten seconds, in the appropriate box—teacher talks, student talks or silence. Totaling the tallies at the end of a lesson or portion thereof will give you an indication of the time spent in each of the three types of activities.

If you are watching a teacher in person or on video tape, you can use Part Two which deals with facial expressions. Again at a fixed time interval tally what the teacher is doing. Is he smiling? Is he frowning? Or does he have a neutral expression?

The teaching method can be observed and recorded in Part Three. The tally system records when the teacher is lecturing, asking questions and directing students or giving instructions. This system is described in detail in a book by Allen, Barnes, Reece and Roberson entitled *Teacher Self-Appraisal: A Way of Looking Over Your Own Shoulder*.[2]

---

[2] *Ibid.*

Interaction Analysis

Interaction analysis offers teachers a tool which can provide objective data about teaching behavior. Various scales have been developed to quantify the interaction which takes place in a classroom.

FLANDERS SYSTEM OF INTERACTION ANALYSIS

Flanders has developed a system of analysis to observe and record student-teacher interaction in the classroom. It is a method of recording and analyzing teacher and student statements.

There are ten categories in the Flanders system. Seven are assigned to teacher talk, two to student talk and the remaining category denotes silence or confusion (see Figure 8–2). Each category is mutually exclusive, but the ten together are totally inclusive. Each verbal communication in the classroom will fit into one and only one of the ten categories.

The system can be used by an independent observer or by the teacher listening to a tape recording of a class session. The procedure involves the classification of the verbal communication every three seconds or at a rate of twenty to twenty-five entries per minute.

In order to analyze the classroom interaction, the data can be tallied to determine what percentage of the time each of the ten types of communication was taking place. It is also possible to calculate the ratio of teacher talk to student talk or the ratio of indirect teacher influence to direct teacher influence. For more elaborate analysis a ten by ten matrix can be used. (See the first two Flanders references at the end of this chapter for a more complete discussion.)

VERBAL INTERACTION CATEGORY SYSTEM

The Verbal Interaction Category System (VICS) is based upon the Flanders system, but is a second generation scale refined by Amidon and Hunter to overcome some of the limitations of the earlier system. VICS has seventeen categories rather than ten, making it more accurate, but also more difficult to use (see Figure 8–3).

The VICS system breaks down the "Asks Questions" category into "Asks Narrow Question" and "Asks Broad Questions." "Accepts or Uses Ideas of Student" is divided into three categories "5(a) Accepts Ideas," "5(b) Accepts Behavior," and "5(c) Accepts Feeling." Other differences will be noted if you study and compare Figures 8–2 and 8–3.

As in the Flanders system, tallies are made every three seconds. Similarly the tallies can be entered on a seventeen row by seventeen column matrix and analyzed. Rather than direct and indirect influence as in Flanders, VICS is concerned with initiation of talk and verbal response. Is the communication initiated by the teacher or a student? Who provides the response?

Fig. 8–2   **Flanders Interaction Analysis Categories** [3]

Teacher Talk	Response	1. *Accepts feeling.* Accepts and clarifies an attitude or the feeling tone of a pupil in a nonthreatening manner. Feelings may be positive or negative. Predicting and recalling feelings are included.
		2. *Praises or encourages.* Praises or encourages pupil action or behavior. Jokes that release tension, but not at the expense of another individual; nodding head, or saying "Um hm?" or "go on" are included.
		3. *Accepts or uses ideas of pupils.* Clarifying, building, or developing ideas suggested by a pupil. Teacher extensions of pupil ideas are included but as the teacher brings more of his own ideas into play, shift to category five.
		4. *Asks questions.* Asking a question about content or procedure, based on teacher ideas, with the intent that a pupil will answer.
	Initiation	5. *Lecturing.* Giving facts or opinions about content or procedures; expressing *his own* ideas, giving *his own* explanation, or citing an authority other than a pupil.
		6. *Giving directions.* Directions, commands, or orders to which a pupil is expected to comply.
		7. *Criticizing or justifying authority.* Statements intended to change pupil behavior from nonacceptable to acceptable pattern; bawling someone out; stating why the teacher is doing what he is doing; extreme self-reference.
Pupil Talk	Response	8. *Pupil-talk—response.* Talk by pupils in response to teacher. Teacher initiates the contact or solicits pupil statement or structures the situation. Freedom to express own ideas is limited.
	Initiation	9. *Pupil-talk—initiation.* Talk by pupils which they initiate. Expressing own ideas; initiating a new topic; freedom to develop opinions and a line of thought, like asking thoughtful questions; going beyond the existing structure.
Silence		10. *Silence or confusion.* Pauses, short periods of silence and periods of confusion in which communication cannot be understood by the observer.

Note: *There is no scale implied by these numbers. Each number is classificatory; it designates a particular kind of communication event. To write these numbers down during observation is to enumerate, not to judge a position on a scale.*

[3] Ned A. Flanders, *Analyzing Teaching Behavior* (Reading, Mass.: Addison-Wesley Publishing Company, 1970), p. 34.

Fig. 8–3 The Verbal Interaction Category System (VICS) [4]

Teacher-Initiated Talk	1. Gives Information or Opinion: presents content or own ideas, explains, orients, asks rhetorical questions. May be short statements or extended lecture. 2. Gives Direction: tells pupil to take some specific action; gives orders; commands. 3. Asks Narrow Question: asks drill questions, questions requiring one or two word replies or yes-or-no answers; questions to which the specific nature of the response can be predicted. 4. Asks Broad Question: asks relatively open-ended questions which call for unpredictable responses; questions which are thought-provoking. Apt to elicit a longer response than 3.

Teacher Response	5. Accepts: (5a) Ideas: reflects, clarifies, encourages or praises ideas of pupils. Summarizes, or comments without rejection.
	
	           (5b) Behavior: responds in ways which commend or encourage pupil behavior.
	
	           (5c) Feeling: responds in ways which reflect or encourage expression of pupil feeling.
	
	 6. Rejects: (6a) Ideas: criticizes, ignores or discourages pupil ideas.
	
	           (6b) Behavior: discourages or criticizes pupil behavior. Designed to stop undesirable behavior. May be stated in question form, but differentiated from category 3 or 4, and from category 2. Gives Direction, by tone of voice and resultant effect on pupils.
	
	           (6c) Feeling: ignores, discourages, or rejects pupil expression of feeling.

Pupil Response	7. Responds to Teacher:
	
	           (7a) Predictably: relatively short replies, usually, which follow category 3. May also follow category 2, i.e. "David, you may read next."
	
	           (7b) Unpredictably: replies which usually follow category 4.
	
	 8. Responds to Another Pupil: replies occurring in conversation between pupils.

[4] Reprinted from Table II, "The Verbal Interaction Category System (VICS)," from Edmund Amidon and Elizabeth Hunter, *Improving Teaching: The Analysis of Classroom Verbal Interaction* (New York: Holt, Rinehart & Winston, Inc., 1966), by permission of the publisher. Copyright © 1966 by Holt, Rinehart & Winston, Inc.

Pupil-Initiated Talk	9. Initiates Talk to Teacher: statements which pupils direct to teacher without solicitation from teacher.
	10. Initiates Talk to Another Pupil: statements which pupils direct to another pupil which are not solicited.
Other	11. Silence: pauses or short periods of silence during a time of classroom conversation.
	Z. Confusion: considerable noise which disrupts planned activities. This category may accompany other categories or may totally preclude the use of other categories.

Evaluation of Specific Competencies

1. EVALUATION OF YOUR USE OF INTELLECTUAL DEVELOPMENT STAGES

Are you aware of the stages of intellectual development of the students in your classroom? Have you actually tested each student's level? Did you take into account the types of conservation which your students can demonstrate? Are you using this information in a conscious attempt to individualize instruction?

2. EVALUATION OF PERFORMANCE OBJECTIVES

In order to evaluate your objectives, it is best that you actually write them down rather than just trying to remember them. You can then use the following performance objective checklist:

A. Does the objective possess a situation, a behavioral term, and an acceptance level statement?
B. Does the situation give the conditions for testing so that they might be established by another person?
C. Does the objective contain a behavioral term which can be measured?
D. Does the objective contain an acceptance level statement which maximizes or makes totally clear just how well the student must perform the described behavior?

If your objective does not meet the above criteria, it should be re-written. Do your test items actually measure the performance stated in the objectives?

3.   EVALUATION OF QUESTION-ASKING SKILLS

What kinds of questions do you ask? While listening to your tape, stop the recorder after each question and classify it into one of the categories listed by Cunningham on pp. 101–102. Was the question poorly phrased? If so, try to rewrite it. When finished you should tally the results and evaluate your strategies for question-asking. How many questions did you ask? At what level were they? How long did you give the students to respond before you restated the question or gave the answer? Remember that questioning behavior *can be* changed significantly. And it does have a profound effect on learning!

4.   EVALUATION OF INSTRUCTIONAL SEQUENCING

Evaluation of your instructional sequence does not require a tape recorder or video tape. You must be able to sit down and take an objective look at how you guided your students from their entry behavior to your terminal goal. Did you take into account the learners' entry behavior? Did you utilize an instructional model which was appropriate for what you wanted your students to learn? Did you provide alternative sequences for those students who needed them? Most importantly, did the sequence allow the students to meet your objectives?

5.   EVALUATION OF YOUR EVALUATION TECHNIQUES

Look at your tests and consider how you use them. Evaluation must be a continuous activity that is used as a basis for making decisions in the classroom. Here are some general rules for test item construction:

A. Precise instructions for answering each item should be provided. Otherwise, the student may miss the question only because the directions are not properly stated. Each question should describe clearly what the student is to do.
B. The type of question used to evaluate a specific objective should be appropriate for that objective. There are many different types of test items: multiple-choice, matching, completion, short answer, true-false and actual performance items. You should choose the type which best measures the desired student performance. Avoid using only one kind of test item throughout the entire test.
C. The question should discriminate between the student who has mastered the objective and the student who has not.
D. The reading level of the question should be low compared to the age level for which the test is to be used. Otherwise, language difficulties may prevent the student from demonstrating mastery of the objective.

6. EVALUATION OF YOUR CREATIVITY

Do you use creative approaches in your teaching? Do you seek new solutions to old problems? Do you recognize the creative efforts of your students and reward them? Do you attempt to develop and improve your creativity? Remember creativity *can* be developed!

Do you attempt to develop creativity in your students? When was the last time you participated in a brainstorming session with other teachers? Look at your video tape or listen to your audio tape and identify incidents where you could have been more creative in your interaction with students. What about making your tests more creative?

Do you provide situations in which your students can be creative or must everything be "cut-and-dried"? Do you have a daily creative check-list? Do you use creative questions (divergent) during class discussions? Do you encourage divergent (open-ended) thinking?

7. EVALUATION OF YOUR HUMAN INTERACTION SKILLS

In order to assess periodically your levels of interpersonal transactions, ask yourself the following questions:

A. Are you aware of the impact your behavior has on another person?
B. Are you aware of the association between your internal self (attitudes, values, feelings, and beliefs) and your external self (behavior)?
C. Are you aware of your differential treatment for persons you respect most and for those you respect least? Reread the Respect Scale to confirm your present functioning.
D. Do you understand empathic listening and responding? Can you function at Level 3? If not, you should reread the Empathy Scale and practice until you do function at Level 3.
E. Do you understand concreteness and specificity of communication? Can you function at Level 3? If not, practice until you can function at Level 3.

Summary

In order to be an effective teacher, you must be more than *just aware of* the seven competencies described in this text. You must make a conscious effort to *practice* and *improve* each of the competencies. Only by quantitatively assessing them will you know where you stand and what progress you are making. A number of assessment techniques have been described. Try one!

Selected References

ALLEN, PAUL M., WILLIAM D. BARNES, JERALD L. REECE, AND E. WAYNE ROBERSON, *Teacher Self-Appraisal: A Way of Looking Over Your Own Shoulder*. Worthington, Ohio: Charles A. Jones Publishing Company, 1970.

AMIDON, EDMUND, AND ELIZABETH HUNTER, *Verbal Interaction in the Classroom: The Verbal Interaction Category System*. Unpublished manuscript. (Reprinted in Anderson; see below)

————, AND ELIZABETH HUNTER, *Improving Teaching*. New York: Holt, Rinehart & Winston, Inc., 1966.

AMIDON, E. J., AND N. A. FLANDERS, *The Role of the Teacher in the Classroom*. Minneapolis, Minnesota: Paul Amidon and Associates, 1963.

FLANDERS, NED S., *Teacher Influence, Pupil Attitudes, and Achievement*. Cooperative Research Monograph No. 12. Washington, D.C.: Government Printing Office, 1965. (Reprinted in Raths; see below)

————, *Interaction Analysis in the Classroom: A Manual for Observers*. Ann Arbor, Michigan: School of Education, University of Michigan, 1966.

————, *Analyzing Teaching Behavior*. Reading, Mass.: Addison-Wesley Publishing Co., Inc., 1970.

GENERAL

ANDERSEN, HANS O. (ed.), *Readings in Science Education for the Secondary School*. New York: The Macmillan Company, 1969. (See especially Chapter 2, "Studying Science Teaching" on pages 44 to 83. It contains the first Amidon reference from above on pages 48 to 59)

RATHS, JAMES, JOHN R. PANCELLA, AND JAMES S. VAN NESS (eds.), *Studying Teaching*. Englewood Cliffs, N.J.: Prentice-Hall, Inc., 1967. (See especially Chapter 2, "Interaction in the Classroom" on pages 31 to 87. It contains the first Flanders reference from above on pages 42 to 68.)

Index

317

Roberson Teacher Self-Appraisal System, 308-9
Rogers, Carl R., 294
Rosenblith, Judy F., 294
Rosenthal, Robert, 294

Sanders, Norris M., 82*n*, 129
Schultz, William C., 249, 250, 251, 294
Selective reflection, 258-59
Self, internal *vs.* external, 247-48
Self-evaluation, suggestions for, 40-42
Senior High School Examination Board (Alberta), 196, 206
Sensations, learning and, 141
Sensorimotor stage, 6-8
Serial ordering, 12-18, 42
Serial Order Tiles, 12-18
Short-answer tests, 183-87
Silence, 259
Sime, Max, 137*n*
Situation, performance objectives and, 48, 50, 52-55, 58-62, 69-71
Smith, James A., 244
Smith, Paul, 244
S.P.C.P. model, for sequencing instruction, 141-47
Spotted Lesser Zonks, 3-5
Stanley, Julian C., 178*n*, 206
Statements (*see* Propositions)
Stevens, Barry, 294
Stevens, Romiett, 120, 129-30
Substance, conservation of, 10, 18-21
Synthesis, 175
Systematic combinations, 24-25

Taba, Hilda, 85, 130, 148*n*, 165
"Taba Tri Tram" model, for sequencing instruction, 148-51
Talent *vs.* creativity, 210
Tape recordings (*see* Audio tape recordings; Video tape recordings)
Taxonomy of Educational Objectives (Bloom), 151, 175, 179, 185, 188, 192, 193, 195, 253-54
Taylor, Calvin W., 244
Teacher
  as designer of learning environment, 137-38
  emotional climate and, 251-53, 254-55
  questions and, 82, 84-86
Teacher competency
  evaluating, 307-15
  interaction analysis, 310-13
Teacher Education Program Staff, 121*n*, 123-24, 130

Teacher Self-Appraisal: A Way of Looking Over Your Own Shoulder (Allen, Barnes, Reece, and Roberson), 309
Terminal goal, in sequencing instruction, 133-34
Tests
  constructing, 178-99
  essay, 178-83
  evaluation, 167-68
  matching items, 191-92
  multiple-choice, 193-97
  objective, 183-99
  published, 199-201
  short-answer, 183-87
  true-false, 187-91
  varying, 197-99
Theory *vs.* practice, 27-28
Thinking
  critical *vs.* creative, 211-12
  questions and, 85
Threat, 257
Tippett, James S., 144*n*
Tompkins, Silvan S., 294-95
Topical rationale, for performance objectives, 71-72
Torrance, Paul E., 221-23, 245
Trojcak, Doris A., 165
True-false tests, 187-91

Utterance, length of, 259

Validity
  definition, 168
  reliability and, 173
Values (*see also* Self)
  definition, 257
  in internalization continuum, 253
Van Ness, James S., 316
Variables, formal operations stage and, 25-26
Verbal Interaction Category System (VICS), 310-13
Video tape recordings, 307-8
Volume, conservation of, 18-21, 23

Walbesser, Henry H., 165
Wann, T. W., 295
Weight, conservation of, 18-20
Wiesen, Allen E., 294
Winter, William D., 295

Xerox Corporation, 206